CAMBR
THE HISTORY OF PHILOSOPHY

AUGUSTINE
*On the Free Choice of the Will, On Grace and Free Choice, and Other Writings*

# CAMBRIDGE TEXTS IN
# THE HISTORY OF PHILOSOPHY

*Series editors*
## KARL AMERIKS
*Professor of Philosophy at the University of Notre Dame*

## DESMOND M. CLARKE
*Emeritus Professor of Philosophy at University College Cork*

The main objective of Cambridge Texts in the History of Philosophy is to expand the range, variety, and quality of texts in the history of philosophy which are available in English. The series includes texts by familiar names (such as Descartes and Kant) and also by less well-known authors. Wherever possible, texts are published in complete and unabridged form, and translations are specially commissioned for the series. Each volume contains a critical introduction together with a guide to further reading and any necessary glossaries and textual apparatus. The volumes are designed for student use at undergraduate and postgraduate level, and will be of interest not only to students of philosophy but also to a wider audience of readers in the history of science, the history of theology, and the history of ideas.

*For a list of titles published in the series, please see end of book.*

# AUGUSTINE

# On the Free Choice of the Will, On Grace and Free Choice, and Other Writings

EDITED AND TRANSLATED BY

## PETER KING
*University of Toronto*

CAMBRIDGE UNIVERSITY PRESS

Cambridge, New York, Melbourne, Madrid, Cape Town, Singapore,
São Paulo, Delhi, Dubai, Tokyo

Cambridge University Press
The Edinburgh Building, Cambridge CB2 8RU, UK

Published in the United States of America by Cambridge University Press, New York

www.cambridge.org
Information on this title: www.cambridge.org/9780521001298

First published 2010

Printed in the United Kingdom at the University Press, Cambridge

*A catalog record for this publication is available from the British Library*

*Library of Congress Cataloging in Publication data*
Augustine, Saint, Bishop of Hippo.
[Selections. English. 2010]
On the free choice of the will, On grace and free choice, and other writings / Augustine ;
[edited and translated by] Peter King.
p.   cm. – (Cambridge texts in the history of philosophy)
Includes bibliographical references and indexes.
ISBN 978-0-521-80655-8 – ISBN 978-0-521-00129-8 (pbk.)
1. Free will and determinism.   2. Grace (Theology)
I. King, Peter, 1955–   II. Title.   III. Series.
BR65.A52E6 2010
230′.14–dc22
2010003262

ISBN 978-0-521-80655-8 Hardback
ISBN 978-0-521-00129-8 Paperback

# Contents

# Acknowledgments

Thanks to Anna Greco, Ian Drummond, and Nathan Ballantyne, each of whom read through this volume in various stages of development. Thanks are also due to Desmond Clarke and Hilary Gaskin, who waited patiently for me to finish it. The volume is dedicated to my mother.

# Introduction

## Life and times

Augustine was born on November 13, 354, to a family of hereditary curial rank, in Thagaste (modern Suq Ahras in Algeria) during the latter days of the western Roman Empire. Christianity was the official state religion, but other religions were still tolerated and practiced; Augustine seems to have received at least a nominal Christian upbringing. He was formally educated at Thagaste, Madaura, and Carthage to be a rhetorician, one of the few professions that allowed upward social mobility. Once his education was complete, Augustine taught rhetoric in Carthage and Rome, eventually securing the post of official rhetorician to the imperial city of Milan in 384 – the very year in which the Emperor Theodosius prohibited pagan worship and made Christianity the only religion of the Empire. While resident in Milan, Augustine attended the sermons of Ambrose, Bishop of Milan, and became a catechumen in the Catholic Church. In the latter part of 386, Augustine chose to embrace Catholicism wholeheartedly (which he describes as a kind of "conversion"), and he subsequently resigned his post as rhetorician. To make ends meet he took on private students and began to write and publish dialogues and treatises. Augustine was formally baptized in a public ceremony by Ambrose himself on Holy Saturday, April 24, 387. Returning to Africa, he founded a religious community in Thagaste. On a trip to Hippo (modern Annaba in Algeria) in 391, he was acclaimed priest, and in 395 he became Bishop of Hippo. Shortly thereafter Augustine wrote his *Confessions*, which, among other things, describes his spiritual odyssey to the Catholic faith.

Augustine remained a bishop for the rest of his life, dividing his time between pastoral duties, theological controversies, research, and writing. The influence of his pastoral and episcopal duties is clearly evident in his writings, above all in his attempt to create a unified Catholic Church: politically, in his polemical campaigns against the Manichaeans, the Donatists, and the Pelagians; doctrinally, in his efforts to understand and clarify the Trinity, Original Sin, predestination, salvation, and grace. Augustine's thoughts on these matters shaped the future of the Church.

Yet while Augustine was pursuing political and doctrinal unity within the Church, the world into which he had been born was coming to an end. In 410, Rome was sacked by Alaric and the Visigoths, a shocking event that caused many to question the adoption of Christianity by the Roman state; Augustine's response was his massive *The City of God*, in which he argued that the community of the faithful should not be concerned with the events of this world. Yet, in 429, the Vandals invaded Africa, and by May of 430 had reached Hippo and put the city, with Augustine inside, under siege. Augustine died on August 28 (celebrated as his feast day) while the city was still besieged. The siege of Hippo ended shortly after his death, in 431; by 437 the Vandals had annexed Carthage, and by 442 an independent Vandal kingdom covered all of North Africa, Corsica, and southern Sicily.

## Augustine's intellectual development

Augustine had no formal philosophical training. From Cicero's *Hortensius* he absorbed not only a passion for wisdom and the drive to live his life according to fundamental principles, but also a distrust of the narrow sectarianism that characterized the philosophical schools of late Antiquity. He therefore chose not to align himself with any school, but to pursue philosophy as a syncretistic amateur, taking truth wherever he might find it. In practice, this meant that Augustine's initial knowledge of philosophy was derived from the authors he studied in the course of his rhetorical education, Cicero and Seneca above all, in an eclectic mix heavily influenced by Stoic doctrines. Most of these doctrines Augustine knew in their non-technical popular forms: the unity of the virtues, the rule of reason over the emotions, the identification of virtue and happiness, strength of character as a defense against the vicissitudes of fortune. Yet he occasionally shows some knowledge of the more technical aspects of Stoic philosophy. For instance, in *On the Free Choice of the Will* 3.25.74.255–3.25.76.264 Augustine speaks of the mind accepting or rejecting the impressions with which it is presented in the course of sensory experience – fundamental points of Stoic doctrine, which he handles correctly.

A question that "hounded" Augustine when he was young, as he tells us in *On the Free Choice of the Will* 1.2.4.10, was how a benevolent Deity could permit there to be evil in the world – the philosophical Problem of Evil (discussed in more detail below). Augustine was not satisfied with the traditional philosophical answers, nor with what he took to be the Christian response. Instead, he found the most intellectually satisfactory answer to be given by an illegal gnostic sect, the Manichaeans, who claimed to have uncovered the rational core of religion, to be successively revealed to its disciples as they progressed through various stages of purification and enlightenment. (A further attraction of Manichaeanism for Augustine was that it presented itself as an "improved" version of Christianity, allowing Augustine to maintain some continuity with his nominal religious upbringing.) According to the Manichaeans, there are two fundamental and equal opposed principles in the world: the good principle, manifest in Light; the evil principle, manifest in Darkness. Each is material, as is the world itself, and their struggle gives the world its structure. Human beings are themselves products of the Light, but have been partly corrupted by Darkness. As a result, they properly belong to the Light, and should strive to "return" to it through moral purification. Human beings are the paradigmatic battleground for the conflict of Light and Darkness, a fact reflected in the presence of both good and evil impulses within the human soul. The cosmic struggle between Light and Darkness is played out in miniature within each human being. This is possible because everything, including the human soul, is material, and hence able to be affected by the fundamental principles, Light being very fine particles and Darkness being coarse particles. In short, the Manichaeans were metaphysical and moral dualists who explained evil in the world by the presence of both a benevolent Deity and a malevolent Deity. Augustine found the depth and the comprehensiveness of the Manichaean system persuasive, and he was an active adherent for a decade or so. The Manichaeans helped Augustine promote his career, providing him with contacts in Italy and using their influence to have him win the post of imperial rhetorician in Milan.

In the end, however, Augustine became disillusioned with Manichaeanism, as he tells us in his *Confessions*. It was not because of its answer to the Problem of Evil – that seems to have been what Augustine held on to the longest – but because its claims to comprehensiveness led the Manichaeans to make false claims in astronomy and elsewhere, a fact Augustine found particularly galling since, in his opinion, there was no need to make such claims in the first place. His dissatisfaction with the Manichaean system left Augustine with no systematic answers to his philosophical difficulties. For a period of time he entertained the possibility that there might be no answers, or at least no answers that we can know. This was more than mere despair; Augustine found an intellectual stance ready for him to adopt in (Academic) skepticism, known to him primarily through Cicero's dialogue *The Academicians*. In addition to a wide array of arguments against dogmatic pretensions to knowledge, Augustine also found in skepticism a discussion and defense of the view that the search for knowledge is itself intellectually rewarding and valuable, and that "knowledge" itself might be understood as a dynamic process rather than a static (and perhaps secret) doctrine available only to initiates, as the Manichaeans held. Although Augustine adopted skepticism for only a few years at most, it shaped his later thinking more than he was ready to admit.

The most important philosophical influence on Augustine was not skepticism, though, but rather late neoplatonism. In his *Confessions*, he tells us how an unnamed source gave him some "books of the Platonists" to read – exactly which texts are a matter of ongoing scholarly dispute – and how the experience was an intellectual revelation to him, an experience that so profoundly moved him it changed the way he understood the world like nothing since the *Hortensius*. For one thing, Augustine tells us that it was from neoplatonism that he learned the distinction between the material and the immaterial, and how to conceive properly of the latter. (Augustine was not unusual in this regard; a similar experience is recorded by Justin Martyr.) The arguments and the doubts so effectively raised by the skeptics, as well as the errors of the Manichaeans, were confined to the realm of the material and physical, and simply did not address the kind of knowledge accessible by the mind directly. With the gates opened thereby to a form of knowledge impervious to skeptical doubt, Augustine readily adopted neoplatonic metaphysics, according to which reality is fundamentally hierarchical, structured by three primary cosmological principles: One/Being, Mind/Intelligence, and Soul/Life, which operate as a threefold unity with respect to the rest of the world, the product of its creative "overflow." The relations among these three principles are necessary and eternal, and, at bottom, indescribable, since the One/Being exceeds Mind/Intelligence, and is therefore ineffable. But certain things can be known about their internal relations; Plotinus, for instance, describes the first principle, One/Being, as the "Father" of the second principle, Mind/Intelligence, which it generates (and is therefore its "Son"); the third principle, Soul/Life, follows thereafter. That reality is structured by these three principles in this manner was a claim supported by extensive detailed argument, in a long tradition of Platonist metaphysics. This intelligible world is accessible to human minds, who try to ascend to the One as their goal – unreachable by the logical mind alone, which must transcend mere Being/Intelligence to attain its ineffable union with the One. At the other end of reality we find things that share least in the ultimate principles. They have less being, and are "scattered," taking less part in unity; matter is the least real kind of being, on this account. Since everything that exists, no matter how tenuously, is derived from the One, evil is not itself a positive force in neoplatonism. It is not, strictly speaking, a being at all, but instead a kind of lack of being, an absence or deprivation of what ought to be present, as blindness is the lack of vision in the eyes.

Augustine accepted the sophisticated and powerful metaphysics at the center of late neoplatonism, but he found philosophical shortcomings in its ethical views, broadly speaking. The key ethical point in neoplatonism is the return to the One, in which humans can hope to lose themselves in a mystical ecstasy. The way in which the return to the One is accomplished, though, was generally thought to depend on passing through a series of intermediate stages, in each case engaging in theurgical ritual practices meant to propitiate the daemon resident at each stage. Augustine thought that this view could not succeed, because there cannot be anything that is genuinely "intermediate" between finite being and the radically transcendent One. Instead, what is needed is something that bridges the gap not by being halfway between the human and the divine, but by being simultaneously human and divine – a Mediator, as Augustine calls it. Furthermore, while neoplatonism is clear that the human soul suffers a "fall" away from the One, necessitating its struggle to return, there is no clear account of why this fall takes place. Augustine saw that the explanation of the fall should be logically tied to the possibility of ascent, and combined this with his long-standing worries about evil, to arrive at his first theoretical understanding of Christianity.

For Augustine, Christianity was the *true* philosophy, a clear philosophical improvement on pagan neoplatonism. The neoplatonic triad of principles was straightforwardly assimilated to the Trinity, whose internal relations are necessary and eternal and whose relation to the rest of Creation is contingent. God the Trinity is ineffable, as was the neoplatonic triad of principles, and it is the goal of human striving. The fall of human souls away from the divine is the result of Original Sin (a term coined by Augustine), and the upward ascent to the divine is a matter of "overcoming" sin through Jesus Christ the Mediator, at once human and divine, Whose incarnation makes possible human redemption through grace. These are not mere dogmas of faith, but philosophically defensible views that offer solutions to problems that pagan neoplatonism was not able to solve. Hence Christianity is Platonist philosophy perfected.

Christianity provided Augustine with the philosophical system he had been looking for. The central mysteries of the faith made it possible to advance in the understanding of Christian doctrine without ever exhausting it, and this is how Augustine spent the rest of his life after his dramatic "conversion" to Christianity in 386. In the first flush of his enthusiasm he wrote a series of treatises, for the most part dialogues, which explore the intellectual content of Christian faith as responding to standard philosophical questions: skepticism (*Against the Academicians*), the nature of happiness (*The Happy Life*), the nature of reality (*On Order*), the immortality of the soul (*Soliloquies, The Greatness of the Soul, The Immortality of the Soul*), the possibility of knowledge (*The Teacher*), and the problem of evil (*On the Free Choice of the Will*). After Augustine became a priest, and thereafter a bishop, pastoral and doctrinal concerns dominated his thinking, so that, instead of taking his cue from standard philosophical questions, he would begin with questions posed by faith and then address them with philosophical methods and arguments. From the mysteries of the Trinity (*The Trinity*) to the community of the faithful in this life (*The City of God*), Augustine devoted his efforts to philosophical explorations of Christianity. Along the way he produced a rich stream of textual commentaries and exegesis, sermons, and occasional treatises provoked by inquiries or by controversy. In the end, Augustine wrote some 5 million words that survive from the period after his "conversion": approximately 120 treatises, 300 letters, and 500 sermons.

Augustine formulated some of his most subtle and original doctrines when confronted by views with which he disagreed. Manichaeanism he saw as an intellectual challenge to Christianity, and he wrote several works directed against it: *Against Faustus the Manichaean*, *The Analysis of "Genesis" Against the Manichaeans*, *The Nature of the Good*, *Against the Fundamental Epistle of the Manichaeans*, to name only a few. Donatism, a social movement within the African Church concerning the issue of sacerdotal purity, absorbed Augustine's energies for many years and led him to reflect on the proper role played by the Church as a social institution, an offshoot of his new pastoral vocation. But without a doubt the most sophisticated challenge Augustine had to confront was the movement inspired by the British monk Pelagius, beginning in the early 400s.

Pelagius was what now would be called a "moral perfectionist" – he thought that humans could attain virtue and the good life by their own efforts, making moral progress towards their goal, "perfecting" themselves. After all, Pelagius reasoned, God would not command us to improve ourselves were it not possible to do so – a version of the "*ought* implies *can*" principle. It follows that the opposition between the spirit and the flesh is not irreconcilable; that blaming "human nature" for shortcomings or faults is bad faith; that infants, who do not yet have a will, cannot sin and therefore are not in immediate need of baptism; that God redeems individuals in proportion to their deserts. Pelagius and his followers, notably Caelestius and Julian of Eclanum, offered systematic defenses of these views, which many found appealing and persuasive.

Augustine did not. Instead, he found "Pelagianism" to be a pernicious and dangerous doctrine, because he understood it to deny the need for God's grace in human salvation. That is, he thought that Original Sin effectively made it impossible for postlapsarian human beings to attain virtue in this life, so that direct divine assistance was the only hope we could have for the good life. Human nature was itself damaged in Original Sin, leaving all human beings with an irreconcilable opposition of spirit and flesh, its stain found even in newborn infants as children of Adam (and hence in immediate need of baptism). The deepest of the Pelagian errors, according to Augustine, was the view that God's grace is proportional to individual deserts, which fails to recognize the extent to which human beings are now incapable of genuine deserts on their own, as well as the pure gratuitousness of God's bestowal of grace.

Unlike Manichaeanism, Pelagianism was not generally taken to be heretical. It was a movement born within the Church, the expression of a different view about how Christian doctrine should be interpreted. It was not clearly opposed to orthodoxy. Augustine therefore had to argue against what he took to be the mistaken views about grace at the heart of the Pelagian movement, and in addition to convince people that Pelagianism was not merely a different view but a dangerous heresy. He carried out the former in a series of works, notably *Deserts and the Forgiveness of Sins, Perfection and Human Righteousness, The Spirit and the Letter, Nature and Grace, The Grace of Christ and Original Sin*, and his two works *Against Julian*. Augustine accomplished the latter through some complex and rather shabby political maneuvers, eventually securing papal and imperial decrees against certain aspects of Pelagianism. The result was not what he had foreseen. The defenders of Pelagianism took refuge in the eastern part of the Roman Empire, where the decrees were not considered to have binding force, and continued to argue their case from exile. Nevertheless, the impetus of Pelagianism in the western part of the Roman Empire had been effectively curbed, although not all of Augustine's positions were adopted as authoritative.

Augustine continued his polemics against the Pelagians in their exile, and also against what he considered worrisome Pelagian "tendencies" in the western part of the Roman Empire, until the Vandal siege of Hippo effectively cut him off from the rest of the world. It was his last doctrinal controversy, and he left in its wake a sophisticated and subtle theory of grace.

## Works

The works translated here deal with two major themes in Augustine's thought: will and grace. Each is central to explaining and understanding human responsibility. On the one hand, free will enables human beings to make their own choices, and hence is tied to the possibility of evil as well as the possibility of good. On the other hand, God's grace is required for human choices to be efficacious, though its active assistance does not go so far as to cancel human responsibility. The difficult task of reconciling free will with God's grace occupied Augustine for much of his life.

Augustine wrote *On the Free Choice of the Will* in two stages. Book 1 was written in 387–388, not long after his "conversion" to Christianity, while he and his friend Evodius (his interlocutor in the dialogue) were waiting in Rome for the weather to clear to return to Africa after the death of Augustine's mother, Monica, in Ostia. Books 2–3, and perhaps some revisions to Book 1, were written after Augustine was acclaimed a priest in Hippo in 391. The work as a whole was finished by 395, when Augustine sent a copy to Paulinus of Nola (*Letters* 31.7). In the annotated catalog of his written works he drew up shortly before his death, Augustine says only that the impetus for *On the Free Choice of the Will* was to "inquire through argument into the origin of evil" (*Reconsiderations* 1.9.1). Clearly one of his motives was to show that Christianity had a reply to the Problem of Evil that was philosophically better than the dualist response of the Manichaeans.

The other main selections translated here were written much later and concentrate on grace: *On Grace and Free Choice* (426–427), *On Reprimand and Grace* (426–427), and *On the Gift of Perseverance* (428–429). The first two were written in response to a situation that had arisen among the monks of a monastery at Hadrumetum (modern Sousse in Tunisia). Some of the brothers had been reading Augustine's *Letters* 194 against the Pelagians. From their reading they concluded that there was little scope for human free will – indeed, so little scope that when one of their number misbehaved, they insisted that the proper response was not to reprimand him but instead to pray to God to set the errant brother straight, since God's direct action is necessary to change anyone's behavior: a confession of human weakness. In response, Augustine wrote *On Grace and Free Choice*, and then *On Reprimand and Grace*, to correct the misreadings of these brothers. Addressed to Valentine, the abbot of Hadrumetum, they were meant to be circulated and read by all the members of the monastic community there and elsewhere. The third, *On the Gift of Perseverance*, from which excerpts are translated here, was written for monks in Provence (mainly in Marseilles and Lérins) who had drawn fatalist conclusions from the doctrine of predestination: If God long ago has already selected those who will be saved and those who will be damned, either at the Creation or at the beginning of the human race, they reasoned, then it cannot make any difference what we do, since God's verdict has already been passed. Again, Augustine's response was meant to be circulated and read widely.

Augustine's writings differ in literary style and genre depending on the audiences to which they are addressed. *On the Free Choice of the Will* and the *Confessions* were written for the educated elite of the late Roman Empire. Nominally Christian since the Edict of Milan in 313, this class was steeped in the culture of its classical past, and would have been as attentive to literary style and presentation as to philosophical content, if not more so. Augustine therefore chose to write *On the Free Choice of the Will* as a dialogue – an "open" literary format which invites the reader to become a participant in the discussion – and to make little appeal to Christian doctrine until Book 3, aiming rather at the cultivated intellectuals who were used to reading Cicero's philosophical dialogues for edification. Likewise, the *Confessions* is in its own way a dialogue, namely a dialogue between Augustine and God, meant to be "overheard" by the reader. Here biblical quotation and allusion are common, with the aim of showing that the Bible could sustain as rich a depth of context and meaning as the classical pagan texts it was meant to replace; in essence, Augustine made a literary use of the Bible.

By contrast, the works *On Grace and Free Choice*, *On Reprimand and Grace*, and *On the Gift of Perseverance* were written not for general consumption but instead for devout monastic communities, deeply engaged with the nuances of Christian doctrine. They are shot through with doctrinal details and biblical exegesis, as befits their audience. Augustine appears here, as he does in *On the Free Choice of the Will* Book 3 (and in the latter parts of most of his dialogues), as the voice of orthodox doctrine. Aimed at devout monks unaccustomed to theological speculation for the most part, Augustine is sensitive to monastic practices as well as to subtleties of doctrine. Here the Bible is treated as the ultimate fount of Christian belief, in which declarations and pronouncements of doctrine appear in a literary context that is the background vehicle for their presentation.

Despite these literary differences, Augustine's focus in the works translated here is always on the complex set of issues that are involved in human responsibility.

## Will

For Augustine, the key to moral action is found in the agent's possession and exercise of free will – the psychological faculty of choice and volition, the existence of which Augustine demonstrates in *On the Free Choice of the Will* 1.12.25.82. Although God alone is completely free, angels and human beings have free will. Just as our minds can transcend the mere sensible world and rise to the contemplation of eternal truths, so too our wills can transcend the natural order and are able to resist all external influences.

Augustine spells out his basic conception of the will in three theses. First, he holds that we are responsible only for acts done out of free choice. As early as *On the Free Choice of the Will* 1.1.1.3 Augustine declares that freedom is a necessary condition for the ascription of moral responsibility. It may not be sufficient; other circumstances, such as ignorance of some relevant circumstances, might absolve a free agent of responsibility. But it is at least necessary. This view is widely shared among philosophers, even today.

Second, the will is completely self-determining, or, as Augustine puts the point in 1.12.26.86 and 3.3.7.27, "what is so much in the power of the will as the will itself?" On pain of infinite regress, there cannot be any prior cause or ground that determines the will in its free choices. The freedom involved in free choice must therefore be a radical freedom, such that nothing whatever can determine its choice, including its own nature.

Third, we are responsible for not having a good will, since it is within our power to have one. Augustine proves in two stages that anyone has the power to have a good will. First, he shows that a mind that is properly "in order" (with reason in control) can easily have a good will (*On the Free Choice of the Will* 1.10.20.71–1.11.21.76). Second, and more difficult, is to show that even a disorderly mind, one that is not entirely in control of itself – the more common situation, and the one in which Augustine finds himself in *Confessions* 8.9.21 – is able to have a good will; this is the burden of his "treatise on the good will" (1.11.23.79–1.13.29.97).

The topic of *On the Free Choice of the Will*, the context in which these theses are articulated and defended, is explicitly concerned with the nature of responsibility. Augustine raises the issue in connection with the traditional Problem of Evil, which asks how God's existence can be reconciled with the presence of evil in the world. More exactly, the Problem of Evil holds that the following three claims cannot all be true:

(1) God is omnipotent, omniscient, and purely good.
(2) Someone good will eliminate any evil that can be eliminated.
(3) There is at least one case of genuine moral evil in the world.

There is nothing problematic in [1], which states a straightforward and widely accepted version of theism. Note, however, that the elimination of evil mentioned in [2] is a weaker requirement than the prevention of evil: Firefighters should put out whatever fires exist, but firefighters who set fires for the simple pleasure of then putting them out are less good than firefighters who do not do so, and indeed who try to prevent fires as well as put out whatever fires exist. (The stronger version of [2] that insists on prevention is not taken into account by Augustine.) Finally, the restriction to *moral* evil in [3] is important: Augustine does not discuss cases of so-called "natural evil" such as the suffering and misery produced by earthquakes, tidal waves, disease, and the like, which arguably might not impugn the goodness of God. Nor does [3] require that evil be widespread, or part of human nature, or even very bad. It is enough that there be at least one instance of an eliminable moral evil in the world to challenge the existence of a benign and powerful Deity. Since [2] and [3] seem unassailable as given, it looks as though [1] has to be given up.

Augustine's strategy is to reject, or at least to modify, [2]. It is the classic statement of what has come to be known as "the Free Will Defense" to the Problem of Evil. Augustine holds that:

(4) Every case of genuine moral evil in the world stems from the voluntary choices of free agents.
(5) Since God bestowed free choice of the will on human beings unconditionally, He ought not, and hence He does not, interfere with its exercise.
(6) It is better for there to be a world in which there are beings with free choice of the will, even at the cost of genuine moral evil, than a world in which there is neither.

Taken together, Augustine thinks that [4]–[6] restrict the scope of [2] as follows:

(2*) Someone good will eliminate any evil that it is morally permissible to eliminate.

Since God gave free will unconditionally, He has morally bound Himself not to interfere with its exercise, as [5] declares, and thus is not obliged in all cases to eliminate any evil that can be eliminated; if anything, God is obliged not to interfere with human free choice. Furthermore, [2*] is plausible on its own merits; no one should be obligated to do something morally impermissible. God of course "can" do so, in the sense that He has the power to do so, but He does not permit Himself to – a fact that Augustine takes to be sufficient as a response to the Problem of Evil.

Much of Book 1 is given over to Augustine's defense of [4], the claim that genuine moral evil stems from human free choice (dramatically recognized in the excerpt from *Confessions* 7.3.5). A key part of his argument is to show that free choices must be uncompelled, and hence are "authored" by the agent – they originate in the agent, who is responsible for them, a conclusion drawn explicitly in 1.11.21.76. Augustine's argument is the proof of the third thesis articulated above, that a good will is accessible to any moral agent.

In Book 2, Augustine defends [1] and [6]. His argument for the existence of God takes us the farthest afield from the will. Briefly, Augustine's argument exploits an analogy between perception and thought. Just as we believe that a sensible object exists because it is publicly accessible to our distinct individual senses – you and I can both see it – so too we should conclude that an "intelligible" object exists because it is publicly accessible to our distinct individual minds, in that you and I can both conceive it. This intelligible object is truth, that is, eternal and necessary truth of the sort exemplified in mathematics. What is more, we have to conform our minds to such truths when we conceive of them. We understand mathematical truths only when we recognize that their truth is independent of our minds, and likewise objective, not a matter of dispute or individual opinion. Mathematical truths are true whatever we may think about them, no matter how much we might want them to be otherwise. Augustine thus concludes that truth is "higher" than our minds. Hence something higher than our minds exists, which either is or is a part of God.

Given the nature of free will, Augustine takes [5] to be implicit in the proof of [6]. In Book 2, he derives [6] from two other claims:

(6a)  All things *qua* good come from God.
(6b)  Free will is one such good thing.

Briefly, his argument for [6a] turns on the claim that all things in the world are disposed in accordance with mathematical laws. Augustine in fact holds a stronger claim, namely that things exist only to the extent that they "are numbered" by eternal (mathematical) truths, which must come from God. To articulate his position, Augustine puts forward and separately argues for three subsidiary claims, in perhaps the most abstruse section of *On the Free Choice of the Will*: (*a*) things exist only to the extent that they have form; (*b*) the forms of things are governed by number; (*c*) eternal laws must derive from something eternal. The conjunction of (*a*)–(*c*), Augustine maintains, entails [6*a*].

Augustine's argument for [6*b*], in contrast, turns on the straightforward idea that free will is itself good because it allows a certain kind of good, namely moral good, to exist in the world. Without free will, there cannot be any moral goodness. Now moral goodness is not merely one feature among the many that add to the goodness of the world. Instead, it is an entirely distinct and unique class of goodness, one that is higher than, and incommensurate with, the goodness of the rest of the world. No matter how beautiful or perfect of their kind rocks, trees, and horses might be, they are not capable of moral goodness, which, as Augustine tells us, far "excels" their goodness. The world would be incomplete if it lacked any of the many kinds of goodness. With free will, created beings can reach higher heights; sinking to lower lows is entirely their own doing.

To support this last claim, Augustine turns in Book 3 to the source of the impulse to evil action. He argues that it does not stem from our nature, since if it were natural, it would be necessitated, and hence necessary and not culpable. (This point occasions Augustine's brief but influential discussion of how God's foreknowledge of our free choices does not make them necessary.) The most striking part of his discussion, perhaps, comes in his rejection of the idea that there could be anything determining or restricting the freedom of the will, in 3.17.48.164–3.17.49.169. Instead, Augustine defends the claim that the freedom involved in free will must be radical: Nothing at all can determine the will in its free choice. In particular, the will is not bound to do whatever the agent thinks it best to do. For Augustine, the freedom of moral agents is bound up with their ability to be weak-willed or even perverse, doing the wrong thing for no reason at all. Such is the radical freedom of the will.

The rest of Book 3 revolves around the main dogmatic issue treated in *On the Free Choice of the Will*, namely the extent to which Original Sin has impaired human free choice. Augustine regularly describes human nature as being "damaged and deformed" after the Fall; since human nature is by definition common to all human beings, the damage it has suffered therefore affects all human beings. This takes two forms. On the one hand, each human being is held to be guilty of Original Sin, precisely in virtue of being human. This is a puzzle. The normal way to be in a state of sin is to commit a sin for which one has not been forgiven; it is not clear how a person could be in a state of sin without having done anything, and particularly unclear in the case of newborn infants, who are incapable of any act of will whatsoever. Augustine considers four possibilities in his attempt to explain the transmissibility of Adam's guilt, which depend on an account of the origin of human souls (3.20.56.188–3.21.59.200), though he does not here settle on a solution.

On the other hand, distinct from the guilt involved in Original Sin, there is the punishment it calls forth. In *On the Free Choice of the Will* 3.18.52.177–3.20.55.186, Augustine identifies three distinct penalties inflicted on human nature: (*a*) ignorance, (*b*) mortality, and (*c*) trouble. Now (*a*), ignorance, refers to our difficulty in discerning the principles of right and wrong, which before the Fall were transparently known to us. And (*b*), mortality, is the fact that human beings now grow old and die. But the problematic penalty for human responsibility is (*c*), "trouble," which refers to the fact that postlapsarian human beings are subject to strong and unruly desires that direct us elsewhere than towards God, desires at best only partly under our control and often not even so. Augustine's generic term for such desires is "lust" (*concupiscentia*), which encompasses more than mere sexual appetite, though it certainly includes it; it is the same sense of the word as occurs in the phrase "the lust for power" – a strong, if not irresistible, craving or compulsion. Some of Augustine's statements in his discussion here gave ammunition to his later Pelagian critics, who argued that in *On the Free Choice of the Will* Augustine was at that time himself a moral perfectionist.

Augustine's discussion of Original Sin points the way to his later speculative thinking, in which doctrinal and dogmatic questions would set the agenda for his philosophical inquiries. And without a doubt, the most difficult questions were raised by the doctrine of grace, as it emerged in its final form after the Pelagians had been hounded into exile.

## Grace

The doctrine of grace has surprising philosophical depth and complexity, as Augustine was the first to recognize. Despite its nominal form, "grace" picks out a feature of certain acts, namely that they are supererogatory in their conferral of benefits. That is, acts of grace confer benefits on their recipients; they are good to do, but not wrong not to do. Hence acts of grace are neither obligatory nor forbidden for the benefactor, and not a matter of entitlement for the recipient. Whether there are such supererogatory acts is a matter of dispute, but most philosophers think that there are. Everyday examples include leaving a "tip" or gratuity (etymologically linked to "grace"); giving money to charity; helping an infirm person to cross the street; volunteer work. The conferred benefit is a gift freely given with no strings attached; grace is thus often called a gift.

Augustine is interested in ordinary cases of grace only insofar as they illuminate divine grace. For it is only through divine grace, Augustine holds, that humanity has any hope: human beings have put themselves in a disadvantaged position through Original Sin, and so are not entitled to the benefits God can provide – benefits God is under no obligation to provide, either. Hence any supernatural benefits to which we might aspire are a matter of grace.

The following example may clarify Augustine's position. An employer has given several of his employees positions of trust; upon discovering that two of them have been embezzling funds, he dismisses them. As a result, each is reduced to penury (one is in worse straits than the other) and must beg for their living. Leaving work one evening, the employer is approached by his former employees, each begging for money. It is reasonable to think that the employer is not under any moral obligation to give either of his former employees money, on the grounds that acts of charity are supererogatory, and hence good to do but not obligatory. And it might well be thought that even if there is a general duty to be charitable, the employer is certainly under no obligation to help *these* two beggars. Not only are they in the condition they are in due to their own wrongdoing, and hence deserve their condition; the wrong that they did was done to the employer. Augustine holds the strong view that, in addition to the moral fault involved in wrongdoing, there is separate and additional harm done to the victim of the wrongdoing – here, harm to their benefactor – which is itself a wrongdoing. (Dante much later followed Augustine on this score, reserving the deepest circles of Hell for those who wronged their benefactors.) Hence the employer, more than anyone else, is certainly not obligated to help either of his former employees. Now if he were to give either of them money, though, he would be conferring a benefit on the recipient(s), and he is morally permitted to do so. Giving either, or both, money would be an act of grace.

In Augustine's view, the human race has disadvantaged itself with respect to God in exactly the way the employees did with respect to their employer. Adam's wrongdoing put him, and thereby the human race, in the wrong. (The whole human race is put in the wrong by the doctrine of the transmissibility of Original Sin – an independent doctrine, but one that Augustine holds, as we have seen.) Nor was Adam's sin merely a case of wrongdoing. The wrong that was done was done to God, who is therefore clearly free of any obligations to the human race, like the employer as regards his former employees. Nevertheless, should God choose to bestow benefits on human beings, He is certainly permitted to do so, and the bestowal of such benefits would be an act of grace – or, as Augustine often says in shortened form, it would be "a grace." Grace is thus supererogatory on God's part but a genuine benefit to us, who are its undeserving recipients.

Augustine identifies four fundamental forms of grace:

[G1] salvation;
[G2] good works;
[G3] perseverance;
[G4] the "beginning of faith" (*initium fidei*).

Each form of grace involves its own philosophical issues, discussed individually below.

The first form of grace, [G1], is salvation. This is the ultimate benefit God can confer. God's graciousness in conferring salvation is further magnified by the fact that Original Sin has made damnation the default and deserved postmortem human condition. (Hence damnation is not an instance of gratuitous cruelty, whereas salvation is an instance of gratuitous kindness.) Now it is intuitive and convenient to think of God's choice whether to save a given person as happening at the instant of that person's death, once and for all. Doctrinally, matters are more complex, to be sure; God's conferral of salvation is in some sense "final" only with the Last Judgment. But these refinements do not matter for the point at issue. That said, we need to distinguish God's grace operative in salvation from closely related puzzles about predestination, and then take up Augustine's claims about residual justice.

Augustine notoriously adopts a strong doctrine of predestination, according to which God has foreordained whom He will gratuitously save (the lucky few known as the "elect"). From the point of view of grace, it makes no difference when God confers the benefit; it is an undeserved good that God is at liberty to bestow whenever He sees fit. The doctrine of predestination, though, has often been thought to conflict with human freedom, on the following grounds: If God has already foreordained, long before my birth, whether I shall belong to the elect, then nothing I do will affect God's choice, and so my free will is inefficacious – it will have no effect on whether I am saved or not, a matter that was settled before I was born, and indeed before the universe was created. This seems to have been the line of reasoning that troubled the monks of Provence, on whose behalf Augustine wrote *The Predestination of the Saints* and *On the Gift of Perseverance*. Yet other philosophers, Augustine among them, held that God would not have foreordained you to the elect if you were freely going to commit evil, and so His choice *is* sensitive to your behaviour. Each side seems to have good reasons for its view: the fatalists because causation does not run backwards in time, the optimists like Augustine because God has genuine foreknowledge.

Yet puzzling as the problems of predestination may be, they are not problems with the fact that God bestows salvation as an act of grace. Instead, they ultimately have to do with the compatibility of free will and foreknowledge (which is closely related to foreordainment), discussed in *On the Free Choice of the Will* Book 3.

Philosophical problems that are specific to [G1], salvation, come to the fore in problems of residual justice. We can best introduce them by returning to the analogy with the employer and his former employees. Since the employer has no moral obligations towards his former employees, helping either would be supererogatory. Suppose he helps one but not the other. Given that he is not obligated to help either, is there any unfairness in helping one but not the other? Suppose further that the one he does not help is the one who has the greater need. Given that he is not obligated to help either, if he does help, is he obligated to help the one with greater need?

These are questions of residual justice, the former focusing on the justice of an act of grace to one (undeserving) recipient and not to the other, the latter on whether such acts of grace, if performed at all, must be at least conditionally proportional to the status of their recipients. The answers to these questions are logically independent of one another, and not entailed by the mere fact that conferring the benefit is supererogatory. One might hold, for instance, that the benefactor is not required to help either of the potential recipients, but that *if* he helps either, he has to help each equally (or if this is not possible then he must select the recipient in an equitable manner).

Augustine takes an uncompromising position on residual justice. He argues that there is no injustice in conferring benefits on one rather than another, and further that no issue of proportionality arises. More exactly, Augustine holds that distinct cases are strongly independent (the moral permissibility of conferring the benefit on one recipient is independent of how anyone else is treated) and that the benefactor need not have a reason to pick one recipient over another. In support of his position he cites in *On the Gift of Perseverance* 8.17 the Parable of the Vineyard (Mt. 20:1–16), in which workers who have labored for different times in the vineyard are nevertheless paid the same amount by the owner. Augustine declares that the owner's "generosity towards some was such that there was no inequity towards the others." Each person receives his due, and further benefits, such as those bestowed by generosity, are not subject to considerations of fairness.

Augustine's position is at least partly motivated by his concern to safeguard divine freedom. He might be thought to go too far. It is enough to avoid Pelagianism to say that God is not obligated to help anyone, that no one deserves divine assistance. Yet that seems compatible with the weaker claim that, if God assists any of the (admittedly undeserving) recipients, He should do so in proportion to their (admittedly inadequate) deserts, or at the very least He should have a reason to bestow grace upon one recipient rather than another. The reason need not be known to us; it is enough to conclude that there must be such a reason. Nor does this obviously impinge on divine freedom. God can bind Himself in all sorts of ways, and bestowing grace in proportion to deserts is not obviously more freedom-canceling than His refusal to interfere with acts of free choice.

The second form of grace, [G2], is the grace involved in human good works. Augustine holds that there is an asymmetry in human action: We do evil all on our own (as established by *On the Free Choice of the Will*), but we can do good only with God's help as a grace. If we grant Augustine the asymmetry – he takes it to be a consequence of the Fall – we need to clarify how God helps humans to do good works, and whether God's help vitiates human freedom, or responsibility, since we cannot perform those works on our own.

An agent brings about a good action, then, only because God graciously comes to his assistance. This can happen in two ways. First, God can make an outcome attainable that would not otherwise be attainable, much the way the pilot makes it possible for me to fly from Amsterdam to Toronto, which I cannot otherwise do. In such a case God's assistance is direct. Second, God can act on the agent's powers, not directly on the outcomes. This is what happens when God "strengthens" the human will, for instance, so that it has the necessary force to reach its object. Augustine holds that in neither of these cases does God's assistance render the outcome a joint product. Rather, God's assistance enables the human agent to accomplish an end, while the accomplishment and the responsibility for the accomplishment remains with the agent, despite the need for God's assistance. Contrast these cases with, say, the differential contributions of the members of a string quartet. Their performance is truly a joint product, since each adds something different; in such a case each contributor adds something distinct but necessary to the performance as a whole, which is genuinely a joint production. But even when God enables a human being to attain an end, He is not merely cheering from the sidelines, so to speak. According to Augustine, God's contribution is necessary, but it does not detract from the agent's responsibility. After all, *I* am the one who flies from one city to another, for all that the pilot controls the plane, the maintenance crew stocks it with fuel, and so on. Likewise, *I* am the one responsible for the (result of the) exercise of my abilities, whether they be increased, diminished, or otherwise affected by another agent. Augustine's substantive thesis, then, is that good works always involve God's gracious assistance in a way that fully preserves human responsibility.

Augustine's thesis might be challenged on the grounds that even in the case in which God merely acts in concert with human abilities, thereby augmenting them, it is not clear why we should assign the responsibility for the action to the human partner – which is all the less tempting when God's contribution is anything more than minor. At the least, it seems as though God should be counted as a joint partner in the action. And so much the more so in the first case, where the outcome is simply unattainable without God's assistance. Why not count God as joint partner?

One reply open to Augustine is that in each kind of case, God's assistance is strongly independent of the human agent. Not only can the human agent not bring it about that God assist him; he cannot influence the kind or nature or degree of assistance God may bestow. From the point of view of the agent, God's "standing offer" of assistance is merely a fact of the situation, a fact of which he may choose to take advantage, much as he might take advantage of a snowfall to ski, or of the high tide to put to sea. What is shared from a metaphysical point of view might yet be chalked up to individual responsibility from a moral point of view.

The third form of grace, [G3], is perseverance. Augustine thinks of this as the personal quality of tenacity more than anything else. An agent cannot be said to persevere in the will-to-φ, according to Augustine, unless he never fails in his will-to-φ. So much holds for the sobriety of reformed alcoholics, too. But Augustine endorses a stronger thesis: he holds that if an agent ever fails to will-to-φ (in the appropriate circumstances), then the agent never really had the will-to-φ in the first place. Steadfastness of will is the model here: unless it is maintained "up to the end," as Augustine likes to say, then the agent never had the will-to-φ.

It is tempting to construe Augustine's notion of perseverance of the will as a kind of policy, a "meta-will" or second-order will about future acts of will. The will-to-φ is an occurrent act, whereas the policy to will-to-φ is distinct from any individual instance of the policy – with Augustine's additional proviso that one does not have the policy if there is ever a lapse from it. Because of the distinction between occurrent action and policy, Augustine can maintain that the bestowal of perseverance is separate from and additional to having the will in question. Yet, tempting as it is, this construal is problematic as an interpretation of Augustine's view. For Augustine holds that perseverance is a feature of the very act of willing that is directed at its object. The person on a diet wills not to eat certain foods, which, at least on the surface, appears to be a volitional act directed at those foods, not at future acts of will and choice, as the second-order interpretation would have it.

A better approach is to think of an act of will as a *resolve*. The agent resolves – wills – to do or not to do such-and-so, and the "strength" of the resolve is measured by its efficacy. The vegetarian resolves not to eat meat; the sybarite resolves to enjoy the pleasures of life. In each case the agent's future behavior is plausibly seen as the operation of the selfsame resolve, rather than as a new act of will that may or may not be in conformity with a prior policy decision. Furthermore, a resolve must endure for some period of time. If not, we suspect that there was no resolve in the first place, a fact that at least approximates Augustine's stronger thesis mentioned above. And finally, it is clear that a resolve is just a particular act of will. Augustine can be understood as holding that every act of will really is a resolve – that acts of will that do not endure over time are not really acts of *will* at all, but better understood as whims, or wishes, or something else that falls short of resolve. There is little discussion of such matters in contemporary philosophy; Augustine's remarks are a useful point at which to start thinking about them afresh.

The fourth and final form of grace, [G4], is the "beginning of faith": the initial impulse to believe in Christian doctrine. It is perhaps the most challenging to reconcile with freedom. Augustine holds that the "beginning of faith" is itself due to the grace of God. Under this heading he includes two very different kinds of cases. On the one hand, God may strengthen a person's faith to make it, or to help make it, wholehearted. On the other hand, God may simply make one a believer, as Saul of Tarsus, on the road to Damascus, seems to have been infused with faith, independent of his will.

The first case is similar to [G2] and [G3]: God "strengthens" the faith that the agent already has or wills to have. It is relatively unproblematic.

The second case is more difficult to reconcile with human freedom and responsibility. It seems wrong to say that Saul is "responsible" for his conversion. It also seems wrong to think that coming to have proper Christian faith, as Augustine would say, is entirely out of our control. If so, accepting Christ as savior seems not to be in our power. Yet radical conversion of the sort Augustine envisions seems in God's power rather than ours. How can this form of grace be compatible with free choice?

A possible reconciliation is as follows. The cases of radical conversion Augustine discusses are cases in which there is, arguably, voluntary or culpable lack of faith – that is, a lack of faith on the part of those who, like Saul, should have known better. (According to Augustine, Saul should have known better because his Jewish heritage gave him the relevant information to recognize Christ as the messiah.) God's conversion of Saul, then, merely brings Saul to a point at which he *should* have arrived on his own. It is clearly a gift from God and, while it does not depend on a prior free act of will on Saul's part, it might reasonably be said to accord with how Saul should comport his will. That is, God's action removes Saul's perverse and blameworthy refusal to believe, and allows his will to believe freely. This is in keeping with Augustine's remarks about the Jews and the Gentiles, as well as those to whom the gospel has been preached, whom he declares are culpable for their lack of faith. In short, God removes an *obstacle* from the individual, and the belief that follows upon its removal is as free as any other. Removal of an obstacle or an impediment does not cancel freedom. Instead, it makes it possible: untying someone frees him from constraint and allows him to act freely thereafter. So too in the case of radical conversion. God's action removes an (internal) obstacle to faith, which the agent may then embrace freely. It would be different if God directly infused faith. But even in the case of Saul, the best-known and most dramatic radical conversion, He did not; He merely appeared to Saul on the road to Damascus and asked Saul why he persecuted Him – a question, leaving Saul's subsequent conversion to Paul a matter of his free choice.

Augustine regarded his reconciliation of human free will and divine grace as one of his crowning achievements. The subsequent history of theories of free will and moral responsibility, and the extremely acrimonious history of theological discussions of grace, have confirmed the accuracy of that assessment. Although the metaphysical assumptions within which he articulated his account of free choice have changed over time, Augustine's intuition about the will as a self-determining power or faculty has been developed and defended for fifteen centuries as one of the classical statements of what is involved in human choice. Augustine's influence on the theology of grace has been equally dominant. It would not be an exaggeration to say that all discussions of grace and salvation within the Christian tradition, including those that occurred in reformed churches following the Reformation, were influenced by Augustine's legacy and in many cases reduced to alternative readings of his work. This applies to the work of Calvin and to those within the Calvinist tradition who disagreed about the necessity of grace for salvation, predestination, and the efficacy or otherwise of free will when not supported by grace. It applies equally to Jansenist theologians in the seventeenth century and their vociferous opponents among the Jesuits; the most famous and influential theological exposition of the Jansenist position was called, simply, *Augustinus* (1640), in recognition of its debt to Augustine. The texts translated in this volume are among those that helped define the terms within which all subsequent philosophical and theological discussion of human responsibility took place.

# Chronology

426–427    *On Grace and Free Choice, On Reprimand and Grace.*
427    *Reconsiderations.*
428–429    *On the Gift of Perseverance.*
430    [August 28]: Death of Augustine.

# Further reading

Augustine's life is well known in general and in its details, though particular bits of chronology and development continue to exercise scholars. The first biography was written by Possidius, who claims to have known Augustine for more than forty years: *Vita Augustini*, edited by A. A. R. Bastiaensen in C. Mohrmann (ed.), *Vite dei Santi*, vol. III: *Vita di Cipriano, Vita di Ambrogio, Vita di Agostino* (Milan: Mondadori, 1975), 127–241, translated by F. R. Hoare as *The Western Fathers* (London: Sheed & Ward, 1954). The standard modern biography is Peter Brown's *Augustine of Hippo* (Berkeley: University of California Press, 1967). A lively complement to Brown is James J. O'Donnell's *Augustine: A New Biography* (New York: HarperCollins, 2005). The best brief introduction is Henry Chadwick's *Augustine* (Oxford University Press, 1986). A good picture of Augustine's life as a full-time bishop, focusing on Church controversies and politics, is Gerald Bonner's *St. Augustine of Hippo: Life and Controversies* (Norwich: Canterbury Press, 2002).

There are several scholarly journals devoted to Augustine, *Augustinian Studies, Recherches augustiniennes, Revue des études augustiniennes*, and *Agostino* among them. Many articles and studies are published in other journals, of course. There are also monograph series, such as the Marquette Augustine series, the Villanova 'St. Augustine Lecture' series, and the occasional anthologies *Collectanea Augustiniana*. The *Revue des études augustiniennes* each year publishes a survey of work on Augustine. This annual survey is nicely complemented by the online bibliographical index used by the Würzburg Augustinians in the *Augustinus-Lexikon* project (see below). These resources should be used in conjunction with the four standard modern bibliographical reference works: T. J. van Bavel (ed.),

*Répertoire bibliographique de saint Augustin 1950–1960* (The Hague: Nijhoff, 1963); the *Fichier augustinien* in four volumes (Boston: G.K. Hall, 1972) compiled by the Institut d'études augustiniennes in Paris, along with the fifth volume, *Premier supplément* (Boston: G.K. Hall, 1981); C. Andresen (ed.), *Bibliographia Augustiniana*, 2nd edn. (Darmstadt: Wissenschaftliche Buchgesellschaft, 1973); T. L. Miethe (ed.), *Augustinian Bibliography 1970–1980* (London: Greenwood, 1982). There are specialized bibliographies as well.

A reasonably up-to-date encyclopedic reference work is Allan Fitzgerald (ed.), *Augustine Through the Ages: An Encyclopaedia* (Grand Rapids, MI, and Cambridge: William B. Eerdmans Publishing Company, 1999). This is a stopgap until the completion of Cornelius Mayer (ed.), *Augustinus-Lexikon* (Basel: Schwabe AG, 1986), currently being published in fascicules; articles are in English, French, or German. This massive reference work is the project of the Zentrum für Augustinusforchung, which makes further reference material available online.

The best single-volume overview of Augustine's philosophical thought is John Rist's *Augustine: Ancient Thought Baptized* (Cambridge University Press, 1994). Less comprehensive but rewarding in its own right is Gareth Matthews's *Augustine* (Oxford: Blackwell, 2005); it is written to be accessible to beginners but it is by no means restricted to them. A high-level engagement with Augustine as a philosopher is found in Christopher Kirwan's *Augustine* (London: Routledge, 1989), in the Arguments of the Philosophers series.

The best single-volume overview of Augustine's theological thought, one that is uncommonly sensitive to philosophical questions and arguments, is Eugene TeSelle's *Augustine the Theologian* (London: Burns & Oates, 1970). Any standard history of theology, such as J. N. D. Kelly's *Early Christian Doctrines*, 5th edn. (San Francisco: Harper, 1978) or Jaroslav Pelikan's *The Christian Tradition* (University of Chicago Press, 1975), will present Augustine's views in their historical context.

The study of *On the Free Choice of the Will* by Franco De Capitani, which includes an edition and Italian translation of the text with extensive notes and lengthy investigations covering all aspects of this work, is an advanced work well worth consulting: *Il "De libero arbitrio" di S. Agostino* (Milan: Università Cattolica del Sacra Cuore, 1987).

The long tradition of discussion of Augustine's view of the freedom of the will (he is usually construed as a classic libertarian) has recently been joined by a lively new debate initiated by the claim that Augustine "invented" the will. This claim was proposed in Augustus Dihle's Sather Lectures, published as *The Theory of Will in Classical Antiquity* (Berkeley: University of California Press, 1982). There is a careful response by Charles Kahn in his 'Discovering the Will: From Aristotle to Augustine' in J. Dillon and A. Long (eds.), *The Question of Eclecticism: Studies in Later Greek Philosophy* (Berkeley: University of California Press, 1988), 234–259. Kahn's views are examined and discussed in T. D. J. Chappell's *Aristotle and Augustine on Freedom: Two Theories of Freedom, Voluntary Action, and Akrasia* (New York: St. Martin's Press, 1995).

Augustine's theories of grace and will are less often studied, but there is a doctrinal and historical survey worth consulting: Cyril Gorman, "Augustine and High Medieval Theologies of Perseverance," unpublished PhD thesis, University of Notre Dame (2005). A very different approach to grace and its relation to philosophy is presented in Phillip Cary, *Inner Grace: Augustine in the Traditions of Plato and Paul* (Oxford University Press, 2008).

# Note on the texts and translation

I have used the following editions with variant readings as noted:

[1] *On the Free Choice of the Will.* William Green (ed.), *De libero arbitrio* in *Corpus christianorum series latina* 29 (Turnholt: Typographi Brepols editores pontificii, 1970), 211–321.

1.6.14.46: *earum* for *erarum*
1.7.16.55: *quo beluis* for *quod belius*
1.14.30.101: *quo* for *qua*
2.3.8.26: *quoniam bestiis inesse manifestum est*
3.4.11.40: *memoria* for *ememoria*, *praeterierunt* for *praterierunt*
3.5.13.50: *tam* for *tamen*
3.5.14.53: *si* for *is*
3.8.22.76: *debuisse* for *debuise*
3.9.28.103: *angelos sibi* with some manuscripts
3.10.29.107: *et* for *ex*
3.12.35.122: *nihil* for *nihll*
3.14.40.138: *usitate* for *uisitate*
3.23.69.234: *diuisionis* for *diuisiones*

[2] *Reconsiderations.* Almut Mutzenbecher (ed.), *Retractationes* in *Corpus christianorum series latina* 57 (Turnholt: Typographi Brepols editores pontificii, 1984), 23–29.

[3] *Confessions.* Martin Skutella (ed.), corrected by H. Jürgens and W. Schaub, *Confessiones*, Bibliotheca scriptorum graecorum et romanorum Teubneriana (Stuttgart and Leipzig: Teubner, 1984), 169–174 and 127–128.

[4] *On Grace and Free Choice.* There is no critical edition; I have used the Benedictine text of *De gratia et libero arbitrio* as it appears in J. P. Migne, *Patrologia latina* 44 (Paris: Imprimerie Catholique, 1845, reprinted 1865), 881–912.

8.19: *quomodo* for *quoniam*
13.25: *qua* for *quia*
14.29: *ergo* for *ego*

[5] *On Reprimand and Grace.* Georges Folliet (ed.), *De correptione et gratia* in *Corpus scriptorum ecclesiasticorm latinorum* 92 (Vienna: Verlag Österreichischen Akademie der Wissenschaften, 2000), 219–280.

[6] *On the Gift of Perseverance.* Mary Alphonsine Lesousky (ed. and trans.), *The 'De dono perseverantiae' of Saint Augustine* in *The Catholic University of America Patristic Studies* 91 (Washington, DC: The Catholic University of America Press, 1956), 124–156.

I have also taken other translations of these works into account, with special profit from Thomas Williams's version of *On the Free Choice of the Will* (Indianapolis, IN: Hackett, 1993), Henry Chadwick's version of the *Confessions* (Oxford University Press, 1998), Roland Teske's versions of *On Grace and Free Choice* and *On Reprimand and Grace* (New York: City Press, 2000), and Mary Alphonsine Lesousky's version of *On the Gift of Perseverance* (Washington, DC: Catholic University of America Press, 1956). The translations in the *Bibliothèque augustinienne* have also been useful.

Augustine usually used the Old Latin version of the Bible, which predates Jerome's Vulgate and differs from it in a number of ways. I have generally rendered biblical quotations along the lines of the King James translation (somewhat modernized) whenever possible. Where textual differences are important, I have given details in a footnote: Sol. 8:5, Rom. 5:12, Rom. 8:28, Phl. 1:6, 1 Jn. 4:7. There are many lesser variants.

# Abbreviations

The book–chapter–section numbers, given in the margins, are the traditional divisions of Augustine's text, and the basis for cross-references and the indexes. Cross-references within a particular work are given solely by number; references to other works are always given with the name of the work.

The books of the Bible to which Augustine refers are abbreviated as follows:

## Old Testament

| | | | |
|---|---|---|---|
| Gen. | Genesis | Ps. | Psalms |
| Ex. | Exodus | Prv. | Proverbs |
| Lv. | Leviticus | Ecl. | Ecclesiastes |
| Num. | Numbers | Sol. | The Song of Solomon |
| Dt. | Deuteronomy | Wis. | The Wisdom of Solomon |
| Jsh. | Joshua | Sir. | Sirach [Ecclesiasticus] |
| Sam. | Samuel | Is. | Isaiah |
| Kng. | Kings | Jer. | Jeremiah |
| Chr. | Chronicles | Ez. | Ezekiel |
| Est. | Esther | Hab. | Habakuk |
| Mac. | Maccabees | Zch. | Zecheriah |
| Job | Job | | |

## New Testament

| | | | |
|------|-------------|------|-----------------|
| Mt. | Matthew | Ths. | Thessalonians |
| Mk. | Mark | Tim. | Timothy |
| Lk. | Luke | Tit. | Titus |
| Jn. | John | Phm. | Philemon |
| Acts | Acts | Hbr. | Hebrews |
| Rom. | Romans | Jas. | James |
| Cor. | Corinthians | Pet. | Peter |
| Gal. | Galatians | Jn. | John (epistles) |
| Eph. | Ephesians | Jud. | Jude |
| Phl. | Philippians | Rev. | Revelations |
| Col. | Colossians | | |

I refer to 1–2 Samuel and 3–4 Kings, since the form "'1–2 Kings" is ambiguous.

Not all versions of the Bible agree in their numbering of individual chapters and verses. I give the numbers as found in the Vulgate by default, and, when needed, the numbers in the Revised Standard Version (abbreviated "RSV") and in the Septuagint (abbreviated "LXX"). In a few cases there are several variants to choose from, and this is noted as well. A complete index of biblical citations is given, so the reader can easily see how Augustine treats the same passage in different places.

*On the Free Choice of the Will, On Grace
and Free Choice, and Other Writings*

# On the Free Choice of the Will

## Book 1

EVODIUS: Please tell me whether God is not the author of evil.  1.1.1.1
AUGUSTINE: I shall tell you if you make it plain what kind of evil you are asking about. We usually speak of "evil" in two ways, namely when someone has (*a*) done evil; (*b*) suffered something evil.
EVODIUS: I want to know about both kinds.
AUGUSTINE: Well, if you know or believe that God is good (it is blasphemous to think otherwise), then He does not *do* evil. On the other hand, if we grant that God is just (denying it is irreligious), then He rewards the good; by the same token, He hands out punishments to evildoers, punishments that are doubtless evils to those who suffer them. Accordingly,  1.1.1.2 if no one pays penalties unjustly – which we must believe since we believe that the world is governed by divine providence – then God is indeed the author of evils of type (*b*), though not in any way the author of evils of type (*a*).
EVODIUS: Then is there some other author of the evil we have found not to come from God?
AUGUSTINE: Of course! Evil could not occur without an author. But if  1.1.1.3 you ask *who* the author is, no answer can be given, for there is not just a single author – rather, evil people are the authors of their evildoing. If you doubt this, pay attention to my earlier statement [in 1.1.1.1] that evildoings are redressed by God's justice. It would not be just to redress them unless they come about through the will.
EVODIUS: Perhaps no one sins unless he has learned how. But if that is  1.1.2.4 true, I ask: From whom did we learn how to sin?

3

AUGUSTINE: Do you hold that teaching[1] is something good?

EVODIUS: Who would dare to say that teaching is something evil?

AUGUSTINE: What if it is neither good nor evil?

EVODIUS: It seems good to me.

AUGUSTINE: Rightly so, in that knowledge is imparted to us (or awakened in us) through teaching, and nobody learns anything except through teaching. Do you think otherwise?

EVODIUS: I for one think that only good things are learned through teaching.

1.1.2.5 AUGUSTINE: Then draw the conclusion: Evil things are not learned! For "teaching" (*disciplina*) is linguistically derived from "learning" (*discere*).

EVODIUS: Evil things are not learned? Then how does it happen that we do them?

AUGUSTINE: Perhaps because we turn aside and away from teaching, that is, from learning. But whether this is the reason or not, the point is certainly clear: Since teaching is something good, and "teaching" is

1.1.2.6 derived from "learning," evil things cannot be learned at all. For if evil things are learned, they are included in teaching, and thus teaching will not be something good. But it *is* something good, as you yourself declared. Hence evildoing is not learned, and your search for the one from whom we learn to do evil is in vain. (Alternatively, if we do learn evil things, we do so to avoid them rather than to do them.) The conclusion is that evildoing is nothing but turning away from teaching.

1.1.3.7 EVODIUS: All in all I think there are two kinds of teaching: one through which we learn to do right, the other through which we learn to do evil. But when you asked whether teaching was something good, the love of the good itself caught my attention, and so I looked only at the first kind, and thus I replied that it is good. But now I am mindful of the second kind, which I declare without a doubt to be an evil, and whose author I am looking for.

1.1.3.8 AUGUSTINE: Do you at least think that understanding is indeed something good?

EVODIUS: Of course! It is plainly so good that I do not see what could be more excellent in humans. I declare that no understanding can be evil in any way.

---

[1] "Teaching": *disciplina*, the general activity associated with a field of knowledge.

4

AUGUSTINE: Well, if someone were not to understand when he is taught, can he seem to you to have learned anything?

EVODIUS: Not at all.

AUGUSTINE: It follows that if all understanding is good, and no one 1.1.3.9 learns without understanding, then everyone who learns is doing right. For everyone who learns, understands; everyone who understands is doing right. Hence anyone looking for an "author" through whom we learn something is really looking for the one through whom we do right. Accordingly, stop trying to track down some mysterious evil teacher! If he is evil he is not a teacher, and if he is a teacher he is not evil.

EVODIUS: Very well. Now that you have pushed me into admitting that 1.2.4.10 we do not *learn* to do evil, tell me: How is it that we *do* evil?

AUGUSTINE: You are raising a question that hounded me while I was young; when I was worn out it caused my downfall, landing me in the company of heretics.[2] I was so injured by this fall, and so buried under such vast heaps of empty tales, that had the love of finding out the truth not succeeded in requesting and receiving divine succor for me, I would not have been able to dig my way out and breathe again, recovering my earlier freedom of inquiry. And since such pains were taken in my case to 1.2.4.11 set me free from that question, I shall guide you on the same route that I used to escape. God will be at hand and make us understand what we have come to believe. Indeed, we are well aware that this is to take the course prescribed by the prophet Isaiah, who says: "Unless you believe you shall not understand" [Is. 7:9].

Now we believe that everything that exists comes from the one God, although God is not the author of sins. But this is the sore point: If sins come from the souls that God created, and those souls come from God, how is it that sins are not almost immediately traced back to God?

EVODIUS: You have now stated plainly what keeps troubling my 1.2.5.12 thoughts, pushing and dragging me into this very investigation.

AUGUSTINE: Take heart! Believe as you do; there is no better belief, even if the reason why it is so is hidden. Holding God in the highest esteem is surely the most authentic beginning of religiousness. Nor does anyone hold God in the highest esteem without believing that God is omnipotent, not changeable in even the least detail, the Creator of all good things, Who is more excellent than they are, the most just Ruler of

---

[2] The Manichaeans. See *Confessions* 3.7.12–3.10.18 and 8.10.22–24.

all He has created. Nor does God require the assistance of any nature in his creating – as though He were not sufficiently powerful all by Himself! 1.2.5.13 It follows that God created all things from nothing. Yet out of Himself He did not *create* the one whom we call the only Son of God, but rather *generated* him as equal to Himself.[3] When we try to describe the Son of God more plainly we call him "the power of God and the wisdom of God" [1 Cor. 1:24]; through which He made everything that was made from nothing.[4]

1.3.5.14 Now that these points have been settled, let us try with God's help to gain an understanding of the problem you posed, as follows. You are really asking *why* it is we do evil. Thus we should first of all discuss what it is to *do* evil. Declare your view on this topic. If you cannot summarize it briefly, at least acquaint me with your view by calling to mind some particular evil deeds.

EVODIUS: Adultery, murder, and sacrilege – not to mention others that time and memory will not allow me to list. Is there anyone to whom these deeds do not seem evil?

1.3.6.15 AUGUSTINE: Then tell me first of all why you think it is evil to commit adultery. Is it because the law forbids it?

EVODIUS: It is not evil because it is forbidden by the law. Instead, it is forbidden by the law because it is evil.

AUGUSTINE: What if someone were to exaggerate the delights of adultery, pressing us insistently why we judge it to be evil and worthy of condemnation? Do you think that people who now want to understand, and not merely to believe, should take cover in the authority of the law?

1.3.6.16 Well, for my part I believe as you do. I resolutely believe that adultery is evil, and I proclaim that all societies ought to believe so. But now we are trying to know and establish most firmly through understanding what we have already accepted on faith. So think it over as carefully as you can, and tell me the reason by which you know that adultery is something evil.

---

3 The Persons of the Trinity are co-eternal, standing in relations of interdependence: The Father generates the Son; the Father and the Son spirate the Holy Spirit. Neither is a case of "creation" strictly speaking.

4 See Jn. 1:3: "All things were made by [the Word], and without Him was not any thing made that was made" (partially cited in 3.10.30.108). Also 2 Mac. 7:28: "Look upon the heavens and the Earth, and all that is in them, and consider that God made them of things that were not."

EVODIUS: I know that it is evil because I would be unwilling to tolerate it in the case of my wife. Anyone who does to another what he is not willing to have happen to himself is undoubtedly doing something evil.

AUGUSTINE: What if someone's lust (*libido*) leads him to offer his wife   1.3.6.17
to another, freely tolerating her being violated by him, and in turn desiring to have equal license with the other man's wife? Does he then seem to you to have done nothing evil?

EVODIUS: On the contrary, a great evil!

AUGUSTINE: But he does not sin according to your rule, since he does not do what he himself is unwilling to tolerate. Accordingly, you should look for something else to prove that adultery is evil.

EVODIUS: It seems evil to me because I have often seen people con-   1.3.7.18
demned for this crime.

AUGUSTINE: Well, people are often condemned for acting rightly, are they not? Look again at history – and, not to send you to other books, look at the history which stands out by virtue of its divine authority. You will quickly find just how evil we must think the apostles and all the martyrs are if we accept that condemnation is a reliable judgment of evildoing. They were all judged to deserve condemnation by their admission of faith. Accordingly, if everything condemned is an evil, it was evil in those   1.3.7.19
days to believe in Christ and to profess the faith. But if not everything that is condemned is evil, look for something else to establish that adultery is an evil.

EVODIUS: I have no answer to give you.

AUGUSTINE: Then perhaps lust is the evil in adultery, and you will run   1.3.8.20
into difficulties as long as you are looking for evil in the outward visible deed. Now to understand that lust is the evil in adultery, consider the following. If a man does not have the opportunity to sleep with someone else's wife but it is plain somehow that he wants to do so, and that he is going to do so should the opportunity arise, he is no less guilty than if he were caught in the act.

EVODIUS: Nothing could be more obvious. Now I see that there is no   1.3.8.21
need for a long discussion to persuade me about murder, sacrilege, and in fact all other sins. It is clear now that nothing but lust dominates in every kind of evildoing.

AUGUSTINE: You do know, do you not, that lust is also called "desire"?   1.4.9.22
EVODIUS: Yes.

AUGUSTINE: Well, do you think that there is a difference between desire and fear, or that there is not?

EVODIUS: I think there is a great difference between them.

AUGUSTINE: I believe you think so because desire pursues its object whereas fear avoids it.

EVODIUS: That is it exactly.

AUGUSTINE: Then suppose someone were to kill a person, not out of a desire to get something but because of fear that some evil will happen to him. Will he not be a murderer?

1.4.9.23 EVODIUS: He will indeed. Yet his deed is not free from the domination of desire by that token; whoever kills someone in fear surely *desires* to live without fear.

AUGUSTINE: And does living without fear seem like a small good to you?

EVODIUS: It is a great good, but the murderer cannot achieve it in any way through his crime.

1.4.9.24 AUGUSTINE: I am not asking what he can *achieve* but what he *desires*. Anyone who desires a life free from fear certainly desires a good thing. Hence the desire itself ought not to be blamed; otherwise we shall blame all who love the good. The upshot is that we must admit that there are cases of murder in which the dominance of evil desire cannot be found, and either (*a*) it will be false that lust dominates in all sins insofar as they are evil, or (*b*) there will be some kind of murder that can be not a sin.

1.4.9.25 EVODIUS: If murder is killing a human being, it can sometimes happen without sin. For instance, a soldier kills an enemy; a judge or his agent executes a convicted criminal; someone throws his weapon by chance imprudently and against his will. They do not seem to me to be sinning when they kill someone.

AUGUSTINE: I agree. But they are not usually called murderers, either. So tell me: Do you hold that someone who kills his master, at whose hands he fears brutal torture, should be counted among those who kill someone but do not merit the name of murderer?

EVODIUS: I see that this case is quite different. In the earlier cases, the people were acting according to the laws – or at least not against the laws – whereas no law sanctions the crime of this slave.

1.4.10.26 AUGUSTINE: Once again you are calling me back to authority. You must remember that we have now undertaken to *understand* what we believe.

We do indeed believe the laws; hence we should try, if we somehow can, to grasp whether it is not an error for the law to punish the slave's deed.

EVODIUS: The law hardly punishes "in error" since it punishes someone who willingly and knowingly puts his master to death, which none of the others[5] does.

AUGUSTINE: Well, do you recall having said a little while ago that lust 1.4.10.27 dominates in every evil deed, and that a deed is evil due to lust?

EVODIUS: Of course I do.

AUGUSTINE: And have you yourself not also granted that someone who 1.4.10.28 desires to live without fear does not have an evil desire?

EVODIUS: I remember that too.

AUGUSTINE: Then, although the master is slain by the slave on account of his desire, he is not slain on account of a blameworthy desire. Consequently, we have not yet found out why this deed is evil. For we agreed that all evildoings are evil precisely because they come about from lust, that is, from a blameworthy desire.

EVODIUS: It seems to me now that the slave was condemned unjustly. 1.4.10.29 Yet I would not dream of saying so if I had another reply to offer.

AUGUSTINE: Is it so? You convinced yourself that so great a crime should go unpunished before considering whether the slave desired to have no fear of his master so as to gratify his lusts. Surely evil people 1.4.10.30 desire to live without fear, just as good people do. But the difference is as follows. Good people pursue this by turning their love away from things that cannot be possessed without the risk of losing them. Evil people, on the other hand, try to remove hindrances so that they may securely attach themselves to these things to be enjoyed. The end result is that they lead a life full of crime and wickedness, a life which is better called death.

EVODIUS: I have regained my wits now. I am glad to know so plainly 1.4.10.31 the nature of that blameworthy desire referred to as "lust." It has become apparent that lust is the love of things one can lose against one's will. So, 1.5.11.31 if you agree, let us now look into whether lust dominates in sacrilege too – most of the cases of sacrilege we see are committed out of superstition.

AUGUSTINE: Make sure the question is not premature. First of all, I 1.5.11.32 think there should be a discussion whether a charging enemy or a mur-derer attacking from ambush may be killed without lust, but for the sake of one's life, freedom, or chastity.

---

5 The soldiers and judges mentioned in 1.4.9.25.

EVODIUS: How can I think that people are free of lust if they fight ferociously for things that can be lost against their will? On the other hand, if such things cannot be lost, what need is there to resort to killing someone for their sake?

1.5.11.33 AUGUSTINE: Therefore, the law is unjust which grants permission (*a*) to a traveler to kill a highway robber, so as not to be killed himself; (*b*) to any man or woman to slay a rapist in his onslaught, if possible, before enduring rape. Indeed, the law bids a soldier to kill the enemy, and if he holds back from this bloodshed he pays the penalties from his commander. Surely we will not dream of calling these laws unjust – or rather, not to call them "laws" at all, for a law that is not just does not seem to me to be a law.

1.5.12.34 EVODIUS: I see that the law is well protected against this kind of charge. [1] The law gives the people whom it governs permission to do lesser evils in order to avoid greater ones. It is much more civilized that someone who plots against another's life be killed rather than the one who is protecting his own life; it is much more barbarous that someone unwillingly endure a rape than that the assailant be slain by his intended victim.
[2] Furthermore, in killing the enemy a soldier is then acting as an agent of the law, and thus easily does his duty without lust.

1.5.12.35 [3] Besides, the law itself, which was enacted for the protection of society, can hardly be accused of lust – at least assuming that the lawgiver, if he enacted the law at God's bidding (namely as eternal justice prescribes), was able to do so entirely free of lust. However, even if he did decree the law out of some lust, it does not follow that obeying the law must be accompanied by lust. A good law can be enacted by a lawgiver who is not

1.5.12.36 himself a good person. For example, if someone who had seized tyrannical power were to accept a bribe from an interested party leading him to decree that it is illegal to run off with a woman, even for marriage, the law will not thereby be evil merely because the one who enacted it is unjust and corrupt. Therefore, the law that bids enemy force to be repulsed by equal force, to protect the citizens, can be obeyed without lust. The same thing can be said regarding all officials who wield their powers in accordance with law and the established order.

1.5.12.37 Yet even if the law is blameless, I do not see how the people involved can be blameless. The law does not force them to kill, but merely leaves it in their power. Hence they are free *not* to kill anyone for things they can lose against their will, which they should therefore not love. With respect to life,[6] someone could perhaps be in doubt whether it is somehow taken away from the soul when the body dies. Yet if life can be taken away, it should be held of little worth. On the other hand, if it cannot, there is nothing to fear. With respect to chastity, well, seeing that it is a virtue, 1.5.12.38 who would doubt that it is located in the mind itself? Therefore, it cannot be taken away by a violent rapist. Hence anything that was about to be taken away by the one who was killed is not completely in our power. For this reason, I do not understand why it should be called "ours." In the end, I do not find fault with the law that permits such people to be killed. Yet I have not found any way to defend those who do the killing.

AUGUSTINE: I am even less able to find out why you are looking to 1.5.12.39 defend people whom no law finds guilty.

EVODIUS: Well, perhaps no law among those that are public and proclaimed by human beings. I rather suspect they are guilty according to a more powerful and hidden law, if divine providence oversees all things. How indeed are they free of sin in the eyes of divine providence? They have been stained with human blood for the sake of things that should be held of little worth. Therefore, it seems to me that a law drafted to gov- 1.5.13.40 ern society rightly permits these things, and also that divine providence rightly redresses them. The former has in its scope redressing deeds sufficiently to maintain peace among unenlightened people, to the extent that such deeds can be governed by human beings. The other faults, however, have different penalties appropriate to them, from which wisdom alone, it seems to me, can free them.

AUGUSTINE: I approve and endorse this distinction of yours. Even 1.5.13.41 though it is just a beginning and not complete, it confidently aims at exalted heights. For it seems to you that the law that is enacted to govern states tolerates and leaves unpunished many things, which are nevertheless redressed by divine providence (and rightly so). Yet it does not follow that just because the law does not accomplish everything, we should disapprove of what it *does* accomplish.

If you agree, let us look carefully at (*a*) the extent to which retribution 1.6.14.42 for evildoings should be exacted by the law that controls society in this life, and then at (*b*) what remains, which is punished by divine providence in a more unavoidable, yet hidden, fashion.

---

[6] Life and chastity are examples of things that can be lost against one's will, namely by murder and rape.

EVODIUS: Yes. If only we could get to the end of such a great issue! Personally, I think it is endless.

1.6.14.43 AUGUSTINE: Have courage, and set out along the roads of reason with the support of religiousness. There is nothing so demanding or difficult that is not made completely plain and easy with God's assistance. Therefore, let us look into (*a*) and (*b*), trusting in God and praying for His aid. First of all, tell me whether promulgating a written law is helpful to human beings living this present life.

1.6.14.44 EVODIUS: Obviously. States and societies are made up out of these human beings.

AUGUSTINE: Well, these human beings and societies are the same sort of things. Are they eternal and completely unable to change or perish? Or are they instead changeable and subject to time?

EVODIUS: Changeable, plainly, and subject to time; who could doubt it?

1.6.14.45 AUGUSTINE: Suppose that a society were well ordered, responsible, and a watchful guardian of the common welfare, one in which each person regards his private interest as less valuable than the public interest. Then is it not right to enact a law whereby this society is allowed to create its own governing officials, through whom the public interest is overseen?

EVODIUS: Quite right.

1.6.14.46 AUGUSTINE: Well, now suppose that the same society gradually becomes corrupted. Private interest is put before public interest; votes are bought and sold; degraded by those who covet honors, society hands its rulership over to disgraceful criminals. Would it not again be right if a good person were then found, someone more capable than the rest, who would take the power to confer honors away from society and restrict its choice to a few good people, or even to just one good person?

EVODIUS: Rightly so.

1.6.14.47 AUGUSTINE: Then, although these two laws[7] seem to be contrary to one another – one of them vests the power of conferring honors in the society, whereas the other takes it away – and although the latter was enacted so that the two laws cannot both hold simultaneously in one state, are we to say that one of them is unjust and hardly ought to have been enacted?

EVODIUS: Not at all.

---

[7] The law investing society with the right to create its own governing officials (1.6.14.45), and the law restricting that power to only a few people (1.6.14.46).

AUGUSTINE: Then let us call a law *temporal* if, although it is just, it can justly be changed in the course of time. Do you agree? 1.6.14.48

EVODIUS: Fine.

AUGUSTINE: Well, consider the law referred to as "supreme reason."[8] It should always be obeyed; through it good people deserve a happy life and evil people an unhappy one; and finally through it temporal law is both rightly enacted and rightly changed. Any intelligent person can see that it is unchangeable and eternal. Can it ever be unjust that evil people are unhappy while good people are happy? Can it ever be unjust that an orderly and responsible society sets up governing officials for itself while a dissolute and worthless society lacks this privilege? 1.6.15.48

1.6.15.49

EVODIUS: I see that this law is eternal and unchangeable.

AUGUSTINE: I think you also see, along with this, that nothing in the temporal law is just and legitimate which human beings have not derived from the eternal law. If a given society justly conferred honors at one time but not at another, this shift in the temporal law, to be just, must derive from the eternal law whereby it is always just for a responsible society to confer honors and not for an irresponsible one. Is your view different? 1.6.15.50

EVODIUS: No, I agree.

AUGUSTINE: So to explain concisely as far as I can the notion of eternal law that is stamped on us: It is the law according to which it is just for all things to be completely in order. If you think otherwise, say so. 1.6.15.51

EVODIUS: I have no objection. What you say is true.

AUGUSTINE: This law, on the basis of which all temporal laws made to govern human beings are altered [at different times], is one. Therefore it cannot itself be altered in any way, can it?

EVODIUS: I understand that this cannot happen at all. No force, no chance, no disaster could ever make it not just for things to be completely in order.

AUGUSTINE: Very well. Now let us see how a human being may be completely in order within himself. For a society is made up of human beings bound together under one law – a temporal law, as we noted. Tell me whether you are completely certain that you are alive. 1.7.16.52

EVODIUS: What could I say that is more certain?

---

[8] Cicero, *Laws* 1.6.18: "Supreme reason is the law implanted in nature, which enjoins what ought to be done and forbids the contrary."

AUGUSTINE: Well, can you distinguish *being alive* and *knowing yourself to be alive*?

EVODIUS: I know that nobody knows himself to be alive unless he is alive, but I do not know whether everyone alive knows himself to be alive.

1.7.16.53 AUGUSTINE: How I wish you also *knew* what you believe, namely that animals lack reason; our examination would quickly get past this question. But since you say that you do not know, you are initiating a long discussion. The issue is not the sort of thing we can skip over. If we do, we may not succeed in reaching our goal with as tight a chain of reasoning as I think it requires.

1.7.16.54    So tell me this. We often see wild animals dominated by human beings – that is, not merely the animal's body, but even its spirit is so subjugated that it is enslaved to human will by habit and inclination. Do you think it could somehow happen that a wild animal, however ferocious or strong or cunning, could in turn try to subjugate a human being (even though many wild animals are able to destroy the human body either by sheer force or by a surprise attack)?

EVODIUS: This cannot possibly happen.

1.7.16.55 AUGUSTINE: Right you are! But again, tell me this. It is clear that many wild animals easily surpass human beings in strength and in other physical abilities. What is it in virtue of which a human being is superior, so that he can command many wild animals, yet none of them commands him? Is it not perhaps what we usually call *reason* or *understanding*?

1.7.16.56 EVODIUS: I don't find anything else, since that in virtue of which we are superior to animals is in the mind. If they were inanimate, I would say that we are more excellent than them because we are animate. However, since they *are* animate, something is not present in their souls (and so we tame them) that *is* present in ours, so that we are better than they are. Since it is apparent to anyone that this is neither insignificant nor trivial, what else shall I call it more rightly than "reason"?

1.7.16.57 AUGUSTINE: See how easy it becomes, with God's help, to do what people think is most difficult. I for one admit that I thought this question, which I see has now been settled, was going to hold us back for perhaps as long as all the topics we have covered since our discussion began. Therefore, keep it in mind now, so that our reasoning is airtight hereafter. I think you are aware that what we call "knowing" is nothing other than having in reason what was perceived.

EVODIUS: Yes. 1.7.16.58

AUGUSTINE: Then whoever knows himself to be alive does not lack reason.

EVODIUS: That follows.

AUGUSTINE: Yet wild animals are alive and, as is now plainly obvious, they do not have reason.

EVODIUS: That is clear.

AUGUSTINE: Then look! You now know what you claimed, in your [earlier] reply, you did not know.[9] Not everything alive knows itself to be alive, whereas everything that knows itself to be alive necessarily is alive.

EVODIUS: I no longer have any doubts. Continue where you are heading. 1.7.17.59 I have learned well that *being alive* is one thing, *knowing yourself to be alive* quite another.

AUGUSTINE: So which of the two seems to you to be more excellent?

EVODIUS: What do you think? The knowledge of life.

AUGUSTINE: Does the knowledge of life seem better to you than life itself? Or do you perhaps understand knowledge as a higher and more authentic life? For nobody can know except those who have understanding, which itself is nothing but living a more enlightened and perfect life in accordance with the light of the mind. Unless I am mistaken, you have accordingly not rated anything else above life, but a better life above just any life at all.

EVODIUS: You have grasped and explained my view wonderfully well. 1.7.17.60 As long as knowledge can never be evil, that is.

AUGUSTINE: I think there is no way [for that to be so], unless we stretch the word "knowledge" to cover mere experience. Experience is not always good: for instance, experiencing punishments. But how can "knowledge" in the strict and proper sense be evil, since it is acquired by reason and understanding?

EVODIUS: I grasp the distinction. Keep going.

AUGUSTINE: This is what I want to say. That by which humans are 1.8.18.61 ranked above animals, whatever it is, be it more correctly called "mind" or "spirit" or both – we find both terms in Scripture – if it dominates and commands the rest of what a human consists in, then that human being is completely in order.[10]

---

[9] See 1.7.16.52.
[10] Augustine is addressing the question raised in 1.7.16.52, namely "how a human being may be completely in order within himself."

We recognize that we share many common characteristics not only with animals but with trees and plants too. We see that taking bodily nutrition, growing, reproducing, and flourishing are also attributes of trees, and are contained in a lower level of life. We also note that wild animals are able to see, hear, and sense material objects by smell or taste

1.8.18.62 or touch. We admit that their senses are often sharper than ours. Add to this energy, vigor, strength in arms and legs, the swiftness and agility of bodily movements: In all these qualities we are superior to some animals, equal to others, and even surpassed by some. Nevertheless, qualities of this sort are surely shared by human beings and animals, despite the fact that every action in an animal's life is pursuing physical pleasures and avoiding discomforts.

1.8.18.63     There are other features that seem not to occur among animals but are not the highest attributes in human beings. Take joking and laughing. Anyone judging human nature most rightly holds that these features are indeed human, but the least important part of a human being. Next, there is the love of praise and of glory, and the drive to dominate. Although absent in animals, we should not be thought better than animals because

1.8.18.64 we lust after these things. When the pursuit of these things is not controlled by reason it makes us unhappy, and no one ever thought to rank himself above others on account of unhappiness.

    Thus a human being should be called "in order" when these selfsame impulses of the soul are dominated by reason. For it should not be called the right order, or even "order" at all, when the better are controlled by the worse. Do you not think so?

1.8.18.65 EVODIUS: It is clear.

AUGUSTINE: Therefore, when reason (or mind or spirit) governs irrational mental impulses, a human being is dominated by the very thing whose dominance is prescribed by the law we have found to be eternal.

EVODIUS: I understand and agree.

1.9.19.66 AUGUSTINE: Then a human being who is arranged in order in this way seems to you to be wise, is that not so?

EVODIUS: I do not know who could seem wise if not this person!

AUGUSTINE: I believe you also know that most people are fools.

EVODIUS: That is true enough.

1.9.19.67 AUGUSTINE: Well, if fools are the opposite of the wise, since we have ascertained who is wise, you surely now understand who the fool is too.

16

EVODIUS: Is it not obvious? The fool is someone in whom the mind does not have supreme power.

AUGUSTINE: Then what should we say when people are so afflicted? That they have no mind, or that they do have a mind but it lacks dominance?

EVODIUS: The latter.

AUGUSTINE: I would very much like to hear from you the grounds on which you hold that there *is* a mind in someone when it does not exercise its sovereignty!

EVODIUS: I hope you are willing to do your share as well. It is not easy for me to shoulder the burden.

AUGUSTINE: It should at least be easy for you to recall what we said a    1.9.19.68
bit earlier. Just as wild animals are broken by human beings and then remain tame, so too humans would suffer the same from animals in their turn, as the argument proved, were they not somehow superior to them. Now we did not find this superiority in the body; therefore, since it is apparent that it is in the soul, we found that it should be called "reason." We later remembered that this is also dubbed "mind" and "spirit"; even if reason and mind are not the same, surely only mind can make use of reason, and hence it follows that whatever has reason cannot be without mind.[11]

EVODIUS: I do remember these points and still hold them.    1.9.19.69

AUGUSTINE: Well, do you believe that only the wise can tame animals? (I call "wise" those whom truth bids be so called, namely those who have attained peace by subjugating lust to the mind's full governance.)

EVODIUS: It is silly to regard as wise those people who are commonly called "animal trainers" – or likewise shepherds or cowboys or horsemen, all of whom we see controlling tame animals and working to control untamed animals.

AUGUSTINE: See! You therefore have compelling evidence to make it    1.9.19.70
clear that mind may be present in a human being without being dominant. It is present in these people, for they do things they could not do without mind. Yet it does not govern, for they are fools, and we know quite well that mind's governance is characteristic only of the wise.

EVODIUS: I am astonished that we already reached this conclusion earlier and yet I was not able to think of what to say to you. Well, let us take    1.10.20.70

---

[11] See 1.8.18.61 and 1.8.18.65 for the first point, and 1.9.19.67 for the conclusion.

up other matters, for now we have found out that human wisdom is the governance of the human mind, and also that it might not govern.

I.10.20.71 AUGUSTINE: Do you think that lust is more powerful than the mind itself, which we know has been granted governance over lusts by eternal law? I do not myself think so. The weaker commanding the stronger would not be a case of being completely in order. Accordingly, I think the mind must be more *powerful* than desire for the very reason that it rightly and justly dominates desire.

EVODIUS: I think so too.

I.10.20.72 AUGUSTINE: Well, are we going to hesitate over putting every virtue ahead of every vice, such that virtue is stronger and more unbeatable to the extent that it is better and more exalted?

EVODIUS: Not at all.

AUGUSTINE: Then no vice-ridden mind overcomes a mind equipped with virtue.

EVODIUS: That is completely true.

AUGUSTINE: Now I think you will not deny that any kind of mind at all is better and more powerful than every physical object.

EVODIUS: Nobody denies this who sees, as is easily done, that a living substance is more valuable than a non-living one, and that a substance imparting life is more valuable than one receiving it.

I.10.20.73 AUGUSTINE: Then so much the less does a physical object of any sort overthrow a mind endowed with virtue.

EVODIUS: Most evidently.

AUGUSTINE: Well, can a just mind (*animus*) – a mind (*mens*) safeguarding its proper right and command – cast down from its stronghold and subjugate to lust another mind governing with equal justice and virtue?

EVODIUS: By no means. Not only is there the same degree of superiority in each, but a mind that attempts to do this to another will fall away from justice and become vice-ridden, and thereby will be weaker than the other.

I.10.21.74 AUGUSTINE: You understand quite well. Consequently, it remains for you to declare, if you can, whether you think anything is more excellent than a wise and rational mind.

EVODIUS: Nothing but God, I think.

AUGUSTINE: That is also my view. Yet even though we hold this view with the strongest faith possible, the matter is difficult, and it is not appropriate to look into it now with a view to understanding it; we should

18

complete a careful and diligent treatment of the question at hand. For the    I.II.21.75
time being, we *are* able to know that, whatever the nature may be that is
appropriately superior to a mind powerful in virtue, it cannot be in any
way unjust. Thus even this nature, despite having the power, will not
enslave a mind to lust.

EVODIUS: Surely everyone would unhesitatingly go along with your
argument up to this point.

AUGUSTINE: Therefore, since (*a*) anything equal or superior to a gov-    I.II.21.76
erning mind possessed of virtue does not make it the servant of lust, on
account of justice, and since in addition (*b*) anything inferior to it could
not do this, on account of weakness, as the points we have agreed on
between us establish, we are left with this conclusion: Nothing makes the
mind a devotee of desire but its own will and free choice.

EVODIUS: I see no other conclusion so necessary to draw.

AUGUSTINE: It follows, as you might already think, that such a mind    I.II.22.77
justly pays the penalties for so great a sin.

EVODIUS: I cannot deny it.

AUGUSTINE: Well, then, should we count this as a *light* penalty? Lust
dominates the mind and drags it back and forth, despoiled of the richness
of virtue, poor and needy; at one moment taking falsehoods for truths
and even making a practice of defending them, at another rejecting what
it had previously accepted and nonetheless rushing to other falsehoods;
now withholding its assent and often in dread of clear lines of argument;
now despairing of the whole enterprise of finding the truth, lingering
deep within the shadows of foolishness; now struggling towards the
light of understanding but again falling back from it due to exhaustion.
All the while, that reign of desires savagely tyrannizes and batters a    I.II.22.78
person's whole life and mind with storms raging in all directions. On
this side fear, on that desire; on this side anxiety, on that empty spuri-
ous enjoyment; on this side torment over the loss of something loved,
on that ardor to acquire something not possessed; on this side sorrows
for an injury received, on that the burning to redress it. Whichever way
one turns, greed can pinch, extravagance squander, ambition enslave,
pride puff up, envy twist, laziness overcome, stubbornness provoke,
submissiveness oppress – these and countless others throng the realm of
lust, having the run of it. Can we think that this penalty, which (as you
recognize) all who do not hold fast to wisdom must suffer, is in the end
trivial?

I.11.23.79    EVODIUS: I do judge this penalty to be harsh. But it is completely just if someone currently at the heights of wisdom were to choose to descend from there and to be the slave of lust. However, it is uncertain whether there can be anyone who has willed or who does will to do this. We believe that human beings were so perfectly created by God and established in a happy life that it was only by their own will that they fell from this condition to the afflictions of mortal life.[12] Yet even though I hold this with the firmest faith, I have not yet arrived at an understanding of it. If you think that we should defer a careful investigation into this matter for now, you do so against my will.

I.12.24.80    However, what bothers me the most is why *we*, who are certainly fools and have never been wise, should suffer such bitter penalties. Yet we are said to suffer these things deservedly, for abandoning the stronghold of virtue and choosing to be the slave of lust. Were you to clear this up through careful reasoning, should you be able, I would not allow you to postpone doing so.

I.12.24.81    AUGUSTINE: Up to now, you have talked as though you had plainly found out for certain that we have never been wise, paying attention only to the time since we were born into this life. But since wisdom is in the mind, there is a deep question (and a deep mystery) whether the mind had lived some other kind of life before its partnership with the body, and whether it lived wisely at some point. This question should really be addressed in its proper place.[13] In any event, it does not prevent clarifying

I.12.25.82    as much as possible what we now have on our hands. So tell me: We have a will, do we not?

EVODIUS: I do not know.

AUGUSTINE: Do you not want to know this?

EVODIUS: I do not know this either.

AUGUSTINE: Then from now on ask me no more questions!

EVODIUS: Why not?

AUGUSTINE: Because I am not required to answer your questions unless you are willing to know what you are asking about. Henceforth, unless you want to attain wisdom, I should not discuss these matters with you. Finally, you cannot be my friend unless you want my well-being. Then

---

[12]   The reference is to Adam and Eve in Paradise, and their Fall.
[13]   Augustine returns to the question of the soul's antenatal existence in 3.20.58.198–3.21.59.202, though he never arrives at a settled view.

you, for your part, will see in respect of yourself whether you have no will for the happy life.[14]

EVODIUS: That we have a will cannot be denied, I admit. Go on; let us see what you are going to do with this.  1.12.25.83

AUGUSTINE: I shall do so. But first tell me whether you think you have a good will.

EVODIUS: What is a good will?

AUGUSTINE: A will by which we seek to live rightly and honorably, and to attain the highest wisdom. Now see whether you do not seek a right and honorable life, and whether you do not passionately want to be wise – or at least whether you would venture to deny that we have a good will when we want these things.

EVODIUS: I deny none of these things. Accordingly, I grant not only that I have a will, but also that it is good.  1.12.25.84

AUGUSTINE: How much regard do you have for this will, I ask you? Do you think that riches or honors or bodily pleasures, or all of these together, are to be compared to it in any respect?

EVODIUS: God forbid such horrendous madness!

AUGUSTINE: Should we then not rejoice a little that in the mind we have something – I am speaking of the good will itself – in comparison with which all the things we have mentioned are completely unimportant, things in pursuit of which we see many people spare no efforts or avoid no dangers?  1.12.25.85

EVODIUS: We should rejoice a great deal.

AUGUSTINE: Well, do you think that those who do not feel this rejoicing suffer a slight loss when deprived of so great a good?

EVODIUS: On the contrary, they suffer the greatest loss.

AUGUSTINE: Then I think you see now that it lies in our will to enjoy or to lack such a great and genuine good. For what is so much in the power of the will as the will itself? When anyone has a good will, he surely has something to be put far ahead of all earthly kingdoms and all bodily pleasures. Anyone who does not have a good will certainly lacks the very thing the will alone would provide through itself, something more excellent than all the goods not within our power. Thus while someone will  1.12.26.87

---

[14] In this exchange, "want" and "will" are versions of the same Latin word: *uelle*, "to will" or "to want" or even "to wish (for)" in its verbal form; *uoluntas*, "the will" or "(a) want" or "wish" in its nominal form.

21

judge himself thoroughly unhappy if he has lost his glorious reputation, great wealth, and whatever bodily goods, will you not by contrast judge him to be thoroughly unhappy even if he *has* all such things in abundance? For he holds fast to things that can easily be lost, and he does not have them when he wants to. Furthermore, he lacks a good will, which is not to be compared with these things – and, even though it is so great a good, it is only necessary to will in order to have it.

I.12.26.88    EVODIUS: Quite true.

AUGUSTINE: Then even if foolish people have never been wise – an uncertain and very obscure point[15] – they are rightly and deservedly afflicted with these sorts of miseries.

EVODIUS: I agree.

I.13.27.89    AUGUSTINE: Now consider whether prudence[16] seems to you to be knowledge of things to be pursued and avoided.

EVODIUS: It does.

AUGUSTINE: Well, is bravery not the psychological state by which we attribute little value to all hardships and losses of things that are not within our power?

EVODIUS: So I hold.

AUGUSTINE: What is more, moderateness is the state that checks and restrains the appetite from things it pursues disgracefully. Do you think otherwise?

EVODIUS: Quite the contrary; I think it is as you say.

I.13.27.90    AUGUSTINE: Then what should we say justice is but the virtue by which each receives his due?

EVODIUS: I have no other conception of justice.

AUGUSTINE: Therefore, anyone who has a good will (whose superiority we have been discussing for a long time now) would embrace this one thing[17] as an unsurpassable delight – on the one hand pleasing himself, on the other hand taking complete satisfaction and rejoicing to think of it, judging how great it is and how it cannot be stolen or taken away against

---

[15] Augustine is leaving open the possibility that foolish people were "wise" in the sense that their souls, before birth, were acquainted with wisdom: a clear allusion to the doctrine of Recollection in Plato's *Meno*. See I.12.24.81.

[16] Prudence, bravery, moderateness, and justice are the traditional four cardinal virtues; Augustine takes them up here in order.

[17] "This one thing": the good will. Augustine's initial "therefore" suggests that he is speaking about the virtue of justice, but I.13.27.93 makes it plain that it is the good will here.

his will. Can we have any doubt that he is going to set himself against anything inimical to this one good?

EVODIUS: He must set himself against it completely.

AUGUSTINE: Do we think someone is *not* equipped with prudence if he sees that this good should be pursued and things that are opposed to it should be avoided? 1.13.27.91

EVODIUS: It does not seem to me that anyone can do this without prudence.

AUGUSTINE: Right! But why do we not attribute bravery to this person too? He cannot love or value highly all those things that are not in our power. They are loved by the evil will, which he must resist as inimical to his own most cherished good. But since he does not love them, he is not pained by their loss and holds them as utterly worthless. As we declared and agreed earlier,[18] this is the work of bravery.

EVODIUS: Let us indeed attribute bravery to him. I do not think I could more truly call anyone brave than a person who bears with equanimity the loss of things that it is not in our power to get or keep, which we have found this person necessarily does. 1.13.27.92

AUGUSTINE: Now see whether we can deprive him of moderateness, since this is the virtue that restrains our lusts. What indeed is as harmful to a good will as lust? From this you surely recognize that the person who loves his own good will resists lusts in every way and sets himself against them, and so is rightly called moderate.

EVODIUS: I agree. Go on.

AUGUSTINE: Justice remains. I do not see at all how this person could lack it. Someone who possesses and takes delight in the good will, standing against whatever is inimical to it, as mentioned, cannot have ill-will towards anyone. Therefore, it follows that he would do injury to no one. This can happen only if he gives to each his due – and when I said that this pertains to justice, I think you remember that you agreed. 1.13.27.93

EVODIUS: I do remember, and I agree that all four virtues you sketched a little while ago, with my agreement, are found in anyone who takes delight in his own good will and regards it highly.

AUGUSTINE: Then does anything prevent our granting that his life is praiseworthy? 1.13.28.94

---

[18] See 1.13.27.89.

EVODIUS: Absolutely nothing. Quite the opposite; all these points encourage and even compel us to do so.

AUGUSTINE: Well, is there any way you can avoid judging that the unhappy life should be avoided?

EVODIUS: No. That is exactly what I think should be done.

AUGUSTINE: But surely you do not think that a praiseworthy life should be avoided, do you?

EVODIUS: If nothing else, it should be eagerly pursued.

AUGUSTINE: Therefore, a praiseworthy life is not unhappy.

EVODIUS: That does indeed follow.

AUGUSTINE: Then as far as I can tell, no further difficulty stands in the way of your acknowledging that a life which is not unhappy is happy.

EVODIUS: That is completely clear.

1.13.28.95 AUGUSTINE: Hence we agree that someone is happy when he takes delight in his own good will, and on account of it he attributes little worth to anything else that is called good but can be lost even when the will to retain it remains.

EVODIUS: Of course. That logically follows from the points we granted earlier.

AUGUSTINE: You have understood quite well. But please tell me: Is not taking delight in one's own good will, and valuing it as highly as we described, *itself* the good will?

EVODIUS: That is true.

AUGUSTINE: If we correctly judged that this person [who has and takes delight in his own good will] is happy, is it not correct that anyone having a contrary will is unhappy?

EVODIUS: Quite correct.

1.13.28.96 AUGUSTINE: Therefore, is there any reason for us to hesitate in thinking that even if we have never been wise before, nevertheless it is by our will that we have and deserve either a happy and praiseworthy life, or an unhappy and disgraceful one?

EVODIUS: We have reached this conclusion by certain and undeniable steps.

1.13.29.97 AUGUSTINE: Look at this point as well. I think you recall how we described the good will, namely as that by which we seek to live rightly and honorably.

EVODIUS: Yes, I remember.

AUGUSTINE: Hence if it is precisely by a good will that we embrace and take delight in this will, and put it ahead of all the things that we are unable to retain just by willing to do so, then, as the argument has shown, our mind will possess those very virtues whose possession is the same thing as living rightly and honorably. The upshot is that anyone who wills to live rightly and honorably, if he wills himself to will this instead of transient goods, acquires so great a possession with such ease that having what he willed is nothing other for him than willing it.

EVODIUS: To tell the truth, I can scarcely keep myself from shouting for joy, when such a great and easily acquired good has suddenly sprung up before me! 1.13.29.98

AUGUSTINE: If indeed the joy occasioned by acquiring this good elevates the mind calmly, peacefully, and steadfastly, this is called the happy life. You do not think that living happily is something other than rejoicing in genuine and certain goods, do you?

EVODIUS: No, I agree with you.

AUGUSTINE: Quite right. But do you think there is anyone who does *not* will and decide upon the happy life in all ways? 1.14.30.99

EVODIUS: Who doubts that everyone wills it?

AUGUSTINE: Then *why do they not all attain it*? We had said and agreed that it is by the will that people deserve the happy life, and it is also by the will that they deserve the unhappy life; the end result is that people deserve what they get. But now some sort of contradiction has cropped up, and, unless we look into the matter carefully, it will work to undermine the earlier carefully crafted and solid argument. How does anyone suffer an unhappy life by his will, since absolutely no one wills to live unhappily? That is, how does someone gain the happy life through the will, when everyone wants to be happy and yet so many are unhappy? 1.14.30.100

Does it happen because it is one thing to will in a good or evil manner, another to deserve something due to a good or evil will? Those who are happy (who must also be good) are not happy simply because they willed to live *happily*. Even evil people will this. Instead, it is because they willed to live *rightly*, which evil people are unwilling to do. For this reason, it is no wonder that unhappy people do not attain what they will, namely the happy life. They do not likewise will what goes along with it, namely living rightly, and without willing this no one is worthy of the happy life or attains it. The eternal law – it is now time for us to consider it again – established firmly with unchangeable stability that deserts are 1.14.30.101

in the will, whereas reward and punishment are in happiness and unhap-
1.14.30.102  piness.[19] Thus when we say that people are unhappy due to the will, we
are not thereby saying that they will to be unhappy, but rather that they
are in a condition of will upon which must follow unhappinesses, even
against their will. Accordingly, the fact that all people will to be happy
and yet are not able to be happy does *not* contradict our earlier argument,
because not all will to live rightly; the happy life is due to this one will.
Do you have anything to say against these claims?

1.15.31.103  EVODIUS: Nothing. Instead, let us see now how they are related to the
question at hand about the two kinds of law [temporal and eternal].

AUGUSTINE: Yes, but first tell me this. Does not someone who takes
delight in living rightly – enjoying it so that the life not only is right for
him but also is pleasant and agreeable – does he not, I ask, love and hold
most dear the law by which he sees that the happy life is bestowed upon
the good will, and the unhappy life is bestowed upon the evil will?

EVODIUS: He loves it completely and wholeheartedly, for it is in following the selfsame law that he lives as he does.

1.15.31.104  AUGUSTINE: Well, when he loves the law, does he love something
changeable and temporal, or something stable and everlasting?

EVODIUS: Surely eternal and unchangeable.

AUGUSTINE: What about those who persist in their evil will but nonetheless desire to be happy? Are they able to love the law by which people
such as themselves are deservedly punished by unhappiness?

EVODIUS: Not at all, I think.

AUGUSTINE: They do not love anything else, do they?

EVODIUS: On the contrary, many things – namely the things their evil
will is bent on acquiring or keeping.

1.15.31.105  AUGUSTINE: I think you are talking about riches, honors, pleasures,
physical beauty, and all the other things that they can fail to acquire
despite willing to, and can lose against their will.

EVODIUS: Those are the very things.

AUGUSTINE: Surely you do not think that *these* things are eternal? You
see that they are subject to the vicissitudes of time.

EVODIUS: Who but a madman would hold this?

---

[19] Augustine is perhaps thinking of 1.6.15.48–1.6.15.49, although the view that deserts are in the
will is expressed more clearly in 1.11.21.76–1.11.22.77.

AUGUSTINE: Then since it is clear that some people love eternal things and others temporal things, and since we have agreed that there are two laws, one eternal and the other temporal – if you know anything about fairness, which group do you judge should be subject to the eternal law, and which to temporal law? 1.15.31.106

EVODIUS: I think the answer to your question is obvious. I hold that happy people dwell under the eternal law, due to their love for eternal things, whereas temporal law is imposed on unhappy people.

AUGUSTINE: You are right, provided you hold resolutely what our argument has already established explicitly: People subservient to temporal law cannot be free from the eternal law, from which we said all things that are just, or are justly altered, are derived. You understand well enough that people who hold fast to the eternal law through their good will have no need of temporal law, as is apparent. 1.15.31.107

EVODIUS: Yes.

AUGUSTINE: Hence the eternal law commands us to turn our love aside from temporal things and to turn it, purified, towards eternal things. 1.15.32.108

EVODIUS: It does.

AUGUSTINE: Now when people, through desire, hold fast to things that can be called ours only for a time, do you not think that the temporal law prescribes that they possess them by right – namely the right by which peace and human intercourse are preserved, to the extent they can be preserved in the case of these things?

These things are as follows: (*i*) this body and what are called its goods, such as sound health, keen senses, strength, beauty, and whatever other goods there may be, some of which are necessary for good skills and should therefore be more highly valued, while others should be considered less valuable; (*ii*) freedom, which is genuine only if it belongs to happy people who adhere to the eternal law, but for now I am discussing the "freedom" by which people who have no human masters think of themselves as free and which those who want to be set free by their human masters desire; (*iii*) parents, brothers, a spouse, children, neighbors, relatives, friends, and anyone else bound to us by some close relationship; (*iv*) the state, which typically has the role of a parent; (*v*) honors and praise and what is called "celebrity"; and finally (*vi*) property, under which single name we classify everything we control by right and appear to have the power to sell or give away. 1.15.32.109 1.15.32.110

1.15.32.111   It is difficult and tedious to explain how the law distributes each of these things to those to whom they are due, and plainly it is unnecessary for the task at hand. It is enough to recognize that the power of the temporal law to redress deeds does not extend further than taking these goods (or some of them) away from the one being punished, depriving him of them. Therefore, temporal law restrains through fear. It twists and turns the minds of the people, for whose governance it was designed, to what it wants. As long as people are afraid to lose these goods, they maintain a certain mode of conduct in using them, one appropriate to holding together whatever kind of state can be set up with such people. 1.15.32.112 Retribution for sin is not exacted when they love these goods, but rather when they are taken away from others through dishonesty.

Accordingly, see whether we have now reached the end of what you thought endless, for we meant to investigate how far the law governing earthly societies and states has the right to exact retribution.

EVODIUS: We have.

1.15.33.112   AUGUSTINE: Then you also see that there would be no penalty, whether imposed on human beings through injury or some kind of redress, if they did not love things that can be taken away against their will.

EVODIUS: I see that too.

1.15.33.113   AUGUSTINE: Hence the selfsame things are used in a good manner by one person and in an evil manner by another. The person who uses them in an evil manner holds fast to them with love and is tangled up with them. That is to say, he is controlled by things that he ought to control, and, in setting them up as goods for himself that need to be put in order and treated properly, he holds himself back from the [true] good. However, the person who uses them rightly shows that they are goods, but not his own goods, for they do not make him good or better. Instead, they become good or better due to him. Hence he does not attach himself to them with love. Nor does he make them like the limbs of his mind (which happens through loving them), so that when they start to be cut off again he is not ravaged by pain and corruption. Rather, he is completely above them, possessing and governing them when there is need; he is ready to lose them, and more ready not to have them.

Since this is how things are, then, do you think we should censure silver and gold because of greedy men, food because of gluttons, wine because of drunkards, attractive women because of fornicators and adulterers, and so on? Especially since you recognize that the physician makes good use of fire whereas the poisoner makes evil use of bread!

EVODIUS: You are absolutely right that the things themselves should not be blamed, but rather the people who use them in an evil manner.

AUGUSTINE: Correct. We have now begun to see, I think, the power of eternal law, and to discover how far temporal law can extend in redress. We have also explicitly and adequately distinguished two kinds of things, the eternal and the temporal, and again two kinds of people: some who follow and take delight in eternal things, and others who follow and take delight in temporal things. We have established that what each person elects to pursue and embrace is located in the will, and that the mind is not thrown down from its stronghold of dominance, and from the right order, by anything but the will. It is also clear that when a person uses something in an evil manner, the thing should not be blamed, but rather the person using it in that evil manner. 1.16.34.114

Let us return then, if you please, to the question posed at the beginning of our discussion, and see whether it has been solved.

We set out to investigate what it is to do evil, and everything we have said we said to this end. As a result, we are now ready to turn our attention to consider whether evildoing is anything other than pursuing temporal things and whatever is perceived through the body (the least valuable part of a human being), which can never be fixed, as though they were great and wonderful, having neglected eternal things, which the mind enjoys through itself and perceives through itself and which it cannot lose while loving them. For all evildoings – that is to say, all sins – seem to me to be included under this one heading. But I am waiting to know what you think. 1.16.34.115

EVODIUS: It is as you say. I agree that all sins are contained under this one heading, when someone turns aside from divine and genuinely abiding things and towards changeable and uncertain things. Although the latter are rightly located in their proper place and attain a certain beauty of their own, it is the mark of a twisted and disordered mind to be subject to pursuing those things he was set above, to be in charge of as he might so command, in accordance with divine order and right. 1.16.35.116

I also see that we have simultaneously resolved and answered what we planned to look into after the question what it is to do evil, namely why 1.16.35.117

we do evil.[20] Unless I am mistaken, we do it out of free choice of the will, as the argument we dealt with here has established.

However, I ask whether free choice itself, through which we are found guilty of having the ability to commit sin, ought to have been given to us by Him who made us.[21] It seems that, if we lack it, we would not be bound to sin. My fear is that in this way God will also be reckoned as author of our evildoings.

1.16.35.118  AUGUSTINE: Do not worry on that score. But we shall have to find another time to look into this again more carefully, for our current discussion should now conclude. I would like you to believe that in this discussion we have, so to speak, been knocking at the door of profound and abstruse matters that need to be explored. Once we begin to enter into their inner recesses, with God's help, you surely will judge how much distance there is between this discussion and those to follow, and how much the latter surpass the former, not only in the sagacity of the investigation but also in the grandeur of the issues and the most resplendent light of the truth. May there be enough religiousness in us that divine providence allows us to hold to and complete the course we have plotted!

EVODIUS: I bow to your will, and quite freely join mine to it in judgment and in prayer.

# Book 2

2.1.1.1  EVODIUS: Now if possible, explain to me *why* God gave human beings free choice of the will. If we had not received it, we surely would not be able to sin.

AUGUSTINE: Do you already know for sure that God gave us something which you think we should not have been given?

EVODIUS: As far as I seemed to understand matters in Book 1, we have free choice of the will, and we sin through it alone.

AUGUSTINE: I too remember that this was made evident to us then. But I have just asked you whether you know that God clearly gave us what we have and through which we sin.

2.1.1.2  EVODIUS: No one else, I think. We have our existence from God; whether we sin or act rightly, we deserve penalty or reward from Him.

---

[20] See 1.3.5.14: "You are really asking *why* it is we do evil." This is the main question of Book 1.
[21] This is the main question of Book 2: see 2.1.1.1.

AUGUSTINE: I would also like to know whether you know this unequivocally, or you are induced by authority to believe it readily, even though you do not know it.

EVODIUS: I grant that at first I believed this on authority. But what is more true than that every good is from God, that everything just is good, that a penalty for sinners and a reward for those acting rightly is just? From this it follows that it is God who bestows unhappiness on sinners and happiness on those acting rightly.

AUGUSTINE: I do not disagree, but I am asking about the *other* point, 2.1.2.3
namely: How do you know that we have our existence from God? You did not explain this now. Instead, you explained that we deserve penalty or reward from God.

EVODIUS: The answer to this question also seems to be clear, precisely on the grounds that God redresses sins – at least, if all justice comes from Him; for while conferring benefits on strangers is a sign of someone's goodness, redressing [the wrongdoings] of strangers is not thereby a sign of someone's justice. Accordingly, it is clear that we belong to God, since 2.1.2.4
He is not only most generous to us in His excellence, but also is most just in redressing [wrongdoing]. In addition, I proposed and you granted that everything good is from God; human beings can also be understood to be from God on this score. For a human being *qua* human being is something good, since he can live rightly when he wills to.

AUGUSTINE: Obviously, if these things are so, the question you raised[22] 2.1.3.5
has been solved, [as follows].

[1]  If a person is something good and could act rightly only because he willed to, then he ought to have free will, without which he could not act rightly. We should not believe that, because a person also sins through it, God gave it to him for this purpose. The fact that a person cannot live rightly without it is therefore a sufficient reason why it should have been given to him.

[2]  Free will can also be understood to be given for this reason: If anyone uses it in order to sin, the divinity redresses him [for it]. This would 2.1.3.6
happen unjustly if free will had been given not only for living rightly but also for sinning. How would God justly redress someone who made use of his will for the purpose for which it was given? Now,

---

[22]  See 2.1.1.1.

however, when God punishes the sinner, what does He seem to be saying but: "Why did you not make use of free will for the purpose for which I gave it to you?" – that is, for acting rightly.

2.1.3.7 [3] If human beings lacked free choice of the will, how could there be the good in accordance with which justice itself is praised in condemning sins and honoring right deeds? For what does not come about through the will would neither be sinning nor acting rightly. Consequently, penalty and reward would be unjust if human beings did not have free will. There ought to be justice in punishment and in reward, since justice is one of the goods that are from God.

Hence God ought to have given free will to human beings.

2.2.4.8 EVODIUS: I grant that God gave it. But I ask you: If free will was given for acting rightly, does it not seem that it should be unable to be turned towards sinning, as justice itself was given to people for living correctly? Who in the world can live in an evil manner through justice? Likewise, no one could sin through the will if the will was given for acting rightly.

2.2.4.9 AUGUSTINE: God will enable me to answer you, I hope. Or rather, He will enable you to answer yourself, when the greatest teacher of all, truth itself, instructs you from within.[23] But if you hold that God gave us free will – which I had asked you about – as something that is known for certain, I want you to tell me briefly whether we should say that God ought not to have given what we acknowledge he gave.

2.2.4.10 [1] Now if it is *uncertain* whether God gave it, we rightly ask whether it was well given. Then if we find that (*a*) it was well given, we also find that it was given by Him from whom all goods are given to the soul; or if we find that (*b*) it was not well given, then we realize it was not given by Him Whom it is blasphemous to blame.

[2] On the other hand, if it is *certain* that God gave it, then, no matter how it was given, we must recognize that it should neither (*a*) not have been given, nor (*b*) have been given otherwise than it was given. For it was given by Him Whose deed cannot be faulted in any way.

2.2.5.11 EVODIUS: While I hold this with resolute faith, I do not yet hold it with knowledge. So let us examine it as though all these points were uncertain.

---

[23] See *The Teacher* 14.45, where Augustine puts forward his view that knowledge is inner illumination. He identifies the recognition of truth with Christ as the Teacher, Who is Truth.

From the uncertainty whether free will was given for acting rightly, on the grounds that we can also sin through it, I see that it also becomes uncertain whether He ought to have given it. For if it is uncertain whether [2.2.5.12] it was given for acting rightly, it is also uncertain whether it ought to have been given. Consequently it will also be uncertain whether God gave it. For if it is uncertain whether it ought to have been given, it is uncertain whether it was given by Him Whom it is blasphemous to believe gave something that ought not to have been given.

AUGUSTINE: You are certain that God exists, at least.

EVODIUS: I hold this resolutely, too, but by believing it rather than by having a theoretical grasp of it.

AUGUSTINE: Then suppose one of those fools of whom it is written: [2.2.5.13] "The fool has said in his heart: There is no God" [Ps. 13:1 (14:1 RSV), 52:1 (53:1 RSV)] were to say this to you, and further that he did not want to join you in merely believing what you believe, but instead wanted to know whether what you believe is true. You would not turn your back on him, would you? Would you not think he should somehow be *convinced* of what you hold resolutely, especially if he eagerly wanted to know it rather than to persist in quarreling with you?

EVODIUS: Your last remark suggests to me exactly what answer I should [2.2.5.14] give him. Even if he were quite unreasonable, he would surely admit that one should not discuss anything at all with an insincere and truculent person, in particular not such an important topic. After this initial admission, he would press me to believe that he is raising the question in the right spirit, and not hiding any insincerity or truculence in himself that pertains to this undertaking. I would then point out – something that I [2.2.5.15] think is quite easy for anyone to do – that, since he wants another person to believe him about things that he admits are hidden in his own mind, when the other person does not know these things, it would be much more reasonable for him also to believe that God exists, from the books written by the great men who left behind their written testimony that they lived with the Son of God – for (*a*) they wrote that they saw things that could not have happened if [Jesus] were not God, and (*b*) he would be quite the fool himself if he were to find fault with me for believing these men, since he wants me to believe *him*. But then, since he could not rightly find fault with me, he would find no reason why he also should be unwilling to follow my example.

2.2.5.16 AUGUSTINE: If you hold that it is sufficient for determining whether God exists that we judge with care that such great men are to be believed, then tell me *why* you think we do not likewise believe the authority of these selfsame men regarding the other matters we have set out to explore, as though they were uncertain and plainly not known,[24] so that we labor no more in investigating them?

EVODIUS: Well, we want to know and understand what we believe.

2.2.6.17 AUGUSTINE: You remember aright. We cannot deny what we held even at the very beginning of Book 1: Believing is one thing, understanding another; we should first believe the great and divine matter that we desire to understand.[25] Otherwise, the prophet's words, "Unless you believe

2.2.6.18 you shall not understand" [Is. 7:9], would be in vain. Our Lord Himself also encouraged belief in those whom He called to salvation with both His words and His deeds. But afterwards, when speaking about the gift He was going to give to those who believe, He did not say "This is life eternal, that they might *believe*..." but rather: "This is life eternal, that they might *know* you, the true God, and Jesus Christ, the one whom You have sent" [Jn. 17:3]. Then He said to those who already believed "Seek, and you shall find" [Mt. 7:7]. For something that is believed but not known cannot be said to be 'found.' Nor is anyone made suitable for the task of finding God unless he first believes what he will later know.

2.2.6.19 Consequently, let us obey the Lord's precepts in pressing our inquiry. What we seek with His encouragement we shall find when He Himself shows it to us – at least insofar as these things *can* be found in this life by people such as ourselves. For we must believe that better people – even some who dwell in this world, and certainly all good religious people in the afterlife – grasp and recognize these things more evidently and completely. We must hope that we are going to be so, desiring and taking delight in such things, disdaining worldly and human things completely.

2.3.7.20 Let us pursue our inquiry in this order, if you agree:

[1] How is it clear that God exists?
[2] Do all things, insofar as they are good, come from God?
[3] Is free will to be counted among these goods?

Once we have answers to [1]–[3], I think it will be quite apparent whether free will was given to humans rightly.

---

[24] See 2.2.5.11.  [25] See 1.2.4.11–1.2.5.13.

So, to start off with what is clearest, I ask first whether you yourself exist. Are you perhaps afraid that you might be deceived in this line of questioning? Surely if you did not exist, you could not be deceived at all.

EVODIUS: Go on.

AUGUSTINE: Therefore, since it is clear that you exist, and it would not 2.3.7.21 be clear to you unless you were alive, this too is clear: You are alive. Do you understand that these two points are absolutely true?

EVODIUS: Yes indeed.

AUGUSTINE: Then this third point is also clear, namely: You understand.

EVODIUS: Clearly.

AUGUSTINE: Which of these three do you think is superior?

EVODIUS: Understanding.

AUGUSTINE: Why do you think so?

EVODIUS: Because existing, living, and understanding are three [dis- 2.3.7.22 tinct] things. A stone exists and an animal is alive, yet I do not think a stone is alive or an animal understands. However, it is quite certain that one who understands both exists and is alive.[26] Accordingly, I have no hesitation in judging superior that in which all three features are present rather than that in which even one is missing. For anything alive surely 2.3.7.23 exists too, but it does not follow that it also understands. This is the sort of life an animal has, I think. Furthermore, from the fact that something exists it does not follow that it is alive and understands. I can grant that corpses exist, but nobody would say that they are alive! And what is not now alive understands so much the less.

AUGUSTINE: Hence we hold that a corpse lacks two of the three, an 2.3.7.24 animal one, and a human being none.

EVODIUS: Yes.

AUGUSTINE: We also hold that the most excellent feature among these three is what human beings have in addition to the other two: under- standing. For it follows that someone having understanding also is alive and exists.

EVODIUS: Yes indeed.

AUGUSTINE: Now tell me whether you know yourself to have the ordi- 2.3.8.25 nary bodily senses: sight, hearing, smell, taste, and touch.

EVODIUS: I know that.

---

[26] See 1.7.17.59, where Evodius explains why the knowledge of life ranks higher than life as such.

AUGUSTINE: What do you think pertains to the sense of sight? That is, what do you think we sense by seeing?

EVODIUS: Any physical object.

AUGUSTINE: Do we also sense hard and soft by seeing?

EVODIUS: No.

AUGUSTINE: Then what pertains strictly to the eyes, which we sense through them?

EVODIUS: Color.

AUGUSTINE: What pertains to the ears?

EVODIUS: Sound.

AUGUSTINE: To smell?

EVODIUS: Odor.

AUGUSTINE: Taste?

EVODIUS: Flavor.

AUGUSTINE: Touch?

EVODIUS: Hard and soft, rough and smooth, and lots of such things.

AUGUSTINE: Well, do we not sense the shapes of physical objects – large or small, round or square, and the like – by touching *and* by seeing? Hence they cannot be assigned strictly either to sight or to touch, but rather to both.

EVODIUS: I understand.

2.3.8.26 AUGUSTINE: Then do you understand that while individual senses have proper objects on which they report, some [also] have common objects?

EVODIUS: Yes.

AUGUSTINE: Can we settle what pertains to each sense by means of any of these senses? Or what they all have in common with one another, or some of them?

EVODIUS: Not at all. These matters are settled by something internal.

AUGUSTINE: This is not by any chance reason itself, which animals lack, is it? For I think it is by reason we grasp these things and know that they are so.

2.3.8.27 EVODIUS: I think instead that by reason we grasp that there is an "internal sense" to which the familiar five senses convey everything. Surely that by which an animal sees is one thing, whereas that by which it pursues or avoids what it senses by seeing is another. The former sense is in the eyes, the latter within the soul itself. By it, animals either pursue and take up as enjoyable, or avoid and reject as offensive, not only what they

2.3.8.28 see but also what they hear or grasp by the other bodily senses. Now this [internal sense] cannot be called sight, hearing, smell, taste, or touch, but something else, whatever it may be, that presides over them all in common. We do grasp it with reason, as I pointed out, but I cannot call it reason itself, since it is clearly present in animals.

AUGUSTINE: I recognize it, whatever it is, and I do not hesitate to name it the 'internal sense.' Yet unless what the bodily senses convey goes beyond it, we cannot arrive at knowledge. We hold anything that we know as something grasped by reason. But we *know* that colors cannot be sensed by hearing, nor spoken words by sight, to say nothing of the others. Although we know this, we do not know it by the eyes, nor the ears, nor by the internal sense which animals also have. Nor should we believe that they know that light is not sensed by the ears nor an utterance by the eyes, since we single these things out only by rational attention and thought. 2.3.9.29

2.3.9.30

EVODIUS: I cannot say that I quite get the general idea. What if animals also settle this question – that they cannot sense colors by hearing nor spoken words by sight – through the internal sense, which you admit they also have? 2.3.9.31

AUGUSTINE: Do you also think they can single out from one another (1) the color that is sensed; (2) the sense in the eye; (3) the internal sense in the soul; (4) reason, by which each of these is defined and enumerated?

EVODIUS: Of course not.

AUGUSTINE: Well, could reason single (1)–(4) out from one another and explicate them with definitions unless color were conveyed to it through the sense in the eyes, and this [sense] again through the internal sense that presides over it, and the selfsame internal sense through itself – at least if nothing else intervenes? 2.3.9.32

EVODIUS: I do not see how it could do so otherwise.

AUGUSTINE: Well, do you see that color is sensed by the sense in the eyes, whereas the selfsame sense is not sensed by the same sense? That is, you do not also see seeing itself by the same sense by which you see color. 2.3.9.33

EVODIUS: Absolutely not.

AUGUSTINE: Try to settle these points too. I believe you do not deny that the following differ: (*a*) color; (*b*) seeing color; (*c*) having the sense by which color could be seen if present, even when color is not present.

EVODIUS: I too distinguish (*a*)–(*c*), and I grant that they differ from one another.

2.3.9.34 AUGUSTINE: With regard to (*a*)–(*c*), do you see anything with your eyes other than color, that is, (*a*)?

EVODIUS: Nothing else.

AUGUSTINE: Then tell me: How do you see (*b*)–(*c*)? You could not single them out unless they were seen.

EVODIUS: I have no idea. I know that they are, nothing more.

AUGUSTINE: Then you do not know whether it is reason itself, or the life we call the 'internal sense' superior to the bodily senses, or something else?

EVODIUS: No.

2.3.9.35 AUGUSTINE: Yet you do know that it is not possible to *define* these things except by reason. And reason can do this only in the case of things presented to it for examination.

EVODIUS: Certainly.

AUGUSTINE: Hence the whatever-it-is by which we can sense everything we know is an *agent* of reason. It presents and reports to reason anything with which it comes into contact. As a result, the things sensed can be singled out within their limits and grasped not only through sensing but also through knowing.

EVODIUS: Yes.

2.3.9.36 AUGUSTINE: Reason itself singles its agents out from the things they deliver. Again, it recognizes the difference between these things and itself, and it confirms that it is more powerful than they are. Surely reason does not grasp itself by anything other than itself (*i.e.* by reason), does it? How would you know that you had reason unless you perceived it by reason?

EVODIUS: Quite true.

2.3.9.37 AUGUSTINE: Thus when we sense a color, we do not likewise also sense our sensing by the selfsame sense.[27] When we hear a sound we do not also hear our hearing it. When we smell a rose something is fragrant for us, but it is not our smelling. In tasting anything, the taste itself does not have a flavor in our mouth. In touching something we cannot also touch the very sense of touch. In short, it is clear that none of the five senses can be sensed by any of them, even though all physical objects are sensed by them.

EVODIUS: That is clear.

---

[27] See 2.3.9.33.

AUGUSTINE: I think this point is also clear: The internal sense not only 2.4.10.38
senses the things it receives from the five bodily senses, but also senses
*that* they are sensed by it. Animals would not move themselves to either
pursue or avoid something unless they sensed themselves sensing – not
for the sake of knowledge, for this belongs to reason, but only for the sake
of movement – and they surely do not sense this by any of the five bodily
senses.

If this is still obscure, it may shed some light to consider what is suf- 2.4.10.39
ficient in the case of a single sense, for instance sight. An animal could
not even open its eyes or turn its gaze to what it wants to see unless
it sensed that it did *not* see [the object] when its eyes were closed, or
not turned in that direction. But if the animal senses that it does not
see when it does not see, it must also sense that it sees when it *does*
see: When it sees, it does not turn the eyes with the desire with which
it turns them when it does not see. This shows that the animal senses
itself sensing in each case.

Now it is not clear whether this life, a life that senses itself sensing 2.4.10.40
corporeal things, senses *itself*, unless it is for the following reason.
Anyone putting the question to himself realizes that every living thing
avoids death. Since death is contrary to life, life must also sense itself, for
it avoids its contrary.

But if this is still not apparent, disregard it, so that we may press on to 2.4.10.41
what we want solely on clear and certain grounds. The following points
are clear: (*a*) physical objects are sensed by bodily sense; (*b*) the same
sense cannot be sensed by the selfsame sense; (*c*) physical objects are
sensed by the internal sense through bodily sense, as well as bodily sense
itself; (*d*) reason acquaints us with all the foregoing, as well as with reason itself, and knowledge includes them. Do you not think so?
EVODIUS: I do indeed.
AUGUSTINE: Very well. Now tell me the state of the question. We have
been trudging along the road for a long time, wanting to arrive at its
solution.
EVODIUS: As far as I remember, we are now discussing the first of 2.5.11.42
the three questions we put forward a little while ago to structure the
discussion,[28] namely, how can it be made clear that God exists? (Even
though this should be *believed* most firmly and strongly.)

[28] See 2.3.7.20.

AUGUSTINE: You recall this correctly. But I also want you to recall the following with some care. When I asked you whether you knew yourself to exist, it was apparent to us that you knew not only this but also two other things.[29]

EVODIUS: I recall that too.

2.5.11.43 AUGUSTINE: Then look now: To which of the three, do you think, belongs everything that the bodily senses come into contact with? That is, under what heading do you think we should classify whatever our senses come into contact with through the eyes or any other bodily organ – (a) what merely exists; (b) what is also alive; (c) what also understands?

EVODIUS: Under (a).

AUGUSTINE: Well, under which of (a)–(c) do you think sense falls?

EVODIUS: Under (b).

AUGUSTINE: Then which of these two do you judge to be better: sense itself, or what sense comes into contact with?

EVODIUS: Sense, of course.

AUGUSTINE: Why?

EVODIUS: Because what is also alive is better than what merely exists.

2.5.12.44 AUGUSTINE: Well, what about the internal sense? We found earlier that it is lower than reason, though common to human beings and animals. You will not hesitate to rank the internal sense above the [external] senses – through which we come into contact with physical objects, and which you just declared should be ranked above physical objects themselves – will you?

EVODIUS: Absolutely not.

2.5.12.45 AUGUSTINE: I want to hear you explain *why* you do not hesitate. You cannot say that the internal sense should be classified under (c), but rather along with what exists and is alive, though it lacks understanding. The internal sense is also present in animals, where understanding is not present. Since this is so, I am asking why you rank the internal sense above the senses by which physical objects are sensed, for each falls 2.5.12.46 under (b). You ranked the senses, which come into contact with physical objects, above physical objects, because the latter fall under (a) and the former under (b). Since the internal sense is also found in (b), tell me why you think it better. If you say because the one senses the other, I do not believe you are going to find a rule by which we can trust that whatever

29 See 2.3.7.21.

senses is better than what it senses. Otherwise, we might be forced to say on this basis that whatever understands is better than what it understands, and this is false, since a human being understands wisdom and is not better than wisdom itself. Accordingly, see why it seems to you that the internal sense is superior to the sense by which we sense physical objects. 2.5.12.47

EVODIUS: Because I know that the internal sense controls and judges the bodily senses. If the latter miss anything while carrying out their job, the internal sense demands what its agent owes it (so to speak), as we argued it through a little while ago.[30] The sense in the eyes does not see that it sees or does not see – and since it does not, it cannot judge what is missing or what is enough – but rather the internal sense does, which prompts even an animal's soul to open its closed eyes or to fill in what it senses is missing. But nobody doubts that what judges is better than what it judges. 2.5.12.48

AUGUSTINE: Then do you also recognize that the bodily senses somehow judge physical objects? Pleasure and pain pertain to the bodily senses, namely when the bodily senses come gently or roughly into contact with a physical object. Just as the internal sense judges what is missing or what is enough for the sense in the eyes, so too the sense in the eyes itself judges what is missing or what is enough in the case of colors. Again, just as the internal sense judges whether our hearing is attentive enough, so too hearing itself judges which spoken words gently flow in or roughly grate [on our ears]. There is no need to run through the other bodily senses. I think you anticipate what I want to claim: Just as the internal sense judges the bodily senses when it approves their completeness or demands what is lacking, likewise the bodily senses themselves judge physical objects, taking in from them their 'gentle touch' and rejecting the opposite. 2.5.12.49 2.5.12.50

EVODIUS: I understand quite well, and I agree that these claims are entirely true.

AUGUSTINE: Consider now whether reason also judges the internal sense. I am not asking whether you have any doubt that reason is *better* than the internal sense. I am sure you hold that it is. In fact, I do not think we need even to raise the question whether reason judges the internal sense. Surely in the case of things lower than reason – physical 2.6.13.51

---

[30] See 2.4.10.39–2.4.10.41.

objects, the bodily senses, the internal sense – what else but reason itself, in the end, declares how one is better than another, and how much more excellent reason itself is than the rest? Yet reason could only do this if it were to judge them.

EVODIUS: That is clear.

2.6.13.52 AUGUSTINE: Therefore, a nature that only exists and neither lives nor understands, such as an inanimate physical object, is inferior to a nature that not only exists but also lives, but does not understand, such as the soul of animals. This nature is in turn inferior to one that at once exists and lives and understands, such as the rational mind in human beings. Do you think you can find anything in us, that is, find anything among the features that complete our nature as human beings, that is more excellent 2.6.13.53 than understanding?[31] It is clear that we have a body, as well as some sort of life that animates and enlivens the body. We also recognize these two features in animals. There is a third feature, something like the 'head' or 'eye' of our soul – or whatever term is more suitable for reason and intelligence – which animal nature does not have. So please see whether you can find anything more exalted in human nature than reason.

EVODIUS: I see absolutely nothing better.

2.6.14.54 AUGUSTINE: Well, suppose we were able to find something that you had no doubt not only exists but also is more excellent than our reason. Would you hesitate to say that *this*, whatever it is, is God?

EVODIUS: Even if I could find something better than what is best in my nature, I would not immediately say it was God. I do not call 'God' that to which my reason is inferior, but that to which none is superior.

2.6.14.55 AUGUSTINE: Plainly so, since He gave your reason the ability to think about Him so accurately and religiously. But I ask you: If you find nothing above our reason except what is eternal and unchangeable, will you hesitate to say that *this* is God? For you know that physical objects are changeable; it is clear that the life by which a body is animated is itself changeable through various states; and reason is surely proved to be itself changeable when at one time it strives to reach the truth and at another it does not, and at one time it reaches truth and at another it fails.

2.6.14.56 Suppose that reason sees something eternal and unchangeable through itself, without recourse to any bodily organ – not through touch, taste, or smell; not through the ears or the eyes, nor through any sense inferior

---

[31] Literally: "than what we have listed third among these three [features]?"

to itself. Reason must then admit itself to be inferior, and the eternal and unchangeable being [that it sees] to be its God.

EVODIUS: I will plainly admit that this being, to which we agree none is superior, is God.

AUGUSTINE: Very well. It will be sufficient for me to show that there is   2.6.14.57
something of this sort that you will admit is God – or, if there is something higher, you grant that *it* is God. Accordingly, whether there is something higher or not, it will be clear that God exists when, with His help, I show as promised that He is higher than reason.

EVODIUS: Then prove it! Make good on your promise.

AUGUSTINE: I shall. First, I ask whether my bodily senses are the same   2.7.15.58
as yours, or whether mine are mine alone and yours are yours alone. Of course, if this were not the case, I could not see anything through my eyes that you would not also see.

EVODIUS: I fully agree that, despite being of the same kind, we each have   2.7.15.59
our own sense of seeing, hearing, and so on. This is why: One person can not only see but also hear what someone else does not hear. In fact, anyone can sense something with any sense that another person does not sense. Accordingly, it is clear that your senses are yours alone and mine are mine alone.

AUGUSTINE: Will you give the same answer in the case of the internal   2.7.15.60
sense?

EVODIUS: Exactly the same. Surely mine senses my senses and yours senses yours. This is why I am often asked by someone who sees something whether I see it too. I am the one who senses that I see or do not see, not the person who asks.

AUGUSTINE: What about reason? Each person has his own, does he   2.7.15.61
not? Sometimes it happens that I understand something when you do not understand it, and you are not able to know whether I understand, whereas I do know.

EVODIUS: It is clear that each person has his own rational mind.

AUGUSTINE: Can you also say that we each have our own Suns that we   2.7.16.62
see, or Moons, or morning stars, and so on, even though each person sees these things with his own individual sense [of sight]?

EVODIUS: I would not say anything of the sort.

AUGUSTINE: Therefore, many of us can see one thing simultaneously,   2.7.16.63
even though each of us has his own senses with which we each sense the single thing that we see simultaneously. The upshot is that, although one

sense is mine and the other is yours, it can happen that what we see is not one thing as mine and another as yours, but instead a single thing in front of each of us, seen simultaneously by each of us.

EVODIUS: Quite clearly.

2.7.16.64 AUGUSTINE: We can also hear one spoken word simultaneously. Although my hearing is different from yours, the word we hear simultaneously does not differ as mine and as yours. Nor does my hearing take one part of it and yours another. Instead, whatever sound it makes is present simultaneously to both of us as a single whole to be heard.

EVODIUS: That is clear too.

2.7.17.65 AUGUSTINE: Note that what we have said about the eyes and the ears
2.7.17.66 does not fit the rest of the bodily senses exactly. Yet it is not completely off the mark, either. You and I can breathe one air and sense its state by odor. Again, we can both taste one honey, or any other kind of food or drink, and sense its state by flavor – even though the former is one, whereas we each have our own senses, you yours and me mine. Yet we sense one odor or one flavor in each case. You do not sense it with my sense, nor I with yours, nor with any sense which can be ours in common. Instead, my sense is mine completely and yours is yours, even if each senses the same odor or flavor. On this score, then, we find that the senses [of smell and taste] have something in common with the senses in the case of see-
2.7.17.67 ing and hearing. However, insofar as they are relevant to the point now at issue, they differ. For, although we breathe one air and take one food to taste, I nevertheless do not breathe the same part of the air as you, nor do I take the same part of the food as you. I have my part; you have yours. Hence when I breathe, I inhale a part of the whole air that is enough for
2.7.17.68 me, and you likewise inhale a different part that is enough for you. And although we eat one food as a whole, nevertheless the whole cannot be eaten by me and the whole by you, the way I hear a word as a whole and you do too simultaneously, or the way I see some appearance and you see it as much as I do simultaneously. Instead, some part of the food or drink must go to me and another to you. You understand these matters a little, do you not?

EVODIUS: Indeed, I agree that it is remarkably clear and certain.

2.7.18.69 AUGUSTINE: You do not hold that the sense of touch should be compared to the senses associated with the eyes and the ears on the point now at issue, do you? Through the sense of touch not only can we both sense a single physical object, but you can even touch the same part I have touched. As a result, by touch we can both sense not only the same physical object but also the same *part* of it. This is not like the case of food, where we both eat it but we cannot each take it as a whole. In the case of touch, you can touch one and the same whole that I touched. We both touch it: Each person touches it, not in individual parts, but as a whole.

EVODIUS: The sense of touch is quite similar to the first two senses[32] on this score, I admit. But I see that they differ in the following respect. We can both see and hear one whole thing simultaneously, that is, at a single moment, whereas both of us can touch some whole thing at a single moment, but distinct parts of it. We can only touch the same part at different times: I can touch any part you touch, but only when you are no longer touching it.

AUGUSTINE: An acute reply! But note this point as well. Among the things we sense, some we both sense, and others we sense individually. However, we sense our own senses themselves individually, so that I do not sense your sense nor you mine. Now among the things we sense through the bodily senses (*i.e.* among physical objects), what is there that we can sense only individually, not both together? Only what becomes our own in such a way that we change and transform it into ourselves. Food and drink, for instance: You cannot taste any part that I have tast-ed.[33] Even if nurses give babies food that has already been chewed, any food the nurses have taken that they first taste and then have transformed into [their own] by digestion cannot in any way be called back to use in feeding the baby. When the palate tastes something pleasing, no matter how small, it claims part of it for itself as something that cannot be called back, forcing it to become suited to the body's nature. If this were not so, no flavor would remain behind in the mouth once the food had been chewed and then spat out.

The same point holds for the parts of the air that we breathe. Even if you can inhale some of the air I have exhaled, you still cannot inhale that which has gone to nourish me, since that cannot be exhaled. Physicians teach that we take nourishment even with the nose. I am the only one who can sense the nourishment while breathing, and I cannot exhale it for you to inhale and sense with your nose.

2.7.18.70

2.7.18.71

2.7.19.72

2.7.19.73

2.7.19.74

2.7.19.75

---

[32]  Seeing and hearing, discussed in 2.7.16.63–2.7.16.64.
[33]  "Tasted": *percipio*, here straddling the words "to take" (*capio*) and "to perceive" (*percipio*).

2.7.19.76     There are other sensible items that we sense without destroying them in the process of changing them into our body. These are things we can both sense, whether at one time or at different times in turn, where you also sense the whole or the part that I sense. Such are light, sound, and physical objects with which we come into contact but which we do not damage.

EVODIUS: I understand.

2.7.19.77    AUGUSTINE: Therefore, it is clear that things we sense with our bodily senses but do not transform (*a*) do not pertain to the nature of our senses, and so (*b*) are the more common to us, since they are not changed and converted into our own "private property" (so to speak).

EVODIUS: I agree completely.

2.7.19.78    AUGUSTINE: You should understand "private property" as whatever is each person's own, which he alone senses in himself, because it pertains strictly to his own nature, and "common public property" as what is sensed by all who sense it without destroying or transforming it.

EVODIUS: Yes.

2.8.20.79    AUGUSTINE: Very well. Pay attention now. Tell me: Do we find anything that all reasoning beings, each one using his own reason or mind, see in common? That is, something that is present to all, but is not changed into the [private] use of those to whom it is present, the way food and drink are; instead, it remains incorrupt and intact whether they see it or not. Perhaps, though, you think that there is nothing of the sort.

2.8.20.80    EVODIUS: On the contrary, I see that there are many! It is enough to mention just one: The intelligible structure[34] and truth of number is present to all reasoning beings. Everyone who calculates tries to apprehend it with his own reason and intelligence. Some do this with ease; others, with difficulty. Yet it offers itself equally to all who are capable of grasping it. It is not changed and converted into its perceiver when anyone perceives it, the way food is. Nor is there a flaw in it when anyone makes a mistake; it remains true and intact while the person is all the more in error the less he sees it.

2.8.21.81    AUGUSTINE: Quite right. I see that you quickly found an answer, as befits one experienced in these matters. Yet suppose someone were to object that numbers are stamped on our mind not from some nature of theirs,

---

[34] "Intelligible structure": *ratio*. Note that the term has a clear connection with the psychological faculty of reason, even though the Greek term of which it is the equivalent, λογός, has no such overtones.

46

but instead from the physical objects we come into contact with through bodily sense, as though they were some sort of "images" of visible things. What reply would you make? Or do you agree with the objection?

EVODIUS: I don't think so at all. Even supposing I *had* perceived num- 2.8.21.82 bers through the bodily senses, that would not then enable me to perceive the intelligible structure of numerical addition or subtraction through the bodily senses. Rather, it is by the light of the mind that I prove that someone who makes a mistake in adding or subtracting is wrong. I do not know how long anything I touch with the bodily senses will last, for example when I sense the Earth or the sky or any physical objects in them. But seven and three are ten not only at the moment, but always; it 2.8.21.83 never was and never will be the case that seven and three are not ten. I therefore declared that this incorruptible numerical truth is common to me and to any reasoning being.

AUGUSTINE: I am not opposed to your reply, which is completely true 2.8.22.84 and certain. But you will easily see that numbers have not been drawn in through the bodily senses if you realize that any given number is so called from how many times it includes *one*. For instance, if it includes *one* twice it is called "two" and if three times "three"; if it includes *one* ten times then it is called "ten." Any given number whatsoever derives its name and is so called from as many times as it includes *one*.

Furthermore, anyone who thinks accurately surely realizes that *one* 2.8.22.85 cannot be sensed with the bodily senses. Anything such a sense comes into contact with is shown to be *many* rather than *one*, [as follows]: It is a physical object, and hence has innumerable parts; but – not to go over every tiny and hardly discernible part – no matter how small a given physical object may be, it surely has a right and a left side, a top and a bottom, a near and far side, a middle and two ends; we must admit that 2.8.22.86 these parts are present in any physical object, no matter how small it is, and as a result we concede that no physical object is truly and simply one. Yet so many parts could not be enumerated in it but for a distinct under-standing of *one*. When I look for *one* in a physical object and am sure that I have not found it, surely I know what I was looking for and did not find there; and I know that it cannot be found, or, rather, that it is not there at all.

Then how do I know *one*, which is not a physical object? If I did not 2.8.22.87 know *one*, I could not enumerate *many* in a physical object. But no matter how I know *one*, I surely do not know it through bodily sense, since I only know physical objects through the bodily senses, and we have truly and simply proved that *one* is not a physical object.

Besides, if we do not perceive *one* with the bodily senses, we do not perceive any number with the senses. At least, we do not perceive any of those numbers we single out with the understanding. Every one of these is so called from how many times it includes *one*, and there is no perception of *one* with the bodily senses. Half of any given physical object (no matter how small), since two [halves] make up a whole, itself includes its own half. These two parts are therefore in the physical object in such a way that they are not simply *two*: The number called "two," since it includes twice what is simply *one*, cannot be half of [a whole] – that is, what is simply *one* cannot include a half or a third or any fraction, since it is simple and truly *one*.

2.8.23.89    Next, if we keep to the orderings of numbers, we see that after *one* comes *two*. We found this number to be related to *one* as its double. The double of *two* doesn't follow right away, though. Instead, the triple is interposed, and then the quadruple (which is the double of *two*) follows.

2.8.23.90    This intelligible structure extends through all the rest of the numbers by the most certain and unchangeable law.[35] The first [number] after *one*, *i.e.* the next after the first of all the numbers, includes its double, since *two* follows. But after the second, *i.e.* next after *two*, it is the second which includes its double, for after *two* the first is the triple and the second is the quadruple, the double of the second. The third after *three*, *i.e.* next after the triple, is its double, for after *three* (*i.e.* after the triple) the first is the quadruple, the second the quintuple, and the third the sextuple, which is the double of *three*. And thus the fourth next after *four* includes its double, for after *four* (*i.e.* the quadruple) the first is the quintuple, the second the sextuple, the third the septuple, and the fourth the octuple, which is the double of *four*. And so will you find it in all the rest as we have found in the first linkage of numbers (*i.e.* that we found in *one* and *two*), so that by whatever amount any given number is from the beginning, the same amount after it is its double.

2.8.23.92    So how *do* we recognize what we recognize to be firm and uncorrupted for all numbers? We do not come into contact with all numbers through any bodily sense; they are innumerable. How then do we know that it is

2.8.23.91 (margin)

2.8.22.88 (margin)

---

[35] The "law" is that for any number *n*, the *n*th number after it is its double, 2*n*. Augustine's discussion shifts between the cardinal and the ordinal attributes of number.

so for all numbers? By what imagination or image is so firm a numerical truth recognized so confidently, for innumerable cases, if not in the inner light – a truth the bodily senses do not know?

Those inquirers to whom God has granted the ability and who are not blinded by stubbornness are compelled by these and many such examples to admit that the intelligible structure and truth of numbers does not pertain to the bodily senses. It remains pure and unchangeable, and is seen in common by all who reason. Accordingly, although many other things could occur to us that are common and "publicly available" (so to speak) for all reasoning beings – things each person discerns with his own mind and reason while they remain inviolate and unchangeable – nevertheless, I am glad to see that the intelligible structure and truth of number struck you as the best example when you wanted to answer my question. It is no accident that number is linked to wisdom in Scripture: "My heart and I have gone around so that I might search out and think about and know wisdom and number" [Ecl. 7:26 (7:25 RSV)].

Yet I ask you: What view do you think should be held about wisdom itself? Do you think that each person has his own personal wisdom, or instead that there is one wisdom common to all so that the more someone participates in it the wiser he becomes?

EVODIUS: I do not yet know what you mean by "wisdom," for I see that people have various views about what is said or done wisely. Those in the military seem to themselves to be acting wisely; those who spurn the military and devote their work and care to farming praise it instead, rating it as wisdom. Those who are shrewd at concocting money-making schemes seem to themselves to be wise; those who disregard or renounce all these things and everything temporal, putting all their efforts into the search for truth so as to know God and themselves, judge that this is the gift of wisdom. Those who are unwilling to give themselves over to the leisure of searching for and reflecting on the truth but instead are involved with burdensome cares and duties so that they take counsel with people, caught up in running and supervising human affairs justly, think themselves to be wise. Those who are involved with both and live partly in the contemplation of the truth, partly in the burdensome duties which they think are owed to human society, seem to themselves to grasp the prize of wisdom. I pass over countless sects, in which each one puts its own proponents before the rest, holding them alone to be wise.

Accordingly, since we have agreed for now to answer not what we merely believe but instead what we grasp with clear understanding, I cannot answer your question at all unless I also know by reflection and reasoning what I grasp by believing, [namely] what wisdom is.

2.9.26.100 AUGUSTINE: You do think wisdom is the truth in which the highest good is recognized and grasped, do you not? All the people you mentioned, who follow different things, pursue good and avoid evil. Yet because different things seem good to one person and to another, they follow different things. Thus anyone pursuing what should not have been pursued – even though he pursues it only because it appears good to him – nevertheless is in error. On the other hand, a person who pursues nothing cannot be in error, nor can someone pursuing what he ought to 2.9.26.101 pursue. To the extent that all people pursue the happy life, then, they are not in error. But people are in error to the extent that they stray from the road of life that leads to happiness, even if they profess and protest that they only want to attain happiness; "error" means following something that does not lead where we want to reach.

2.9.26.102 The more someone is in error in the road of his life, so much the less is he wise. For he is to that extent farther from the truth, in which the highest good is recognized and grasped. But anyone who has pursued and attained the highest good becomes happy, which everyone uncontroversially wants. Therefore, just as we want to be happy, so too we want to be wise, for nobody is happy without wisdom. Nobody is happy except by the highest good, which is recognized and grasped in 2.9.26.103 the truth we call wisdom. Thus just as we have had stamped on our minds the notion of happiness before we are happy, for it is through this notion that we know and confidently declare without hesitation that we want to be happy, so too we have had stamped on our mind the notion of wisdom before we are wise; it is through this notion that any one of us, if asked whether he wants to be wise, will reply without the shadow of a doubt that he does.

2.9.27.104 Accordingly, we now agree what wisdom is. Perhaps you were unable to explain it in words. But if your mind could not recognize it at all, you would not at all know that you want to be wise and that you ought to so want, which I do not think you are going to deny. Therefore, I want you to tell me now whether you think that wisdom, like the intelligible structure and truth of number, offers itself in common to all reasoning beings, or, instead, since there are as many human minds as there are human beings (whereby I do not discern anything in your mind nor you in mine), you think that there are as many "wisdoms" as there could be wise persons.

EVODIUS: If the highest good is one for all, the truth in which it is recognized and grasped, namely wisdom, must also be one and common to all. 2.9.27.105

AUGUSTINE: Do you doubt whether the highest good, whatever it is, is one for everyone?

EVODIUS: Yes, I do, for I observe that different people rejoice in different things as their own highest goods.

AUGUSTINE: I only wish that nobody were in doubt about the highest good, the way nobody doubts that, whatever the highest good is, human beings can become happy only when it is possessed. But since this is an important question and might call for lengthy discussion, let us suppose that there are exactly as many different highest goods as there are different things that are sought by various people as the highest good. Surely it does not follow that wisdom itself is not one and common to all, just because the goods that they discern and elect in it are many and diverse? 2.9.27.106

If you think this, you can also doubt that the Sun's light is one, since there are many different things we discern in it. Each person voluntarily elects which of these many things to enjoy through the sense of sight: One gladly looks at a mountain peak and takes pleasure in the sight; another at the level plain; another at the hollow of the valley; another at the green forest; another at the shifting surface of the sea; another brings all these or some of them together for the pleasure of looking at them. Consequently, there are many different things that people see in the Sun's light and elect [to look at] for their enjoyment, despite the fact that the light itself is one – the light in which the person's gaze sees and grasps the sight of any one of them. Likewise, there are many different goods from which a person elects what he wants and, by seeing and grasping it for his enjoyment, sets up the highest good for himself rightly and truly. Yet it can still happen that the light of wisdom itself, in which these things can be seen and retained, is one and common to all wise people. 2.9.27.107 2.9.27.108

EVODIUS: I admit that this can happen. Nothing prevents one wisdom from being common to all, even if there are many diverse highest goods. But I would like to know whether it is so. We granted that it is *possible* that it be so, but we do not thereby grant that it *is* so. 2.9.27.109

AUGUSTINE: We hold for now that wisdom exists. But whether it is one and common to all, or whether each has his own wisdom the way each has his own mind or soul – this we do not yet hold.

EVODIUS: Yes.

2.10.28.110 AUGUSTINE: Well, we hold that wisdom exists, or at least that everyone wants to be wise and happy. Where do we see this claim? For I have no doubt whatsoever that you see it and that it is true. Therefore, do you see that this is so as you see your own thoughts, of which I am completely ignorant unless you declare them to me? Or do you see it in such a way that you understand that this truth can be seen by me too, even if you do not speak to me?

2.10.28.111 EVODIUS: I have no doubt that you can see it too, even against my will.

AUGUSTINE: Then is not the one truth we each see with our individual minds common to both of us?

EVODIUS: Quite clearly.

AUGUSTINE: Likewise, I believe you do not deny that wisdom should be pursued, and you grant that this is true.

EVODIUS: I have no doubt at all.

2.10.28.112 AUGUSTINE: Can we deny that this truth likewise is both one and common to all who know it for being seen, even though any given person recognizes it with neither my mind nor yours nor anyone else's other than his own, since what is recognized is present in common to all who recognize it?

EVODIUS: Not at all.

2.10.28.113 AUGUSTINE: Likewise, won't you admit that the following:

One should live justly
Lesser things should be subordinate to better things
Equals should be compared to equals
To each his own

are the most true, and are present in common to me, to you, and to all who see the truth?

EVODIUS: I agree.

2.10.28.114 AUGUSTINE: Well, can you deny that the incorrupt is better than the corrupt, the eternal better than the temporal, the inviolable than the violable?

EVODIUS: Who can?

AUGUSTINE: Therefore, can anyone say that this truth is his own, while it is there to be unchangeably regarded by all who are able to regard it?

EVODIUS: Nobody will truly claim it to be his own. It is as one and common to all as it is true.

AUGUSTINE: Likewise, does anyone deny that the mind should be turned away from corruption and turned towards the incorruptible – that is, that we should love the incorruptible and not corruption? And once this is admitted to be true, does anyone not also see that he understands the unchangeable, and that it is present in common to all minds able to look upon it? 2.10.28.115

EVODIUS: Entirely true.

AUGUSTINE: Well, does anyone doubt that a life which is *not* thrown off its firm moral stance by any misfortunes is better than one which is easily shattered and undercut by temporary inconveniences?

EVODIUS: Who could doubt it?

AUGUSTINE: I won't look for more examples now. It is enough that you grant that it is completely certain and that you see equally along with me that, insofar as they are the rules and beacons of the virtues,[36] they are true and unchangeable, and they are present, whether singly or collectively, for the regard of those who are capable of recognizing them, each by his own mind and reason. But I do in fact ask whether these rules seem to you to pertain to wisdom. For I believe that it is apparent to you that someone who has acquired wisdom is wise. 2.10.29.116

EVODIUS: Yes indeed.

2.10.29.117

AUGUSTINE: Well, take someone who lives justly. Could he live in this way unless he saw which lower things to subordinate to which more valuable things, and which equal things to link to each other, and which things to assign to their proper groups?

EVODIUS: He could not.

AUGUSTINE: Surely you will not deny that someone who sees these things sees wisely?

EVODIUS: I do not deny it.

AUGUSTINE: Take someone who lives prudently. Does he not elect the incorrupt, recognizing that it should be preferred to the corrupt?

EVODIUS: Quite clearly.

AUGUSTINE: Therefore, since he elects to turn his mind to that which nobody doubts should be elected, it cannot be denied that he elects wisely, can it?

---

[36] See 2.10.28.113.

EVODIUS: Not at all.

AUGUSTINE: Therefore, when he turns his mind to what he elects wisely, he surely turns it wisely.

EVODIUS: Certainly.

AUGUSTINE: And someone who is not deflected by any terrors or penalties from what he wisely elects, and to which he wisely turns, doubtless acts wisely.

EVODIUS: Exactly.

2.10.29.118 AUGUSTINE: Hence it is completely clear that everything we called "rules and beacons of the virtues" pertains to wisdom. The more someone uses them in living his life and lives his life in accordance with them, the more he lives and acts wisely. But it cannot properly be said that what is done wisely is independent of wisdom.

EVODIUS: Yes indeed.

2.10.29.119 AUGUSTINE: Therefore, just as there are true and unchangeable rules of numbers, whose intelligible structure and truth you declared to be unchangeably present in common to all who recognize them,[37] so too are there true and unchangeable rules of wisdom. When asked about a few of them individually just now you replied that they are true and evident, and you granted that they are present and common to be contemplated by all who are able to look upon them.

2.11.30.120 EVODIUS: No doubt. But I would very much like to know whether wisdom and number are classified under a single heading, since, as you reminded us,[38] they are linked even in Scripture; or one is derived from the other; or one consists in the other, for instance number from wisdom

2.11.30.121 or in wisdom. For I would not presume to claim that wisdom derives from number, or that it consists in number. I do not know how that could be, since I know many people who are skilled in numbers (by whatever name people who calculate wonderfully well should be called), but I know very few – perhaps none – who are wise. So wisdom strikes me as being much more worthy of admiration than number.

2.11.30.122 AUGUSTINE: You are describing something I often wonder about too. For when I reflect on the unchangeable truth of numbers and their lair (so to speak) and their inner sanctuary or realm – or any other suitable name we can find to refer to the dwelling-place and residence of numbers – I am far removed from the body. Perhaps I even find something

---

[37] See 2.8.20.80–2.8.24.94.     [38] See 2.8.24.95.

to think about, but not something I could put into words. Eventually I return in exhaustion to familiar things, so that I am able to say something or other, and I talk in the usual way about the things right in front of me. This also happens to me when I think as carefully and intently as I can about wisdom. Thus I am quite surprised, since wisdom and number are linked together in the most hidden and certain truth (with the approval of the scriptural passage I mentioned in which they are conjoined), I am quite surprised, as I said, why wisdom is precious to most people and number of little value. Yet it is indisputable that they are one and the same thing. Still, since it is nonetheless said of wisdom in Scripture that it "reaches from one end to the other strongly and puts all things in order sweetly" [Wis. 8:1], perhaps the power that "reaches from one end to the other strongly" is number, while the power that "puts all things in order sweetly" is then called wisdom in the strict sense, although both powers belong to one and the same Wisdom. 2.11.30.123

2.11.30.124

He[39] gave numbers to all things, even to the lowliest placed at the very end. All physical objects have their own numbers even though they are the last among things. However, He did not give wisdom to physical objects, nor even to all souls, but only to rational souls – as if He had established in them a home for [wisdom], in accordance with which He puts all things in order, even the lowliest to which He gave numbers. Therefore, since we easily make judgments about physical objects *qua* things ordered below us, in which we discern the numbers that have been impressed on them, we also think that numbers themselves are below us, and as a result we hold them to be of little value. But once we begin to turn ourselves upward again (so to speak), we find that numbers transcend our minds too and remain unchangeable in truth itself. Then, since few people can be wise but even fools are given the ability to count, people admire wisdom and think little of numbers. Yet learned and studious people, insofar as they are removed from the taint of wordly things, consider to that extent number and wisdom the more in truth itself, and hold them precious. In comparison with that truth, they rank not only gold and silver and the other things people struggle for as worthless, but even themselves. 2.11.31.125

2.11.31.126

It should not surprise you, then, that people value wisdom and belittle numbers because they can count more easily than they can be wise, 2.11.32.127

---

[39] "He": Wisdom (= God).

since you see they hold gold more precious than lamplight – compared to which gold is laughable. But an inferior thing is much more honored because even a beggar can light himself a lamp, whereas few people have gold.

Enough of wisdom's being found inferior in comparison with number! They are the same, but this calls for an eye able to discern it. Now one senses the brightness and the heat in a fire as "consubstantial,"[40] so to speak, nor can they be separated from one another. Yet the heat affects only what is moved close to it, whereas the brightness is diffused far and wide. Likewise, the power of understanding that is present in wisdom warms those close to it, such as rational souls, whereas things that are farther away, such as physical objects, are not affected by the heat of wisdom but are [merely] suffused with the light of numbers.

Well, perhaps this is still obscure to you, since no analogy drawn from what is visible can apply in every respect to something invisible. Merely pay attention to this point, which is enough for the investigation we have undertaken and is obvious even to humbler minds like ours: Even if we cannot be clear whether number is in wisdom or derives from wisdom, or whether wisdom itself derives from number or is in number, or whether each can be shown to be the name of a single thing, it is certainly evident that each is true, and unchangeably true.

Consequently, you will not deny that there is unchangeable truth, containing everything that is unchangeably true. You cannot call it yours or mine or anyone else's. Instead, it is present and offers itself in common to all who discern unchangeable truths, like a light that is miraculously both public and hidden. Who would claim that everything present in common to all who reason and understand pertains to the nature of any one of them in particular? You recall, I think, our discussion of the bodily senses a little while ago.[41] We said that those things that we touch in common with the senses belonging to the eyes or to the ears, such as colors and sounds (which you and I see simultaneously or hear simultaneously), do not pertain to the nature of our eyes or ears but rather are common objects for us to sense. The same applies to those objects you and I recognize in common, each with his own mind. You would never say that they pertain to the nature of my mind, or to the nature of your mind.

---

[40] Augustine takes "consubstantial" from Trinitarian theology, where it is used to describe how the Persons of the Trinity are the same substance.

[41] See 2.7.15.58–2.7.19.78.

You cannot say that what two people see with their eyes simultaneously belongs to one set of eyes or the other, but rather some third thing at which the gaze of each is directed.

EVODIUS: That is perfectly evident and true.

AUGUSTINE: Then, in regard to this truth we have long been talking about and in which we recognize so many things: Do you think it is (*a*) more excellent than our mind is, (*b*) equal to our minds, or even (*c*) inferior? If (*c*) were the case, we would make judgments about it rather than in accordance with it, the way we make judgments about physical objects because they are lower than us – we often say not only that they are so or not so, but that they ought to be so or not so. So too with our minds: We know not only that the mind is so, but that it ought to be so. We make judgments about physical objects in this fashion when we say that something is less bright than it ought to be, or less square, and so on, and about minds when we say that one is less well disposed than it ought to be, or less gentle, or less forceful, as we are wont to do by reason. We make these judgments in accordance with the inner rules of truth that we discern in common. But nobody makes judgments about the rules themselves. When anyone says that eternal things are more valuable than temporal things, or seven and three are ten, no one says that it *ought* to be so; he simply knows that it *is* so. He is not an inspector making corrections but merely a discoverer taking delight [in his discovery].

Now if (*b*) were the case, that this truth is equal to our minds, then it would itself also be changeable. For our minds sometimes see more of the truth and sometimes less. And for this reason, they acknowledge themselves to be changeable. The truth, remaining in itself, neither increases when we see more of it nor decreases when we see less, but instead it is intact and uncorrupted, bringing joy with its light to those who turn towards it and punishing with blindness those who turn away from it. We even make judgments about our own minds in accordance with [the unchangeable truth], although we are not able to make any judgment about it at all. For we say that a mind understands less than it ought to, or that it understands just as much as it ought to. Furthermore, the closer a mind is able to approach the unchangeable truth and hold fast to it, the more it ought to understand.

Consequently, if the truth is neither inferior nor equal, it follows that it is superior and more excellent.

2.12.34.133

2.12.34.134

2.12.34.135

2.12.34.136

2.13.35.137    Now I had promised you, if you recall, that I would show you that there is something more exalted than our mind and reason.[42] Here you have it: the truth itself! Embrace it if you can and enjoy it; "Take delight in the Lord and He will give you your heart's longings" [Ps. 36:4 (37:4 RSV)]. What do you long for more than to be happy? And who is happier than one who enjoys the unshakeable, unchangeable, and most excellent truth?

2.13.35.138    People cry out that they are happy when they embrace with passionate desire the beautiful bodies of their wives, or even of prostitutes. Shall we doubt that people are happy in the embrace of the truth? People cry out that they are happy when, with throats parched from the heat, they arrive at a plentiful and wholesome spring, or, when hungry, they come upon a well-supplied sumptuous lunch or dinner. Shall we deny that we

2.13.35.139    are happy when we are refreshed and nourished by the truth? We often hear the voices of people crying out that they are happy if they recline among roses and other flowers, or even delight in the most fragrant perfumes. What is more fragrant or more agreeable than drawing in the gentle breath of truth? Do we hesitate to say we are happy when we draw in its breath? Many put the happy life for themselves in the music of voices, strings, and flutes; they declare themselves miserable when such music is absent but thrill with joy when it is present. When our minds are free of any din (so to speak), and the melodious and eloquent silence of truth flows in, do we seek any other happy life and not enjoy the one that is

2.13.35.140    present to us and so secure? People, taking delight in agreeable splendor – for instance the light of gold and silver, the light of gemstones and other colors, whether of the very light that belongs to these eyes,[43] or in earthly fires, on in the stars or the Moon or the Sun – as long as people are not called away from these delights by any poverty or problems, they think themselves happy and always want to live for these things. Are we afraid to set up the happy life in the light of truth?

2.13.36.141    Instead, since the highest good is known and possessed in the truth, and this truth is wisdom, let us recognize and possess the highest good in it and enjoy it completely, since anyone who enjoys the highest good is happy. This truth reveals all true goods, which people elect for themselves to enjoy – either one or many of them – in accordance with their capacity

---

42  See 2.6.13.53 and 2.6.14.57.
43  Augustine holds an "extromission" theory of vision, according to which the eyes see physical objects by emitting rays of light.

for understanding. Consider the following analogy. There are people who 2.13.36.142
elect what they like to look at in the sunlight, and take pleasure in the
sight. And if they were by chance to be supplied with sound, healthier,
and quite powerful eyes, they would like nothing better than to gaze at the
Sun itself, which also sheds its light on the rest of the things that weaker
eyes take pleasure in. Likewise, when the sharp, healthy, and strong sight
of the mind is trained upon many unchangeable truths with its sure reason, it directs [its gaze] on the very truth itself by which all things are
disclosed; holding fast to it as though it were unmindful of the others, it
enjoys them all together in the truth itself. For whatever is agreeable in the
other truths is surely agreeable in virtue of the truth itself.

Our freedom is this: to submit to this truth, which is our God Who set 2.13.37.143
us free from death – that is, from the state of sin. Truth itself,[44] speaking
as a human being among others, said to those believing in Him: "If you
continue in my word, you are truly my disciples; and you shall know the
truth, and the truth shall set you free" [Jn. 8:31–32]. The soul does not
enjoy anything with freedom unless it enjoys it with security.

Now nobody is secure in goods that can be lost against his will. 2.14.37.144
Nobody loses truth and wisdom against his will, however. It is not possible for anyone to be physically separated from it. Instead, what we call
"separation" from truth and wisdom is a perverse will that takes delight
in inferior things, and nobody unwilling wills anything.

Hence we possess something that all can enjoy equally in common. It 2.14.37.145
has no restrictions or defects. It welcomes all its lovers who are not envious of each other: It is common to all and faithful to each. No one says to
the other: "Back off so that I too may approach! Take your hands away so
that I too may embrace it!" All hold fast to it and all touch the selfsame 2.14.37.146
thing. Its food is not divided into portions; you drink nothing from it that
I cannot drink. For you do not change anything from its commonness
into something private of yours, but rather you take something from it
and yet it remains intact for me. When you draw in its breath I do not
wait for you to exhale for me to then draw breath from it. No part of it
ever becomes the property of anyone. On the contrary, it is common as a
whole to all at once.

Therefore, the objects we touch or taste or smell are less analogous to 2.14.38.147
this truth than those we hear or discern. Every word is heard as a whole

---

44 "Truth itself": Christ.

by all who hear it and as a whole at once by each of them; any sight before
2.14.38.148    the eyes is seen at once as much by one person as another. But these analogies [to the truth] are quite remote. No utterance is spoken as a whole at once, for it is brought forth and extended in time, so that one part of it is pronounced before another. Any visible sight is elongated (so to speak) in space, and is not a whole in any one place.

All these things can surely be taken away against our will, and various
2.14.38.149    obstacles prevent us from being able to enjoy them. For example, suppose that someone could sing an everlasting sweet song. His admirers, who eagerly came to hear him, would jostle each other and, the greater the crowd, the more they would fight over places to get closer to the singer. Yet they could not retain anything to keep for themselves in their listen-
2.14.38.150    ing, being only touched upon by all the fleeting sounds. Now suppose I wanted to look upon the Sun itself and were able to do so steadily. It would desert me at sunset, and also when hidden by a cloud or many other hindrances; against my will I would lose the pleasure of seeing it. To cap it off, even if the sweetness of light were always present for me to see, and of sound for me to hear, what great benefit would I gain? This would be common to me and the animals.

2.14.38.151    By contrast, insofar as the will to enjoy it is steadfastly present, the beauty of truth and wisdom does not shut out those coming to it if there is a mob of listeners crammed together; it does not pass with time or change places; nightfall does not interrupt it and shadows do not obscure
2.14.38.152    it; it does not depend on the bodily senses. It is close to all the people in the whole world who take delight in it and have turned themselves to it; it lasts forever for all; it is never absent from any place; outwardly it counsels us and inwardly it teaches us. It changes for the better all those who behold it, and it is not changed for the worse by anyone. No one passes judgments on it, and no one passes judgments rightly without it. And from this it is clear beyond a doubt that it is more valuable than our minds, each of which becomes wise by this one thing and passes judgment, not on it, but on other things through it.

2.15.39.153    Now you had conceded that if I were to show you something above our minds you would admit it to be God, as long as there were nothing still higher.[45] I accepted your concession and said that it would be sufficient if I were to prove this point. For if there is something more excellent,

---

[45] See 2.6.14.57.

that instead is God; but if not, then the truth itself is God. Therefore, in either case you won't be able to deny that God exists, and this was the question we agreed to examine and discuss.[46] (If it bothers you that wisdom has a father, according to the hallowed teaching of Christ that we have accepted in faith, remember that we have also accepted in faith that the Wisdom begotten by the Eternal Father is equal to Him; this is not a matter to be investigated now,[47] but we must hold it with resolute faith.) There is a God who truly *is*, in the highest degree. This we now not only hold free of doubt by faith, I think. We also reach it by a form of understanding that, although as yet very slight, is certain. But it is sufficient for the question we undertook and will enable us to explain other matters that are relevant to it – unless you have some objection to raise.

EVODIUS: I am completely overwhelmed by an unbelievable joy that I cannot express to you in words. I hear what you say and cry out that it is most certain. But I am crying out with an inner voice, which I want to be heard by the truth itself so as to hold fast to it. I grant it to be not only good but also the highest good and the source of happiness.

AUGUSTINE: Quite appropriate! I too rejoice a great deal. But I ask you: Are we now wise and happy? Or are we still trying to arrive at that point?

EVODIUS: I think we are merely trying.

AUGUSTINE: Then how do you grasp these things so that you cry out that you rejoice in them as certain truths, and you grant that they belong to wisdom? Or can someone unwise know wisdom?

EVODIUS: As long as he is unwise he cannot.

AUGUSTINE: Therefore, you are already wise, or you do not yet know wisdom.

EVODIUS: Indeed, I am not yet wise, but I would not say that I am unwise either, insofar as I know wisdom: the things I know are certain, and I cannot deny that they belong to wisdom.

AUGUSTINE: Please tell me: Will you not admit that someone who is not just is unjust, someone who is not prudent is imprudent, and someone who is not moderate immoderate? Or is there some doubt on this score?

EVODIUS: I admit that when a person is not just he is unjust, and I would also say the same for prudence and moderation.

2.15.39.154
2.15.39.155
2.15.39.156
2.15.40.157
2.15.40.158

---

[46] See 2.3.7.20.
[47] Augustine defends the equality of the divine Persons at length in *The Trinity*, written c.400–416.

2.15.40.159    AUGUSTINE: Why then, when he is not wise, is he not unwise?

EVODIUS: I also admit that when someone is not wise he is unwise.

AUGUSTINE: Now then: which of these are you?

EVODIUS: Whichever you call me. I do not yet venture to call myself wise, and I see from what I have granted that I should not hesitate to call myself unwise.

2.15.40.160    AUGUSTINE: Then someone unwise knows wisdom. For, as we have already declared, nobody would be certain that he wills himself to be wise and that he ought to do so unless some notion of wisdom were in his mind. Likewise in the case of those matters belonging to wisdom itself, in whose knowledge you rejoiced when asked about them one by one.

EVODIUS: You have said it exactly.

2.16.41.161    AUGUSTINE: Then what are we doing when we strive to be wise? Nothing but somehow to gather up our whole soul, as quickly as we can, to what we have touched with our mind, to give it a firm foothold there. The upshot is that the soul no longer rejoices in its own private goods that entangle it with ephemeral things. Instead, stripped of all attachments to times and places, it apprehends that which is always one and the

2.16.41.162    same. Just as the soul is the whole life of the body, God is the happy life of the soul. While we are doing this, until we have done it completely, we are on the road [to wisdom].

We have been granted the enjoyment of these true and certain goods, though for now they are but glimmerings along our shadowy path. See whether this is what was written about wisdom, what it does with its lovers when they seek and come to it: "Wisdom shows herself favorably to them along the roads, and in all providence does she meet with them" [Wis. 6:17 (6:16 RSV)].

2.16.41.163    Whichever way you turn, [wisdom] speaks to you by the traces left behind on its works. It calls you back within when you are slipping away into external things through their very forms, so you see that whatever delights you in a body and entices you through your bodily senses is full of number. You search for its source and return into yourself, understanding that you cannot approve or disapprove of what you come into contact with through the bodily senses, unless within you there are some laws of beauty, to which you compare anything beautiful you sense outside yourself.

2.16.42.164    Look upon the heavens, the Earth, and the sea, and at everything in them, whether they shine down or creep below or fly or swim. They have forms because they have numbers. Take the latter away from them and they will be nothing. What is the source of their existence, then, if not the source of the existence of number? After all, they have being precisely to the extent that they are full of numbers.

Craftsmen, who fashion all bodily forms, have numbers in their craft 2.16.42.165 which they apply to their works. They use their hands and tools in designing, until what is formed externally achieves its consummation when it conforms as much as possible to the inward light of numbers and, using sense as the go-between, it pleases the internal judge who looks upon the numbers above.

Next, ask what moves the craftsman's hands. It will be number, for their movements are also full of numbers. If you were to take the work 2.16.42.166 out of his hands and the goal of designing from his mind, and chalk up his bodily movements to pleasure, it will be called "dancing." Ask therefore what pleases you in dancing; number will answer: "Here I am!"

Then inspect the beauty of a sculpted body. Its numbers are held in place. Inspect the beauty of movement in a body: its numbers are involved with time. Enter into the craft from which they proceed and seek in it time and place: It never and nowhere exists, yet number lives in it; it is neither an area of space nor an age of days. Still, when people who want 2.16.42.167 to become craftsmen set themselves to learn their craft, they move their bodies in place and time, but their minds only in time; indeed, as time passes they become more skilled.

So rise above even the mind of the craftsman to see everlasting number! Wisdom will then shine upon you from its inner abode and from the hidden chambers of truth. If it beats back your gaze as still too weak [for such a vision], turn your mind's eye to the road where [wisdom] showed itself favorably.[48] Remember, of course, that you have postponed a vision you will seek once more when you are stronger and healthier.

Wisdom! The sweetest light of a mind made pure! Woe to those who 2.16.43.168 abandon you as guide and wander aimlessly around your tracks, who love indications of you instead of you, who forget what you intimate. For you do not cease to intimate to us what and how great you are. All the

---

[48] See the citation of Wis. 6:17 (6:16 RSV) in 2.16.41.162 and 2.17.45.174. For the gaze being too weak to sustain, see 2.13.36.142. Augustine uses similar language in *Confessions* 7.10.16 to describe his experience of God (addressed to God): "When first I came to know You, You lifted me up so I might see that what I saw *is*, whereas I who saw it not yet was. Shining upon me intensely, You beat back the weakness of my gaze, and I trembled with love and awe."

loveliness of Creation is an indication of you. The craftsman somehow intimates to those who view his work that they not be wholly attached to its beauty. Instead, they should cast their eyes over the appearance of the material product in such a way that they turn back, with affection, to

2.16.43.169 the one who produced it. Those who love what you do in place of you are like people who hear someone wise speaking eloquently and, while they listen too keenly to the sweetness of his voice and the arrangements of his well-placed syllables, they miss the most important thing, namely the *meanings* of which his words were the audible signs.

Woe to those who turn themselves from your light and hold fast with delight to their own darkness! Turning their backs on you (so to speak), they are chained to fleshly labor as to their own shadows. Yet even then, what gives them pleasure shares in the encompassing brilliance of your

2.16.43.170 light. But when a shadow is loved, it makes the mind's eye weaker and less fit to reach the sight of you. Consequently, a man is plunged farther into darkness when he eagerly pursues anything that catches him the more readily in his weakened condition. Due to this, he begins to be unable to see what exists in the highest degree. He starts to think evil anything that deceives him through his lack of foresight, or that entices him in his need, or that torments him in his captivity – although he deservedly suffers these things because he has turned away, since whatever is just cannot be evil.

2.16.44.171 Therefore, if either with bodily sense or with the mind's consideration you cannot get hold of whatever changeable thing you are looking upon, unless you grasp some form of numbers (without which it would lapse back into nothing), do not doubt that there is some eternal and unchangeable form! As a result, these changeable things are not interrupted but instead run their courses through time, with measured movements and a distinct variety of forms, like poetic verses. This eternal and unchangeable form is not contained in and spread out through space; nor is it extended and varied in time. But through it, all [changeable] things are able to be given form, as well as to fulfill and carry out the numbers pertinent to the times and places appropriate to their kind.

2.17.45.172 Every changeable thing must also be formable. (Just as we call what can be changed "changeable," I shall in like manner call what can be given form "formable.") Yet no thing can give form to itself, for the following reason. No thing can give what it does not have, and surely something is given form in order to have form. Accordingly, if any given thing has some form, there is no need for it to receive what it [already] has. But if something does not have a form, it cannot receive from itself what it does not have. Therefore, no thing can give form to itself, as we said. Now what 2.17.45.173 more is there for us to say about the changeability of the body and the mind? Enough was said previously. Thus it follows that mind and body are given form by an unchangeable form that endures forever. To this form was it said: "You shall change them, and they shall be changed; but you are the same and your years shall not fail" [Ps. 101:27–28 (102:26–27 RSV)]. The prophetical figure of speech uses 'years without fail' in place of 'eternity.' About this same form again was it said that "remaining in itself, it makes all things new" [Wis. 7:27].

On these grounds we understand that all things are governed by provi- 2.17.45.174 dence. For if all existing things would be nothing were they completely deprived of form, the unchangeable form through which all changeable things maintain their existence – so that they are fulfilled and are carried out by the numbers pertinent to their forms – is itself their providence. For they would not exist if it did not exist. Therefore, anyone who carefully considers the whole of Creation and takes the road to wisdom senses that "Wisdom shows herself favorably to him along the roads, and in all providence does she meet with him" [Wis. 6:17 (6:16 RSV)]. He will be the more fervent to get along that road to precisely the extent that the road itself is beautiful through the wisdom he is burning to reach.

Now if you find some kind of creature other than (*a*) that which exists 2.17.46.175 but does not live, (*b*) that which exists and lives but does not understand, or (*c*) that which exists and lives and understands – *then* venture to say that there is some good that is not from God![49] These three kinds can also be expressed by two names, if they were called "body" and "life," since that which only lives but does understand, as in the case of brute animals, and that which understands, as in human beings, is quite correctly called alive. These two things, namely body and life, are counted among crea- 2.17.46.176 tures at least – for "life" is said of the Creator Himself, and this is life in the highest degree. Hence, because these two creations, body and life, are "formable" (as shown by what was said previously), and because if the form were completely lost they would lapse back into nothing, they reveal well enough that they maintain their existence from that form which always remains the same. Consequently, all good things whatsoever,

---

[49] The distinction (*a*)–(*c*) was mentioned earlier at 2.3.7.22–2.3.7.24 and 2.5.11.43–2.6.13.53.

2.17.46.177    no matter how great or small, can exist only from God. What can be greater in Creation than intelligent life? What can be less than body? However much these things deteriorate and thereby tend to nonbeing, some form nevertheless remains in them, so that they do exist in some way. Whatever form may remain in a deteriorated thing, it comes from that form which knows no deterioration, and it prevents the movements of these things – as they deteriorate or improve – from transgressing the laws of their own numbers. Hence whatever is found to be praiseworthy in the world, whether it is judged to deserve full or slight praise, should be traced back to the most excellent and inexpressible praise of its Maker. Do you have any objections to raise?

2.18.47.178    EVODIUS: I admit that I am sufficiently convinced – and it has become clear as much as it can in this life among people such as us – (*a*) that God exists, and (*b*) that all goods are from God, seeing that all the things that exist are from God, whether they understand and live and exist, or only live and exist, or only exist.

Now then, let us have a look at whether the third question can be disentangled: Should free will be counted among the goods?[50] Once this has been proved, I shall concede without hesitation that God has given it to us, and that it ought to have been given to us.

2.18.47.179    AUGUSTINE: You have remembered well the questions on the table, and quickly noticed that the second question has now been settled. But you should have seen that the third question has thereby also been resolved. You had declared that it seemed to you that free choice of the will ought not to have been given, on the grounds that it is through it that anyone sins.[51] When I replied to your view that one cannot act rightly except by this selfsame free choice of the will, and maintained that God instead gave it for this reason,[52] you answered that free will should have been given to us the way justice was given, which no one

2.18.47.180    can use except rightly.[53] Your reply forced us to enter into a great roundabout course of argument, in which I proved to you that greater and less good things are from God alone. This could only be shown clearly if, first, against the opinions of irreligious foolishness – in accordance with which "the fool has said in his heart: There is no God" [Ps. 13:1 (14:1 RSV), 52:1 (53:1 RSV)] – whatever kind of reasoning we entered into

---

[50] This is the "third question" raised in 2.3.7.20, the first two having been answered in (*a*) and (*b*).
[51] See 2.1.1.1.    [52] See 2.1.3.5.    [53] See 2.2.4.8.

about so great a matter, fit to our abilities (with God Himself giving us help along this perilous path), were directed at some evident truth. Now although we held these two points – that God exists, and that all good things are from Him – with resolute faith even before, they have nevertheless been discussed in such a way that a third point was quite clearly apparent: that free will should be counted among the good things [as follows]. 2.18.47.181

It has already been made clear from the previous argumentation and we agreed that the nature of the body is at a lower level than the nature of the mind, and, on these grounds, that the mind is a greater good than the body. Therefore, if we find among goods of the body some that could not be used rightly by human beings, but we nevertheless do *not* say as a result that they should not have been given (since we admit that they are goods), then it is not surprising if there are also some goods in the mind that we are also able to not use rightly – but since they are goods, they could not have been given except by Him from Whom all good things come. 2.18.48.182

See how much good is missing in a body that does not have hands! Yet hands are used for evil when someone does cruel or disgraceful things with them. If you saw someone without feet, you would admit that a great good is lacking in his body's wholeness. Yet you would not deny that someone who uses his feet to harm another, or to disgrace himself, uses his feet for evil. With our eyes we see light and distinguish the forms of physical objects; the eyes are the most appealing parts of our body, which is why they are situated in an exalted place of honor, and we use them to oversee our health as well as for many other benefits of life. Yet many people do many disgraceful things with their eyes, enlisting them in the service of lust. You see how much good a face is missing if it does not have eyes. When eyes are present in a face, though, who gave them but the one who generously bestows all goods, God? 2.18.48.183 2.18.48.184

Therefore, just as you approve of these things in the body and praise Him Who gave these good things, disregarding those who use them for evil, you should also admit that free will, without which no one can live rightly, is a good thing and a divine gift – and also that those who use this good for evil should be damned, rather than that He Who gave it ought not to have given it. 2.18.48.185

2.18.49.186    EVODIUS: First, then, I would like you to prove to me that free will is something good; then I will grant that God gave it to us, since I acknowledge that all good things are from God.

2.18.49.187    AUGUSTINE: Did I not in the end prove this with so much effort in the previous argumentation? You admitted that every bodily species and form maintains its existence from the highest form of all things, *i.e.* from truth, and you granted that they are good.[54] Truth itself declares in the gospel that the hairs on our head are numbered.[55] Has it slipped your mind what we said about the supremacy of number, and its power

2.18.49.188    that "reaches from one end to the other" [Wis. 8:1]? How terribly perverse it is to number the hairs on our head among the good things (though among the least and lowly of them), nor to find any author to whom they may be attributed but God as the Maker of all good things (since great and small good things are from Him from Whom every good thing exists), and yet to have doubts about free will – without

2.18.49.189    which even those who live badly grant that we cannot live rightly! Please tell me now which seems better: (*a*) something in us without which we can live rightly, or (*b*) something in us without which we cannot live rightly?

EVODIUS: Stop, stop! I am ashamed of my blindness. Who could doubt that (*b*) is far more excellent?

AUGUSTINE: Then will you now deny that a one-eyed man can live rightly?

EVODIUS: Away with such great madness!

AUGUSTINE: Then since you grant that the eye in the body is a good thing, even though its loss does not prevent one from living rightly, does not free will, without which no one lives rightly, seem to you to be something good?

2.18.50.190    Consider justice, which no one uses for evil. Justice is counted among the highest goods there are in human beings – as well as all the virtues of the mind, upon which the right and worthwhile life is grounded. For no one uses prudence or courage or moderateness for evil. Right reason prevails in all of them, as it does in justice itself (which you mentioned). Without it they could not be virtues. And no one can use right reason for evil.

---

[54] See 2.16.42.164 and 2.16.44.171–2.17.45.173.
[55] Mt. 10:30: "Yet the very hairs of your head are all numbered."

68

Therefore, the virtues are great goods. But you must remember that not only great but even small goods are able to exist from Him alone from Whom all good things are, namely God. The previous line of argument established this, and you agreed to it many times with joy. Hence the virtues by which we live rightly are great goods. The beauties of any given physical objects, without which we can live rightly, are small goods, whereas the powers of the mind, without which we cannot live rightly, are intermediate goods. No one uses the virtues for evil, but the other goods – namely, the intermediate and small goods – can be used not only for good but also for evil. Hence no one uses virtue for evil, because the task of virtue is the good use of things that we can also fail to use for good. But no one uses [something] for evil in using it for good. Accordingly, the abundance and the greatness of God's goodness has furnished not only great goods but also intermediate and small goods. His goodness is more to be praised in great goods than in intermediate goods, and more in intermediate goods than in small goods, but more in all of them than if He had not bestowed them all. {.rightmargin 2.19.50.191 ... 2.19.50.192}

EVODIUS: I agree. But one point bothers me. Our question is about free will; we see that it uses other things for good or not. How is it also to be counted *among* the goods we use? {2.19.51.193}

AUGUSTINE: In the way we know all things of which we have knowledge by reason, and yet reason itself is also counted among the things we know by reason. Or did you forget that when we asked what is known by reason, you conceded that reason is also known by reason?[56] So do not be surprised that even if we use other things by free will, we are able to use free will through free will itself. The will that uses other things somehow uses itself, the same way as reason, which knows other things, knows itself too. Memory does not only embrace all the other things we remember. Since we do not forget that we have memory, memory also somehow grasps memory itself in us, and it remembers not only other things but also itself – or, rather, we remember other things as well as memory itself through it. {2.19.51.194 ... 2.19.51.195}

Thus when the will, which is an intermediate good, holds fast to the unchangeable good as something common rather than private – like the truth, which we have discussed at length without saying anything adequate – a person grasps the happy life. And the happy life, *i.e.* the {2.19.52.196}

---

[56] See 2.3.9.36.

2.19.52.197 attachment of the mind holding fast to the unchangeable good, is the proper and fundamental good for a human being. It also includes all the virtues, which no one can use for evil. Although the virtues are great and fundamental goods in human beings, we thoroughly understand that they are proper to each person, not that they are common. Truth and wisdom, however, are common to all, and people become wise and happy by holding fast to them. Of course, one person does not become happy by the happiness of another. Even if you emulate another in order to be happy, you seek to become happy by means of what you saw made the other person happy, namely through the unchangeable and common truth. Nor does anyone become prudent by another person's prudence, or is made courageous by another's courage, or moderate by another's moderateness, or just by another's justice. Instead, you conform your mind to those unchangeable rules and beacons of the virtues,[57] which live uncorruptibly in the truth itself and in the wisdom that is common, to which the person furnished with virtues whom you put forward as a model for your emulation has conformed and directed his mind.

2.19.52.198

2.19.53.199 Therefore, when the will adheres to the common and unchangeable good, it achieves the great and fundamental goods of a human being, despite being an intermediate good. But the will sins when it is turned away from the unchangeable and common good, towards its private good, or towards something external, or towards something lower. The will is turned to its private good when it wants to be in its own power; it is turned to something external when it is eager to know the personal affairs of other people, or anything that is not its business; it is turned to something lower when it takes delight in bodily pleasures. And thus someone who is made proud or curious or lascivious is captured by another life that, in comparison to the higher life, is death.[58] Even this life is ruled by the oversight of divine providence, which puts all things in order in their appropriate places and distributes to each what is due according to his deserts.

2.19.53.200

Thus it turns out that the good things desired by sinners are not in any way evil, and neither is free will itself, which we established should be numbered among the intermediate goods.[59] Instead, evil is turning the will away from the unchangeable good and towards changeable

---

[57] See 2.10.29.116–2.10.29.118.    [58] See 1.4.10.30.
[59] See 2.19.51.193–2.19.51.195.

goods. Yet, since this "turning away" and "towards" is not compelled but voluntary, the deserved and just penalty of unhappiness follows upon it.

But perhaps you are going to raise the question: Since the will is moved when it turns itself away from the unchangeable good towards the changeable good, where does this movement come from?[60] It is surely evil, even if free will should be numbered among good things on the grounds that we cannot live rightly without it. If this movement, namely turning the will away from the Lord God, is undoubtedly a sin, then surely can we not say that God is the author of sin? Therefore, this movement will not be from God. Then where does it come from?  2.20.54.201  2.20.54.202

If I were to reply to your question that I do not know, perhaps you will then be the sadder, but I will at least have replied truthfully. What is nothing cannot be known. Hold firm with resolute religiousness that you will not encounter, by sensing or understanding or whatever kind of thinking, any good thing which is not from God. Hence there is no nature you encounter that is not from God. Do not hesitate to attribute to God as its Maker everything in which you see number and measure and order. Once you remove these things entirely, absolutely nothing will be left. For even if some inchoate vestige of a form were to remain, where you find neither measure nor order nor number – since wherever these exist the form is complete – you must also take away that vestigial form, which seems to be a sort of material its Maker needs to complete. For if the completion of a form is good, the vestigial form is already something good. Thus if every good were taken away, what will be left is not something, but instead absolutely nothing. Yet every good is from God. Therefore, there is no nature that is not from God. Thus see what the movement of "turning away" pertains to. We admit that this movement is sin, since it is a defective movement, and every defect is from nothing. Be assured that this movement does *not* pertain to God!  2.20.54.203  2.20.54.204

Yet this defective movement, since it is voluntary, is placed within our power. If you fear it, you must not will it; if you do not will it, it will not exist. What then is more secure than to be in that life[61] where what you do not want cannot happen to you! But since we cannot rise of our own accord as we fell of it, let us hold on with firm faith to the right hand of God stretched out to us from above, namely our Lord Jesus Christ; let us  2.20.54.205

---

[60] This is the main question of Book 3.    [61] "That life": the afterlife.

await Him with resolute hope and desire Him with burning charity.[62] If you still think there is something about the origin of sin that should be looked into more carefully, we should defer it until Book 3.

2.20.54.206 EVODIUS: I comply with your will to defer to another time the issues stemming from this, for I agree that we have not yet looked into the matter sufficiently.

# Book 3

3.1.1.1 EVODIUS: It has been made completely clear to me that free will should be counted among good things. Indeed, it is not among the least of them. We are therefore also compelled to admit that free will was given by the divinity, and ought to have been given. If you think the time is right, I want to know this from you:[63] Where does the movement come from by which the will is turned away from the common and unchangeable good and is turned to its private goods, or to goods belonging to another, or to lower goods – all of which are completely changeable?

3.1.1.2 AUGUSTINE: What need is there to know this?

EVODIUS: If free will was given in such a way that it has this movement as something natural, then it is turned to these [lesser goods] by necessity, and no blame can be attached where nature and necessity predominate.

AUGUSTINE: Does this movement please you or displease you?

EVODIUS: It displeases me.

AUGUSTINE: Therefore you find fault with it.

EVODIUS: Certainly I do.

AUGUSTINE: Hence you find fault with a blameless movement of the mind.

EVODIUS: I do not find fault with a blameless movement of the mind. Rather, I do not *know* whether there is any blame in leaving the unchangeable good behind to turn to changeable goods.

AUGUSTINE: Therefore, you find fault with what you do not know.

EVODIUS: Do not push my words too much! I said "I do not know whether there is any blame" in such a way that I wanted it to be understood without a doubt that there *is* blame. In saying "I do not know" I was in fact completely ridiculing doubt about such a clear matter.

---

[62] Here as elsewhere "charity" (*caritas*) means more than simple generosity; it is the unselfish (and nonsexual) love of another, central to Christian doctrine.

[63] See 2.20.54.201.

AUGUSTINE: See how certain the truth is! It has forced you to forget 3.1.1.3
so quickly what you said just a minute ago. If that movement exists by
nature or necessity, it cannot be blameworthy in any way. But you hold so
firmly that it *is* blameworthy that you think doubt about so certain a matter is ridiculous. Therefore, why did it seem to you that what you clearly
demonstrate is false should be affirmed or declared to be certain with no
hesitation? You said: "If free will was given in such a way that it has this 3.1.1.4
movement as something natural, then it is turned to these [lesser goods]
by necessity, and no blame can be attached where nature and necessity
predominate." You should have had no doubts that it was not given in this
way, seeing that you do not doubt that the movement is blameworthy.

EVODIUS: For my part, I called the movement blameworthy, and hence 3.1.1.5
it displeases me. I cannot doubt that we should find fault with it. But I
deny that the soul which is drawn away from the unchangeable good to
changeable goods by that movement should be blamed, if its nature is
such that it is moved by it necessarily.

AUGUSTINE: You grant that this movement surely ought to be blamed. 3.1.2.6
What does it belong to?

EVODIUS: I see it in the mind, but I don't know what it belongs to.

AUGUSTINE: You do not deny that the mind is moved by that movement, do you?

EVODIUS: No.

AUGUSTINE: Then do you deny that the movement by which a stone is
moved is a movement belonging to the stone? I am not speaking of the
movement by which we move the stone, or by which the stone is moved
through some external force (such as when it is thrown upwards). Rather,
I am speaking of the movement by which it directs itself downwards and
falls to the ground.

EVODIUS: I do not deny that the movement by which, as you say, a stone 3.1.2.7
is inclined and strives earthward, is a movement belonging to the stone.
But this movement is natural. If the soul also has its movement in this
way, it too is surely natural, and since it is naturally moved it cannot
rightly incur blame. Even if it were moved to something pernicious, it is
compelled by the necessity of its nature. Since we have no doubt that this
movement is blameworthy, we should henceforth completely deny that it
is natural, and so it is *not* similar to the movement by which the stone is
naturally moved.

AUGUSTINE: Did we accomplish anything in Book 1 and Book 2? 3.1.2.8

EVODIUS: We did indeed.

AUGUSTINE: All right. I believe you recall that in Book I we were in full agreement that the mind becomes a slave to lust only through its own will: it cannot be forced to this ugliness by what is higher or by what is equal, since it is unjust; nor by what is lower, since it is unable.[64]

3.1.2.9 Hence it remains that the movement by which [the mind] turns the will for enjoyment from the Creator to something created is its own. If this movement warrants blame – anyone who doubted it seemed to you to deserve ridicule[65] – then it is surely not natural but voluntary. It is similar to the movement by which a stone is borne downwards, in that just as the movement of the stone is its own, so too the movement of the mind is its own. But it is dissimilar in that the stone does not have it in its power to check the movement by which it is borne in its descent, whereas when the mind does not will, it is not moved to take delight in lower

3.1.2.10 things, leaving higher things behind. Hence the movement of the stone is natural, but the movement of the mind is voluntary. Thus if anyone were to say that the stone "sins" because it tends earthward by its weight, I will not say that he is more stupid than the stone, but rather that he is certainly thought to be a madman. However, we charge the mind with sin when we find it guilty of abandoning higher goods to put lower goods

3.1.2.11 first for its enjoyment. Consequently, what need is there to investigate where the movement of the will comes from, the movement by which it is turned from the unchangeable good to the changeable good? We admit that it is a movement of the mind and that it is voluntary, and therefore blameworthy. All useful teaching that deals with this subject amounts to this: Once we have restrained and condemned that movement, let us turn our will away from its lapse into temporal goods and turn it to the enjoyment of the everlasting good.

3.1.3.12 EVODIUS: I see and somehow grasp and comprehend the true things you are saying. For there is nothing I sense as firmly and intimately as that I have a will and that I am moved by it to the enjoyment of something. Surely I find nothing I might call mine if the will – by which I am willing or unwilling – is not mine! Accordingly, if I do anything evil through it, to whom should it be attributed but me? Since the God who made me is good, and I do nothing good except through the will, it is clearly apparent that it was given to me by God, who is good, for

[64] See 1.10.20.71–1.11.21.76.　　[65] See 3.1.1.2.

74

this purpose.[66] Yet if the movement by which the will is turned one way   3.1.3.13
or another were not voluntary and placed in our power, a man should
neither be praised for swinging with the hinge (so to speak) of his will
to higher things, nor blamed for swinging with it to lower things. Nor
should he ever be admonished to put these things aside and to will to
acquire eternal things, or to be unwilling to live badly and to will to live
well. But anyone who holds that a person should not be so admonished
should be expelled from human companionship!

  Since these things are so, it perplexes me beyond words how it could   3.2.4.14
happen that [1] God has foreknowledge of everything that will happen,
and yet [2] we do not sin by any necessity. Anyone who said that something can turn out otherwise than God previously foreknew would be
trying to destroy God's foreknowledge with his senseless irreligiousness.
Consequently, God foreknew that a good man[67] was going to sin. Anyone   3.2.4.15
who allows that God has foreknowledge of everything that will happen
must grant me this. Thus if this is the case, I do not say that God would
not make him – for He made him good; nor could any sin of his harm
God, Who made him good; instead, He showed His own goodness in
making him, even showing His justice in punishing him and His mercy
in redeeming him – I do not say, therefore, that God would not make
him, but I do say this: Since God had foreknown that he was going to sin,
it was necessary that what He foreknew would be the case would happen.
So how is the will free where such unavoidable necessity is apparent?

AUGUSTINE: You have pounded on the door of God's mercy; may He   3.2.5.16
be within and open it wide! However, I think that most people are bothered by this question because they do not raise it in a religious way: They
are quicker to excuse their sins than to confess them. Alternatively, they   3.2.5.17
are eager to hold that there is no divine providence ruling over human
affairs. While they entrust their bodies and souls to blind chance, they
deliver themselves to be battered and torn apart by lusts. Denying divine
judgments and avoiding human judgments, they think to ward off their
accusers with Fortune as their defense. Yet they usually portray Fortune
as blind, so that either they are better than that by which they think
themselves to be ruled, or they admit that they perceive and declare those
things with the same blindness. Nor is it absurd to grant that they do all

---

[66] "For this purpose": namely, to do good (rather than evil) through the will.
[67] "A good man": Adam.

things by the ways in which chance falls out, when they themselves fall by what they do. But we have said enough in Book 2 against this view,[68] which is filled with foolish and senseless error.

3.2.5.18      There are others, however, who do not dare to deny that God's providence rules over human life. Yet they prefer to believe, in wicked error, that God's providence is weak or unjust or evil, rather than to confess 3.2.5.19 their sins in humble religiousness. If they would all permit themselves to be persuaded so that (*a*) when they think of the best and the most just and the strongest, they would believe that the goodness, justice, and power of God are by far greater than and superior to anything they conceive in their thoughts; and (*b*) considering their own selves, they understood that they owe thanks to God, even if He had willed them to be something lower than they are; and (*c*) from all their bones and the pith of their conscience they cried out: "I said: My Lord, be merciful to me! Heal my soul, for I have sinned against You!" [Ps. 40:5 (41:4 RSV)] – well, *then* they would be led by the certain paths of divine mercy into wisdom. As a result, they would be neither proud when uncovering new things nor disturbed at not uncovering anything. In coming to know, they would become better instructed to see; in being ignorant, they would become 3.2.5.20 the more ready to search. I have no doubt that you are already persuaded of this. See how easily I shall reply to your important question once you answer a few initial queries.

3.3.6.21      Surely what perplexes and upsets you is how these two claims are not opposed and inconsistent:

[1] God foreknows everything that will be
[2] We sin not by necessity but by the will

For if God foreknows that someone is going to sin, you say, it is necessary that he sin; but if it is necessary, then there is no choice of the will in his 3.3.6.22 sinning, but an unavoidable and fixed necessity instead. You fear that by this train of reasoning we infer either the negation of [1], which is irreligious, or, if we cannot deny [1], we infer instead the negation of [2]. Does anything else bother you?

EVODIUS: Nothing else right now.

AUGUSTINE: Therefore, you think: [3] Everything God foreknows happens not by will but by necessity.

---

[68] Augustine argued in 2.16.41.161–2.17.45.174 that all things are governed by divine providence. There is no explicit treatment of chance or fortune in Book 2.

EVODIUS: Yes, exactly.

AUGUSTINE: Wake up and look within yourself for a bit: Tell me, if you can: What kind of will are you going to have tomorrow – to sin, or to act rightly?   3.3.6.23

EVODIUS: I do not know.

AUGUSTINE: Well, do you think God does not know either?

EVODIUS: In no way would I think that.

AUGUSTINE: Therefore, if He knows your will of tomorrow, and He foresees the future wills of all people who either exist now or will exist, so much the more does He foresee what He is going to do with regard to the just and the irreligious.

EVODIUS: If I claim that God has foreknowledge of my deeds, surely I should say with much greater assurance that He foreknows with certainty His own deeds and foresees what He is going to do.

AUGUSTINE: Then are you not worried that someone might raise this objection to you: "Whatsoever God is going to do, He too is going to do not by will but by necessity, given that everything God foreknows happens by necessity and not by will"?   3.3.6.24

EVODIUS: When I said that everything God foreknew to be going to be happens by necessity, I was looking only at what happens in His Creation, not at what happens in Him. For these things[69] do not come to pass; instead, they are everlasting.

AUGUSTINE: Therefore, God does nothing in His Creation.

EVODIUS: He has decreed once and for all how the order He has instituted in the universe is carried out. Nor does He oversee anything by a new will.   3.3.6.25

AUGUSTINE: Does He not make anyone happy?

EVODIUS: He does.

AUGUSTINE: Surely He does so at the time when the person becomes happy.

EVODIUS: Yes.

AUGUSTINE: So if, for example, you are going to be happy a year from now, a year from now He is going to make you happy.

EVODIUS: Just so.

AUGUSTINE: Therefore God already foreknows today what He is going to do a year from now.

---

[69] "These things": what happens in God.

EVODIUS: He always foreknew this. I agree that He also knows it now, if it is going to be so.

3.3.7.26 AUGUSTINE: Tell me, please, whether (*a*) you are not a creature of His, or (*b*) your happiness will not come about in you.

EVODIUS: Quite the contrary: I am His creature, and it will come about in me that I shall be happy.

AUGUSTINE: Therefore, your happiness will come about in you, through God's action, not by will but by necessity.

EVODIUS: His will *is* necessity for me.

AUGUSTINE: Therefore, you are going to be happy against your will!

EVODIUS: If it were in my power to be happy, surely I would already be happy. I will it even now, yet I am not happy, since it is not I but He who makes me happy.

3.3.7.27 AUGUSTINE: How well the truth cries out from within you! You could not perceive anything to be in our power except what we do when we will. Accordingly, nothing is so much in our power as the will itself.[70] Surely it is at hand with no delay as soon as we will. Hence we can rightly say: "We do not grow old by our will but rather by necessity," "We do not become ill by our will but rather by necessity," "We do not die by our will but rather by necessity," and anything else of the sort. But who is so mad 3.3.7.28 as to dare say "We do not *will* by our will..."? Consequently, although God foreknows our future wills, it does *not* follow from this that we do not will something by our will.

As for what you said about happiness, namely that you do not make yourself happy, you said it as if I had denied it. However, I maintain that when you are going to be happy, it will not be against your will but willingly. So although God has foreknowledge of your future happiness – and nothing could happen otherwise than He foreknew, since then it would not be *fore*knowledge – nevertheless, we are not forced to hold on these grounds something quite absurd and far from the truth, 3.3.7.29 namely that you are not willing to be happy. God's foreknowledge of your future happiness (which is certain even today) does not take away your will for happiness at the time when you begin to be happy. Likewise, a blameworthy will, if anything of the sort is going to be in you, will not thereby *not* be your will, merely because God foreknows that it is going to be.

---

[70] See 1.12.26.86.

See how great the blindness is with which the following objection is raised: "If God foreknew what my will is going to be, then, since nothing can happen otherwise than He foreknew, it is necessary that I will what He foreknew; yet if it is necessary, we admit that I do not will it by my will at that time but rather by necessity."   3.3.8.30

What exceptional foolishness! How then can it not happen otherwise than God foreknew, unless there is the will that He foreknew to be your will? I shall pass over the equal monstrousness uttered by this objector that I mentioned a little while ago, namely "It is necessary that I so will."[71] He tries to take away the will by assuming necessity. For if it is necessary that he will, on what grounds does he will when it is not his will?   3.3.8.31

Suppose the objector does not say this but instead says that, since it is necessary that he will, he does not have the will itself in his power. Then the same problem will arise that you yourself ran into when I asked whether you were going to be happy against your will. You answered that if you had the power you would already be happy, for you said that you lacked only the power, not the will. I then added that the truth cries out from within you. For we cannot deny that we ourselves have the power, except while what we will is not present to us. Yet when we will, if we lack the will itself, surely we do *not* will. But if it can happen that we do not will when we will, surely the will is present in those who will; nor is there anything in our power other than what is present to those who will. Hence our will would not be a will if it were not in our power. Quite the contrary: Since it *is* in our power, it is free in us. What we do not have in our power, or what can not be what we have, is not free in us.   3.3.8.32   3.3.8.33

Thus it turns out both that we do not deny that God has foreknowledge of everything that will be, and nevertheless that we do will what we will.[72] For although He has foreknowledge of our will, it is the will of which He has foreknowlege. Therefore, it is going to be our will, since He has foreknowledge of our will. Nor could it be our will if it were not in our power. Therefore, He has foreknowledge of our power. Hence power is not taken away from me due to His foreknowledge – it is thus mine all the more certainly, since He whose foreknowledge does not err foreknew that it would be mine.   3.3.8.34   3.3.8.35

---

[71] See 3.3.7.27.   [72] See [1] and [2] in 3.2.4.14 and 3.3.6.21.

EVODIUS: Look: Now I do not deny that (*a*) it is necessary that anything God foreknows happen, and (*b*) He foreknows our sins in such a way that our will still remains free and placed in our power.

3.4.9.36  AUGUSTINE: Then what bothers you? Did you perhaps forget what we covered in Book 1? Will you deny that, since nothing either higher or lower or equal forces us, it is we ourselves who sin through the will?[73]

3.4.9.37  EVODIUS: I certainly do not presume to deny any of these points. But still, I confess, I do not yet see how these two things are not in conflict with each other: (*a*) God's foreknowledge of our sins, and (*b*) our free will in sinning. For we must allow both that God is just and that He has foreknowledge. Yet I would like to know the following:

[1] How does God justly punish sins that necessarily happen?

[2] How is it that future events God foreknows do not happen necessarily?

[3] How is whatever necessarily happens in His Creation not to be imputed to its Creator?

3.4.10.38  AUGUSTINE: On what grounds does our free will seem to be in conflict with God's foreknowledge? Because it is foreknowledge, or because it is God's foreknowledge?

EVODIUS: Because it is God's foreknowledge.

AUGUSTINE: Well then, if *you* foreknew someone was going to sin, would it not be necessary that he sin?

EVODIUS: It surely would be necessary that he sin. My foreknowledge would not be fore*knowledge* unless I foreknew matters that are certain.

AUGUSTINE: Hence it is not because it is God's foreknowledge that what is foreknown must happen, but merely because it is foreknowledge – which, if it does not know in advance matters that are certain, surely is nothing at all.

EVODIUS: I agree. But where are you going with this?

3.4.10.39  AUGUSTINE: Unless I am mistaken, you would not force someone to sin as a result of foreknowing that he is going to sin. Nor would your foreknowledge force him to sin, despite the fact that he undoubtedly *is* going to sin, since otherwise you would not *foreknow* that it is going to be so. Therefore, just as these two things are not opposed, namely that you know by your foreknowledge what someone is going to do by his will, so

---

[73] See 1.10.20.71–1.11.21.76 (alluded to in 3.1.2.8).

too God, although He does not force anyone into sinning, nevertheless foresees those who are going to sin by their own will.

Why, then, should a God equipped with justice and foreknowledge 3.4.11.40 not redress what he does not force to happen? Just as you do not force past things to have happened by your memory, so too God does not force future things to happen by His foreknowledge. And just as you remember some of the things you have done and yet have not done all the things you remember,[74] so too God foreknows all the things of which He is the author and yet is not the author of all the things He foresees. He is not the evil author of these things; He justly exacts retribution for them.

These are the grounds, then, on which you should understand how God justly punishes sins, namely because He does not do the things He knows will happen. For if He ought not hand out punishments to sinners 3.4.11.41 because He foresaw that they were going to sin, on that account neither should He hand out rewards to those who act rightly, since He foresaw nonetheless that they would act rightly. Instead, let us acknowledge these two points: (*a*) it pertains to His foreknowledge that nothing that will be escapes Him; (*b*) it pertains to justice that sin, which is committed with the will, does not happen unpunished by His judgment, just as much as His foreknowledge does not force it to happen.

Now as for [3] – how whatever necessarily happens in His Creation 3.5.12.42 is not to be imputed to its Creator – it will not easily dislodge the rule of religiousness we agreed to keep in mind,[75] namely that we ought to render thanks to our Creator. His bountiful goodness would be praised most justly even if He had made us for some lower level of His Creation. Although our soul is festering with sins, it is still more exalted and better 3.5.12.43 than if it were turned into mere visible light. See indeed how much even souls given over to the bodily senses praise God for the magnificence of this sort of light! Accordingly, do not let it upset you that sinning souls are blameworthy, so that you are led to say in your heart that it would have been better had they not existed. They are blameworthy in com- 3.5.12.44 parison with themselves, [namely] when one thinks of how they would be had they been unwilling to sin. Still, God their arranger[76] should be

---

[74] "And yet have not done all the things you remember": You can remember that Caesar crossed the Rubicon, for instance, though crossing the Rubicon is not something you yourself have done.

[75] See 3.2.5.19.

[76] God puts things in their proper order, "arranging" them in their places.

given the highest praise that human beings can offer, not only because He justly puts them in order as the sinners they are, but also because He has arranged them so that even when they are stained by sin they are not in any way surpassed in dignity by mere physical light (for which He is nonetheless praised).

3.5.13.45    I also caution you to be careful about the following point. Perhaps you should not claim that it would have been better for them not to have existed. Instead, you should say that they ought to have been made differently. Now whatever may strike you as better in true reason, you should know that God, as the Creator of all goods, has made it. For it is not true reason but envious weakness when you think something should have been made better and then want nothing else lesser to be made, as if you wished the Earth had not been made once you saw the heavens – thor-

3.5.13.46    oughly unreasonable! You would be right in finding fault if you saw that the Earth had been made but the heavens passed by. In that case, you could say that the Earth ought to have been made the way you can think of the heavens. But since you perceive that the object in whose likeness you wanted the Earth to be patterned has also been made, though it is called the heavens rather than the Earth, then you should not be envious at all, I think, that something lesser was made too (and it was the Earth), since you have not been cheated out of something better.

3.5.13.47    Again, there is so great a variety in the parts of the Earth that nothing to do with its appearance occurs to anyone considering it which God, the Maker of everything, did not make [somewhere] in the entire collection. From the most fecund and charming land we arrive by intermediate stages at the most unproductive and barren, so that you would not dare to find any at fault except in comparison with a better. Thus you would ascend through all the levels of praiseworthiness to discover the best kind of land; yet you

3.5.13.48    do not want it to exist all by itself. But how great is the distance between the entire Earth and the heavens! The wet and windy natures are put in between. From these four elements[77] come a variety of other likenesses and forms, uncountable by us though God has enumerated them all.

3.5.13.49    There can be something in the world that you do not think of with your reason, then, but there cannot fail to be something you think of with true reason.[78] Nor can you think of anything better in Creation that has

---

77  "These four elements": earth (land), fire (the heavens), air, and water ("the wet and windy natures").
78  See 3.5.13.45 for earlier appearances of "true reason."

escaped the Maker of Creation. The human soul is naturally linked to the Divine Reasons,[79] upon which it depends when it declares: "It would be better to make *this* rather than *that*." If it speaks the truth and sees what it says, it sees by the [divine] reasons to which it is linked. Therefore, let the human soul believe that God made what it knows by true reason He ought to have made, despite not seeing it among the things that have been made. For instance, even if someone could not see the heavens with his eyes, and yet by true reason were to gather that something of the sort ought to have been made, he should believe that it was made, although he did not see it with his eyes: He would not have seen that it ought to have been made except in these [divine] reasons through which everything was made. No one can see with a truthful thought what is not there, to the extent that [what is not there] is not true.

3.5.13.50

Many people go astray on this score. Although they conceive better things with their minds, they search for them with their eyes in inappropriate places. It is like someone who, grasping perfect roundness in his mind, becomes upset that he does not find it in a nut, never having seen any round object except fruits of this sort. Thus, despite seeing with the most true reason that a creature so devoted to God that it will never sin, even though it has free will, is better, some people are stricken with grief while looking upon people's sins: not so that they stop sinning, but rather because they were made. They declare: "He should have made us such that we always want to enjoy His unchangeable truth and never want to sin." They should not rant and rage! God did not force them to sin merely because he gave to those whom He made the power whether they would so will. Indeed, there are some angels who never have sinned and never will sin. Accordingly, if you take delight in a creature who does not sin due to the perseverance of its will, there should be no question that you rank it by right reason ahead of one that sins. But just as you rank it in thought, so did God the Creator rank it when putting things in order. Believe that there is such a creature in the loftier realms of the heights of the heavens! For if the Maker furnished goodness to a creature whose future sins He foresaw, He would certainly furnish this goodness so as to make a creature which He foreknew would not sin.

3.5.14.51

3.5.14.52

3.5.14.53

3.5.14.54

---

[79] "The Divine Reasons": very roughly, the Platonic Ideas of things as found in God's mind; they are the perfect exemplars of created things, and indeed used in the creation of things. Augustine adopts the Platonic view that knowledge is a matter of grasping these Forms.

3.5.15.55     That exalted [creature][80] has its perpetual happiness in its perpetual enjoyment of its creator, which it deserves for its perpetual will to hold fast to justice. Next, the creature who sins also has his own place. He has lost happiness through his sins, but he has not squandered his ability to regain happiness. Furthermore, the [sinner] surely comes before the creature who is possessed by the perpetual will to sin, [namely the Devil]. Between the [Devil] and the [angels] who remain in the will to justice, the sinner marks out a certain intermediate position. He derives

3.5.15.56  his elevated position from the humility of repentance. For not even from the creature He foreknew not only to be going to sin, but also to be going to persist in the will to sin, did God withhold the bestowal of His goodness, so that He not create it. For just as even a wandering horse is better than a stone that does not wander off because it has no perception or movement of its own, so too a creature that sins through free will is more excellent than one that does not sin because it does not have free will.

3.5.15.57  And just as I might praise wine as good of its kind while faulting someone who got drunk on it, and yet put the same person whom I faulted and who is still drunk ahead of the wine I praised on which he got drunk, so too material creations are rightly praised at their level, although those who turn away from the perception of truth by using them immoderately are to be faulted. The same point holds again. Despite their perversity and "drunkenness" (of its kind), people who are ruined by their greed for material objects, which are praiseworthy at their level, are to be preferred to those selfsame material creations. Not because their vices deserve it, but still because of the worthiness of their nature.

3.5.16.58  Hence every soul is better than any body. No matter how far a sinning soul falls, it is not made into a body by any transformation. Nor is it completely deprived of being a soul. Thus, it does not lose in any way the feature of being better than body. Now light holds the first place among bodies. Consequently, the least soul is put ahead of the first body. It can happen that some other body is put before the body belonging to a given soul, but not in any way before the soul itself.

3.5.16.59  Therefore, why should God not be praised? Let Him be praised with praise that cannot be described! Even though He made those [good angels] who were going to abide in the laws of justice, He also made other souls which He foresaw would sin – indeed, ones which He foresaw

---

[80] The good angel, who never has sinned and never will sin, despite having the free will to do so.

84

would *persevere* in their sins. Yet these souls are better than [things] which cannot sin because they have no rational and free choice of the will. These in turn are still better than the radiance, no matter how splendid, of any physical objects, which some people[81] in great error worship as the substance of God the Highest himself. In the order of bodily creatures 3.5.16.60 from galaxies all the way to the number of hairs on our heads, the beauty of good things at each stage is so interwoven that only the most ignorant say: "What is this, and why is it so?" Everything has been created in its order. How much more ignorant, then, to say this about any given soul, which, no matter how much lessening or defect its loveliness has come to, will undoubtedly exceed the worthiness of all bodies!

Reason and utility evaluate matters differently. Reason performs 3.5.17.61 its evaluations in light of the truth, so that it may subordinate lesser to greater things by right judgment. Utility, however, is generally inclined by being accustomed to convenience, with the result that it evaluates more highly things that truth shows to be the lesser. Although reason puts heavenly bodies ahead of earthly bodies by a great margin, who among us in the flesh would not prefer there to be fewer stars in the heavens over even one less tree in his orchard or cow in his herd? Adults wholly con- 3.5.17.62 demn the judgments of young children (or at least patiently expect them to be corrected), since young children prefer any man, apart from those whose love has delighted them, to die, rather than their pet bird – and so much the more if the man is frightening while the bird is a pretty song-bird! Likewise, those who have made progress towards wisdom by the maturity of their minds, whenever they come across people who evaluate things ineptly, praising God in lesser creatures that are better suited to their carnal senses, whilst in the case of higher and better [creatures] some praise Him little or not at all, others try to blame or correct Him, and others do not believe that He is their Maker – well, they[82] wholly condemn the judgments of such people if they cannot correct them, or they get used to tolerating them and enduring them with equanimity until they are corrected.

Given that these things are the case, it is so far from the truth to hold 3.6.18.63 that the sins of the creature are to be imputed to its Creator, even though what He foreknew to happen must come to pass, that, although you said that you did not find out how not to impute to Him anything that must

---

[81] The Manichaeans.    [82] "They": people who have made progress towards wisdom.

come to pass in His Creation,[83] I, on the contrary, find no way (and I declare that one cannot be found and does not exist at all) in which there is imputed to Him anything in His Creation that must come to pass such that it happen by the will of the sinners.

3.6.18.64    Suppose someone objects: "I would rather not be than be unhappy."

I reply: You lie! For you are unhappy even now: You are unwilling to die for no reason other than in order to exist. Thus, even though you do not want to be unhappy, you nevertheless want to be. Give thanks, then, that you willingly *are*, so that what you unwillingly are, [namely unhappy], is taken away. For you willingly are, and you unwillingly are unhappy. But if you are ungrateful inasmuch as you will to be, you shall rightly be forced to be what you do not will. Hence from the fact that although you are ungrateful you have what you will, I praise the goodness of the Creator; from the fact that you ungratefully suffer what you do not will, I praise the justice of the Lawgiver.

3.6.19.65    Suppose he objects: "I do not want to die, not because I prefer to be unhappy rather than not to be at all, but rather so that I not be more unhappy after death."

I reply: If this is unjust, you will not be unhappy. However, if it is just, we should praise Him by whose laws you will be unhappy.

Suppose he objects: "Why should I presume that if this is unjust I will not be unhappy?"

I reply: Because [1] if you are in your own power, either [1*a*] you will not be unhappy, or [1*b*] by governing yourself unjustly you will justly
3.6.19.66    be unhappy. Alternatively, [2] you are not in your own power, willing to govern yourself justly yet not being able to do so; hence you will be either [2*a*] in someone else's power, or [2*b*] in no one's power – and if you are in no one's power, it is either [2*b*₁] willingly, or [2*b*₂] unwillingly. [Against 2*b*₂]: Well, you cannot be anything unwillingly unless some force has overcome you; yet a person who is in no one's power [as we assumed in [2] above] cannot be overcome by any force. [Against 2*b*₁]: However, if you are in no one's power willingly, the argument comes back to [1]: You are in your own [power], and either [1*b*] by governing yourself unjustly you are justly unhappy, or since, whatever you willingly are, you still have reason to give thanks to the goodness of your Maker.[84]

---

[83]  See 3.2.4.14 and 3.4.9.37.
[84]  There is no refutation of [1*a*], since on that alternative you are not unhappy.

[Against 2*a*]: Now if you are not in your own power, then certainly    3.6.19.67
either [2*a*₁] something stronger will have you in its power, or [2*a*₂] something weaker will. [Against 2*a*₁]: If it is weaker, the blame is yours and
your unhappiness is just, since you can overcome a weaker power if
you want. [Against 2*a*₂]: However, if something stronger has you, as the
weaker party, in its power, you will not rightly think unjust so correct an
order [of things].

Therefore, it was most truly said that, if this is unjust, you will not be
unhappy, whereas if it is just, let us praise Him by Whose laws you will
be unhappy.[85]

Suppose he objects: "I want even to be unhappy more than not to be    3.7.20.68
at all, since I already am, but if before I existed I were able to have been
consulted, I would have elected not to be rather than to be unhappy. Now
the fact that I am afraid not to be, although I am unhappy, is relevant to
that unhappiness due to which I do not will what I ought to will. I ought
to will not to be rather than to be unhappy. But I confess now that I pre-    3.7.20.69
fer even to be unhappy rather than nothing, although the more unhappy I
am, the more foolishly do I will this. Again, the more unhappy I am, the
more truly do I see that I ought not to will this."

I reply: Take care instead that you are not mistaken when you think
you see the truth! For if you were happy, surely you would prefer to be
rather than not. Now, unhappy though you are, you still prefer to be, even
unhappy, than not to be at all, despite being unwilling to be unhappy.
Consider, then, as far as you can, how great a good it is to be, which the    3.7.20.70
happy and the unhappy alike will. If you consider the matter well, you
will see that you are unhappy to the extent that you are not close to Him
Who supremely *is*. You think it is better for someone not to be rather
than to be unhappy to precisely the extent that you do not see Him Who
supremely is. Hence you nevertheless will to be, since you are from Him
Who supremely is.

Thus, if you will to escape from being unhappy, love in yourself the    3.7.21.71
very fact that you will to be. For if you will to be more and more, you
will draw closer to Him Who supremely is. Give thanks that now you
are! Although you are inferior to those who are happy, for all that you
are superior to beings which do not have even the will for happiness.
Regardless, many of them are praised even by those who are unhappy.

---

[85] See 3.6.19.65.

Yet all things should rightly be praised in virtue of the fact that they are! For they are good merely in virtue of the fact that they are.

3.7.21.72    The more you love to be, the more you will desire eternal life. You will long to be trained so that your attachments are not temporary, stamped and branded with the loves of temporal things. Before these temporal things exist they are not; when they are they pass away; once they have passed away they will not be. Thus when they are going to be, they are not yet; when they are past, then they are not. How then can such things be caught so as to remain? For them, beginning to be is setting out to not be. By contrast, someone who loves to be approves of these things insofar as they are, and he loves what always *is*. If he wavered in his love of the former, he will be protected in his love of the latter; if he was dissipated in his love of ephemeral things, he will be made whole in his love of what is permanent, and he will stand fast and gain being itself, which he wanted when he was afraid of not being and, entangled in the love of fleeting things, was not able to stand fast.

3.7.21.73

3.7.21.74    Therefore, do not let it displease you – on the contrary, let it please you most of all! – that you prefer to be, although unhappy, rather than not to be unhappy because you will be nothing.[86] If to this starting-point (namely that you want to be) you add more and more being, you will build yourself up and rise to that which supremely *is*. In this way, you will keep yourself safe from any downfall in which what is lowest passes into nonbeing and, along with itself, undermines the strength of anyone who loves it. Hence, since someone who prefers not to be, in order not to be unhappy, cannot not be, he must therefore be unhappy. However, someone who loves to be more than he hates to be unhappy, shuts out what he hates by adding to that which he loves. For when he begins to be perfectly for one of his kind, he will not be unhappy.

3.7.21.75

3.8.22.76    See how absurd and inconsistent it is to object: "I would prefer not to be rather than to be unhappy." Anyone who says he would prefer one thing to another is electing something. Not-being, on the other hand, is not something but nothing, and so you cannot rightly elect it at all, since what you elect does not exist.

You say that you will to be, although you are unhappy, but that you ought not to have willed this.[87] What then ought you to have willed? You

---

[86]  Alternatively: "rather than, since you are unhappy, to not be, since [then] you will be nothing."
[87]  See 3.7.20.69.

reply "Not to be!" instead. If you ought to have willed this, it is better. But what does not exist cannot be better. Therefore, you ought not to have willed this, and your feeling by which you do not will it is more true than the opinion by which you think you ought to have willed it.   3.8.22.77

Next, when anyone attains what he rightly elects to be pursued, he must become better. But whoever does not exist is not able to be better. Hence nobody can rightly elect not to be. We should not be bothered by the judgment of those who have been driven by their unhappiness to do away with themselves. Either they took refuge in a place where they thought they would be better off, and this is not contrary to our reasoning, whatever they may have been thinking; or, if they believed that they would be nothing at all, so much the less bothersome will be their false election of nothing. How might I follow someone who, when asked what he elects, replies: "Nothing!" For anyone who elects not to be is clearly shown to be electing nothing, even if he is unwilling to say so.   3.7.22.78

Now let me say what I think about this whole matter, if I can. It seems to me that nobody, whether he kills himself or wants to die somehow, has it in mind that he is not going to be after death, even if to some extent he holds this as his opinion. For an opinion, be it in error or in truth, belongs to someone who reasons or believes, whereas feelings hold in virtue of nature or habituation. It can happen that something may differ in opinion and in feeling. This is readily seen from cases in which we believe that one thing should be done but we enjoy doing something else. Now sometimes feeling is more true than opinion, if the feeling derives from nature and the opinion from error. For instance, someone ill often finds drinking cold water pleasant, and it is in fact helpful to him, but he believes instead that it will kill him if he drinks it. At other times opinion is more true than feeling. For instance, if a person were to believe that the art of medicine says that cold water is bad for him, and in fact it is, though drinking it is pleasant. At times both are true, as when what is beneficial is not only believed to be so but is also a source of delight. At other times both are in error, for instance when what is harmful is believed to be beneficial and does not stop being a source of delight. Typically, however, a right opinion corrects perverse habituation, and a perverse opinion perverts right nature, so great is the force in the dominance and sovereignty of reason. Therefore, when anyone is driven by unbearable troubles to desire death wholeheartedly, and, believing that after death he will not be, decides upon death and seizes it – well, he is mistaken in his opinion   3.8.23.79   3.8.23.80   3.8.23.81   3.8.23.82

that he will completely escape, but what he has in his feeling is the natural
3.8.23.83 desire for peace. However, what is at peace is not nothing.

Quite the contrary: it *is*, to a greater extent than something unset-tled. Being unsettled makes our emotions vacillate so that one destroys another. Peace, however, has the constancy in which we best understand what is called "being." Thus, the whole of his pursuit in the wish for death is not meant so that the person who dies is not, but rather so that
3.8.23.84 he is at rest. Thus, although he believes in error that he is not going to be, he still desires by nature to be at peace, that is, to *be* to a greater extent. Consequently, just as it cannot happen that anyone take delight in not being, so too it ought not happen that anyone be ungrateful to the good-ness of the Creator for the fact that he is.

3.9.24.85 Suppose someone objects: "It was not difficult or taxing for God's omnipotence that all things He made, whatever they are, should be placed in their proper order, so that no creature would reach the point of unhappiness. Being omnipotent, He was not unable to do this; being good, He was not envious."

I reply: The ordering of creatures runs from the highest to the lowest by just stages, in such a way that anyone who says "This should not be"
3.9.24.86 is envious, as well as anyone who says "This should be like so." For if he wills something to be like what is higher, the former already is, and it is to the extent that it need not be added to, since it is perfect. Therefore, any-one who objects "This should also be like so" either wants to add to what is higher and perfect, and will be immoderate and unjust, or he wants to
3.9.24.87 destroy the object, and will be evil and envious. Furthermore, anyone who objects "This should not be" will nonetheless be evil and envious, since he does not will it to be, yet is still forced to praise this inferior object. It is as if he were to say "There should be no Moon," though he admits that the brightness of a lamp, while far less, is nevertheless beauti-ful in its own class and appropriate to earthly shadows, suitable for use in the night, and in all these respects praiseworthy in its own small way. (At least, if he does not admit it, his denial will be foolish and contentious.)
3.9.24.88 Therefore, how will he rightly presume to claim "There should be no Moon in the world" since if he claimed "There should be no lamp" he is aware that he should be laughed at? Now if he does not say "There should be no Moon" but instead claims that the Moon ought to be such as he sees the Sun to be, he does not understand that he is saying nothing but "There should be no Moon but there should be two Suns instead"!

He makes a twofold error on this score: he wants to add something to the perfection of things, since he desires another Sun, and he wants to lessen the perfection of things, since he wants the Moon to be taken away.

At this point he may perhaps object that he has no complaint with 3.9.25.89 the Moon, because its lesser radiance does not thereby make it unhappy. Instead, his complaint is with souls: not their darkness, but the unhappiness they suffer.

Let him consider carefully [his claim] that it is not the case that the Moon's radiance is unhappy, just as it is not the case that the Sun's radiance is happy. Although they are celestial bodies, they still are bodies as 3.9.25.90 far as the light that can be sensed through our bodily eyes is concerned. But no bodies *qua* bodies can be either happy or unhappy, although they can be the bodies of those who are happy or unhappy. Yet the analogy 3.9.25.91 drawn from the Sun and Moon does teach us this. As you examine the differences among bodies and see that some are brighter, it is unjust for you to ask that those you noticed to be darker be taken away, or be made the equal of the brighter ones. Instead, if you relate them all to the perfection of the universe, you will realize that they are more or less bright among themselves to precisely the extent that all of them *are* – and the universe will only strike you as perfect because the presence of the greater does *not* result in the absence of the lesser. Likewise, consider the differences among souls. You will find that you realize that the unhappiness you deplore also contributes to the perfection of the universe, for [the universe] does not lack those souls who ought to be made unhappy because they willed to be sinners. Indeed, it is so far from being the case that God ought not to have made them, that He also deserves praise for having made other creatures much inferior to these unhappy souls.

Yet someone who still does not quite understand what we have said 3.9.26.92 has, it seems, an objection to raise against it: "Suppose even our unhappiness completes the perfection of the universe. Then something would be lacking in this perfection if we were always happy. Accordingly, if the soul only comes to be unhappy through sinning, then even our sins are necessary for the perfection of the universe God made. How then does He justly punish our sins? If they were lacking, His Creation would not be complete and perfect!"

Here is my answer. Neither the sins themselves nor our unhappiness 3.9.26.93 is necessary for the perfection of the universe, but rather souls *qua* souls [are necessary] – souls which sin if they so will, and become unhappy if they sin. If unhappiness persists once the sins are taken away, or even if they precede the sins, then the ordering and the oversight of the universe is rightly said to be disfigured. Again, if the sins do occur but our unhappiness is absent, the unfairness nonetheless dishonors the ordering. When people who do not sin are happy, the universe is perfect; when sinners are unhappy, the universe is perfect nonetheless. There is no lack of souls for whom unhappiness follows when they sin, and happiness when they act rightly; the universe is always perfect and filled with all natures. Sin and the punishment for sin are not any kind of nature, but rather states of natures, the former voluntary and the latter a penalty. But the voluntary state that occurs in a sin is disgraceful. The penalty is inflicted to place [the nature] in an ordering where it is not a disgrace for it to be such, and to compel it to be in harmony with the loveliness of the universe, so that the penalty for the sin relieves the ugliness of the sin.

3.9.27.96 As a result, it happens that a higher creature who sins is punished by lower creatures, since the latter are so low that they can be adorned even by disgraced minds, and thereby be in harmony with the beauty of the universe. For what is so great in a household as a human being? And what is so low and detestable as its sewer? Yet a slave, caught in a sin which is such that he is held worthy of cleaning the sewer, adorns the sewer even in his disgrace. Both of these things, the slave's disgrace and the cleaning of the sewer, are joined together and brought into a certain kind of unity, adapted to and woven into an orderly household in such a way as to be suitable to the household as a whole with the most orderly beauty. Yet if the slave had not been willing to sin, the management of the household would not have been lacking some other provision for cleaning the sewer.

3.9.27.98 What then is lower in the world than any earthly body? Yet even a sinful soul so adorns this corruptible flesh that it furnishes it with a fitting appearance and life-giving motion. Therefore, such a soul is not suited for a heavenly abode through its sin, but it is suited to an earthly abode through its punishment, so that whatever it elects to do, the universe, whose maker and overseer is God, is always beautiful and ordered with the most fitting parts. Surely when the best souls inhabit the lowest creatures they do not adorn them with their unhappiness, which they do not have; [they adorn them] by making good use of them. But it is shameful if sinful souls are allowed to inhabit lofty places, since they are not suited for things they neither use well nor bestow any adornment upon.

Hence, although this earthly globe is counted among things corrupt- 3.9.28.100 ible, it still preserves, as far as it can, the image of higher things, and it unceasingly shows us examples and indications of them. Suppose we were to see some great and good man whose body is incinerated by flames while in pursuit of his duty. We do not call this a penalty for sin, but rather evidence of his courage and endurance. We love him more when the horrible corruption consumes his bodily limbs than if he had endured nothing of the sort. In fact, we marvel that the nature of the soul is not changed by the changeability of the body. But when we look upon the body of a 3.9.28.101 ruthless highwayman destroyed with this punishment [of being burned alive], we approve the legal order. Therefore, both men adorn their torments: the former by merit of his virtue, the latter by merit of his sin.

However, if after those flames (or even before them) we saw that excellent man raised up to the stars, transferred to the propriety of a heavenly abode, we would certainly rejoice. But if we saw the wicked highwayman with the same evil will elevated to an everlasting seat of honor, whether before his punishment or after it, who would not be offended? And so it 3.9.28.102 is that both [souls] were able to adorn lower creatures, but one of them higher ones.

From this fact, we are well advised to take note that this mortal flesh adorned even the First Man,[88] so that the penalty would fit his sin. And it adorned our Lord, so that His mercy might free us from sin. For a just person can have a mortal body while remaining in his justice, but a wicked person, as long as he is wicked, cannot likewise attain the immortality of the saints – that is, a sublime and angelic immortality, not the one belonging to those angels of whom the Apostle Paul says: "Do you not know that we are going to judge the angels?" [1 Cor. 6:3] but rather the one belonging to those of whom the Lord says: "They will be the equals of the angels of God" [Lk. 20:36].[89] Those who desire equality 3.9.28.103 with the angels for their own empty glory do not thereby will to be equal to the angels, but instead will the angels to be equal to them. Persevering in such a will, then, they will be equal in their punishment to the fallen angels, who esteemed their own power rather than God's omnipotence. Because they did not seek God through the portal of humility which the

---

[88] "The First Man": Adam.
[89] See also Mt. 22:30: "In the resurrection [human beings] neither marry, nor are given in marriage, but are as the angels of God in heaven."

Lord Jesus Christ displays in himself, and instead were unforgiving and proud in their lives, they will be set upon His left hand and it shall be said unto them: "Depart into the eternal fire that has been made ready for the Devil and his angels" [Mt. 25:41].

3.10.29.104 There are two sources of sins: our own thinking, and persuasion by someone else. I think that the prophet was speaking of these sources when he said: "Cleanse me of my hidden faults, Lord, and spare your servant from those of others" [Ps. 18:13–14 (19:12–13 RSV)]. Each is voluntary – just as someone does not sin by his own thinking unwillingly, so too when one consents to the evil persuasion of another he certainly consents by his will. Yet it is not only more serious to sin by one's own thinking without anyone else's persuasion, it is also more serious to persuade someone else to sin through spite and trickery than it is to be led into sin-

3.10.29.105 ning by someone else's persuasion. God's justice in punishing each kind of sin therefore remains intact. For this point has also been weighed on the scales of fairness:[90] The Devil himself has not been denied power over human beings, whom he made his subjects by his evil persuasion. It was unfair that the Devil not dominate those whom he has captured. Nor can it happen in any way that the perfect justice of the true and supreme God, which encompasses everything, should abandon even those ruined

3.10.29.106 by sin, who need to be put in order. Nevertheless, the fact that human beings sinned less than the Devil did served to win back their salvation. They were awarded to the prince of this world, namely the prince of the lowest and mortal part of things. That is, they were awarded to the prince of all sins and the ruler of death, all the way up to the mortal-

3.10.29.107 ity of their flesh. Made fearful by their awareness of mortality, dreading death and injuries from the least and lowest of beasts (even the smallest), and uncertain of the future, human beings typically embrace and spend themselves in illicit pleasures. Most of all they embrace pride. Cast down by its persuasion, they spit out the medicine of mercy because of this one vice. Who has as much need of mercy as an unhappy person? And who is so unworthy of mercy as an unhappy person who is proud?

3.10.30.108 From this it came to pass that the Word of God, "through which all things are made" [Jn. 1:3] and in which all angelic happiness is enjoyed, extended clemency all the way to our unhappiness: "The Word was made flesh and dwelt among us" [Jn. 1:14]. Though not yet made equal

---

[90] "Weighed on the scales of fairness": has been found to be fair.

to the angles, human beings could in this way eat the bread of angels, seeing that the Bread of Angels[91] deigned to be made equal to human beings. Nor did He abandon the angels in descending to us in this fashion. Instead, He is at once complete with them *and* complete with us. He nourishes the angels from within by the fact that He is God; He counsels us from without by what we are, and by faith renders us fit for Him to nourish equally through his appearance.[92] For the rational creature finds its best "nourishment" (so to speak) in the Word, and the human soul is rational – although it is bound in the chains of mortality as the penalty for its sin, and diminished to the point that it struggles to understand things unseen through conjectures based on things it has seen.[93] The "food" of the rational creature was made visible, not through any change in His own nature, but by donning our nature, to call those who follow visible things back to Himself, Who is invisible. Thus the soul that finds Him in outward humility Whom it had forsaken in its inward pride is going to imitate His visible humility and return again to the heights of the invisible.

3.10.30.109

Clothed in humanity, the Word of God – the only Son of God – subjugated the Devil (whom He always had and always will have under His laws), even to humanity. He did not wrest anything from him by violent domination. Instead, He conquered the Devil by the law of justice. Once the woman was deceived and the man met his downfall through her,[94] the Devil, out of a malicious desire to do harm, yet with a completely legitimate right, laid his claim with the laws of death to all the descendants of the First Man on the grounds of being sinners. His power lasted until he killed the Just One[95] in Whom he could show nothing worthy of death, not merely because He was slain without any crime but also because He was born without any lust, to which the Devil subjugated those whom he held captive, so that he kept whatever was born of lust as though it were the fruit of his own tree – out of a depraved desire to have it, indeed, yet with a not unfair right of possession. Most justly, then, is the Devil forced

3.10.31.110

3.10.31.111

---

91 "The Bread of Angels": Christ.
92 Through faith we may eventually receive the Beatific Vision, which 'nourishes' the angels and which we may learn to live on.
93 See Rom. 1:20: "His invisible things are clearly seen from the creation of the world, being understood by the things that are made." Also Hbr. 11:1: "Faith is the substance of things hoped for, the evidence of things not seen."
94 "The woman" is Eve and "the man" Adam; Augustine is referring to the Fall.
95 "The Just One": Christ.

to relinquish those who believe in Him Whom he killed most unjustly, so that when they die in time, they repay what they owed, and when they live always, they live in Him Who repaid on their behalf what He did not owe. But those whom the Devil has persuaded to persevere in their faithlessness he justly has as his companions in perpetual damnation.

3.10.31.112 Thus did it happen that human beings were not taken away from the Devil by force. Nor did they submit by force, but instead by persuasion. They were justly made humble to serve the one to whom they gave their consent to evil; they were justly made free by Him to Whom they gave their consent to good. For they sinned less in consenting to evil than the Devil did in persuading them to it.[96]

3.11.32.113 Hence God made all natures, not only those who would abide in virtue and justice but also those who would sin – not in order that they sin, but in order that they adorn the universe, whether they willed to sin or not to sin. If there were no souls to occupy the very highest position in the order of the created universe, such that had they willed to sin the universe would be weakened and undermined, something important would be missing from Creation, namely, something the removal of which would 3.11.32.114 disrupt the stability and interconnectedness of things. Such are the best creatures who are the Powers of the heavens and beyond, the holy and sublime creatures whom God alone commands and to whom the whole universe is subject; without their just and perfect roles the universe could not be.[97]

Again, if the universe were to lack natures that would not in any way lessen its order, whether they sin or not, even then something important would be missing. For souls are rational, and they are equal in their nature to those higher beings, even though they are unequal in their role.

In addition to these, there are many levels of things made by the Most High God that are lower yet but still praiseworthy.

3.11.33.115 Therefore, the natures with a more sublime role are the ones which would lessen the order of the universe not only if they did not exist but

---

[96] See 3.10.29.104.

[97] The celestial hierarchy is mentioned in Col. 1:16 and alluded to in Eph. 1:21. Augustine describes the cosmic functions of angels in his *Literal Commentary on "Genesis"* 8.24.45, but elsewhere he candidly admits that he does not have a full account of the hierarchy: "I believe quite firmly that there are Thrones, Dominions, Principalities, and Powers in the heavenly mansions, and I hold with unshaken faith that they differ from one another; but … I do not know what they are like or how they differ from one another" (*Against the Followers of Priscillian* 11.14; see also *Enchiridion* 15.58).

even if they sinned. The natures with a lower role are those which would lessen the universe only if they did not exist, but not if they sinned. The former have been granted the power of maintaining everything with their given role, which cannot be missing from the order of things. They do not persist in their good will because they received this role. Instead, they received it because it was foreseen by Him Who granted it that they would persist. Yet they do not maintain all things by their own majesty, but rather by holding fast to His majesty, and by obeying with the greatest devotion the commands of Him "from Whom and through Whom and in Whom all things have been made" [Rom. 11:36]. 3.11.33.116

The lower natures were also granted the powerful role of maintaining all things, as long as they did not sin. Yet this was not exclusive to them but shared with the higher natures, inasmuch as God foreknew that they would sin. Spiritual beings, in fact, have the feature that they join together with no accumulation and separate with no diminution. As a result, the higher would not be assisted in the easiness of their action when the lower are joined together with them. Nor would it become more difficult for the higher if the lower abandoned their role through sinning. Although spiritual creatures may possess their individual bodies, they can only be joined together by the likeness of their affections or separated by their unlikeness, not by their locations or the mass of their bodies. 3.11.33.117

Ordained to its place among the lower mortal bodies after sinning, the soul rules over its body – not entirely according to its choice, but as the laws of the universe permit. Yet such a soul is not thereby inferior to the heavenly bodies, to which even earthly bodies are subject. The rags of a condemned slave are vastly inferior to the clothing of a well-deserving slave held in high esteem by his master, yet the slave himself is better than any expensive clothes, since he is a human being. Therefore, the higher nature holds fast to God and, in its celestial body, through its angelic power it also adorns earthly bodies and rules over them according to the bidding of Him Whose mere nod it beholds in some inexpressible manner. In contrast, the lower nature, weighed down with its mortal body, scarcely controls from within the body that drags it down. And yet it adorns it as much as it is able. It affects other exterior things around it as it can, but its exterior activity is much weaker over them. 3.11.34.118 3.11.34.119

Thus we may conclude that even if [embodied souls] had been unwilling to sin, completely suitable adornment was not going to be absent from the least of material Creation. For what can govern the whole also governs 3.12.35.120

the part, but what can govern the lesser is not thereby able to govern the greater. A perfect doctor effectively cures a skin rash, but it does not follow that anyone who gives useful advice about a skin rash can provide remedies for every kind of human disease.

3.12.35.121 Furthermore, if we consider the certain argument by which we have made it clear that it was necessary for there to be a creature that never has sinned and never will sin,[98] the same argument also proclaims that it abstained from sin by its free will. Nor was it forced not to sin, but did so 3.12.35.122 voluntarily. Nevertheless, even *if* it were to sin – although it did not sin, as God foreknew that it would not sin – yet even if it were to sin, the inexpressible power of God would be enough power to govern the universe. By assigning to everything what is fitting and appropriate, He would permit nothing to be disgraceful or shameful in the whole of His command. 3.12.35.123 For there are two alternatives: [1] The power of God would rule everything fittingly well by His majesty, not through any of the Powers that He made expressly for this purpose, if every angelic nature had foresaken His precepts through sinning. Nor would God have begrudged spiritual creatures their existence – He Who by the great bestowal of His goodness also fashioned material creatures, which are far inferior even to sinful spiritual creatures. There is no person rationally looking upon the heavens and the Earth, and all the visible natures ordered and measured and formed in their kinds, who either believes that there is some architect of everything other than God or does not admit that He is to be praised beyond words. [2] There is no better order of things than for the angelic Powers, due to the excellence of their nature and the goodness of their will, to be preeminent in the arrangement of the universe. Even if all the angels had sinned they would not cause their Creator any lack of means 3.12.35.124 to govern his realm. For His goodness would not find anything a chore, so to speak, nor His omnipotence meet any difficulty in creating other angels whom He would station at the places they had abandoned through sinning. And no matter how many spiritual creatures were damned on their own merits, they could not hold back the order which appropriately and fittingly imprisons all the damned. And so, directing our attention to either [1] or [2], we find that God is to be praised beyond words, for He is the best Maker of all natures, the One Who oversees them with the greatest justice.

---

[98] See 3.11.32.113–3.11.32.114 and 3.5.14.54–3.5.15.55.

Finally, let us leave contemplation of the beauty of things to those who 3.13.36.125 by a divine gift can see it, and not attempt to bring them with words to look upon matters that are beyond words. Yet on account of people who talk too much, deceitful and weak-minded as they are, let us deal with so great a question with the briefest of reasoning.

Every nature that can become less good is good. Furthermore, every 3.13.36.126 nature becomes less good when it is corrupted. Either corruption does not harm it, and it is not corrupted; or, if it is corrupted, corruption harms it, and if corruption is harmful it takes some good away from it and renders it less good. For if it deprives it completely of all good, whatever remains will not then be able to be corrupted, since there will be no good left for corruption to take away and thereby cause harm. Yet what corruption cannot harm is not corrupted. What is more, a nature that is 3.13.36.127 not corrupted is incorruptible. Thus a nature will be rendered incorruptible by corruption, which is a completely ridiculous claim.

Accordingly, the truth is that every nature *qua* nature is good. For, on the one hand, if it is incorruptible it is better than what is corruptible. On the other hand, if it is corruptible, then, since when it is corrupted it becomes less good, it is undoubtedly good. But every nature is either 3.13.36.128 incorruptible or corruptible. Therefore, every nature is good.

Now I call "nature" what is also usually termed "substance." Therefore, every substance either is God or comes from God, since every good either is God or comes from God.

With these matters settled and guaranteed at the outset of our chain 3.13.37.129 of reasoning, pay attention to what I say. Every rational nature that was made with free choice of the will should without a doubt be praised if it remains fixed in its enjoyment of the highest and unchangeable good. Likewise, every nature that attempts to remain fixed should also be praised. But any nature that does not remain fixed in it and does not will to act so that it remain fixed, inasmuch as it is not there[99] and inasmuch as it does not act so that it be there, should be blamed.

Therefore, if the rational nature that was made is praised, no one 3.13.37.130 doubts that He Who made it should be praised. If it is blamed, no one doubts that its Maker is praised in the blame accorded to it. When we appropriately blame [the rational nature] for not willing to enjoy the highest and unchangeable good (*i.e.* its Creator), we are without a doubt

---

[99] That is, not fixed in the enjoyment of the highest and unchangeable good.

3.13.37.131 rendering praise to Him. How great a good, therefore, is God the Creator of everything! How He should be trumpeted and honored with all our tongues and all our thoughts beyond words to express! We can be neither praised nor blamed without rendering praise to Him. We can only be blamed because remaining fixed in Him is our great, highest, and primary good. And why is this so if not because He is a good beyond words? What grounds can be found in our sins, then, on which to blame God, when blame for our sins is nothing but rendering praise to Him?

3.13.38.132 Well, what does anyone blame in the very things that are blamed but the vice? Yet the vice which belongs to someone is not blamed without praising the nature to which [the vice] belongs. For either (*a*) what you blame is in accordance with the nature and is no vice, and you yourself should be corrected so that you know how to blame rightly, rather than that which you do not blame rightly. Or (*b*) if it is a vice that can 3.13.38.133 be blamed rightly, it must also be contrary to the nature. Every vice, in virtue of the fact that it *is* a vice, is contrary to nature. For if it does not harm the nature, it is not a vice. But if it is a vice precisely because it harms the nature, then it is a vice because it is contrary to the nature.

However, it is unjust to blame a nature if it is corrupted not by its own vice, but through a vice belonging to another nature. We should ask whether the latter nature is not itself corrupted by its own vice through which the former nature was able to be corrupted. But what is it for something to be defective if not to be corrupted by vice? Besides, a nature that 3.13.38.134 is not defective lacks vice, while one whose vice corrupts another nature surely has vice. Therefore, if one nature can corrupt another by its vice, the former is initially vice-ridden and corrupted by its own vice. From all this, it follows that every vice is contrary to nature, even contrary to the nature of the thing of which it is the vice. Accordingly, since in any given thing the only thing blamed is the vice, and it is a vice precisely because it is contrary to the nature of the thing of which it is the vice, the vice belonging to any thing is blamed rightly only if the nature of that thing is praised. For what rightly displeases you in the vice is only that it ruins what pleases you in the nature.

3.14.39.135 We should also see whether it is true to say that a given nature is corrupted by a vice belonging to another nature, with no associated vice of its own. For if the nature that advances with its vice to corrupt another does not find anything corruptible in it, it does not corrupt it. But if it does find something corruptible, it effects its corruption with the addition of this vice. [There are three possibilities.] [1] The stronger is not corrupted by the weaker if it is unwilling to be corrupted. However, if it is willing, it starts being corrupted by its own vice before that of another. [2] An equal likewise cannot be corrupted by an equal if it is unwilling. For any nature with a vice advancing upon one without vice in order to corrupt it does not, by that very fact, advance as an equal, but as weaker due to its own vice. [3] If the stronger corrupts the weaker, this happens either (*a*) through a vice in each of them, if it happens through a depraved desire each of them has; or (*b*) through a vice in the stronger, if its nature has so much more excellence that even when vice-ridden it is more powerful than the lesser nature it corrupts. Who rightly blames the fruits of the Earth because human beings do not use them well and, corrupted by their own vices, corrupt them by misusing them for their luxury? Yet only madmen could doubt that human nature is more excellent and stronger, even when shot through with vice, than any given fruits which are free of vice. Now it can also happen that a stronger nature corrupts a weaker one (*c*) through no vice in either of them, if by "vice" we mean "deserving of blame." But who would dare to blame an abstemious person who tries to get nothing from fruits other than what his nature requires? Or to blame the selfsame fruits because they are corrupted by his use of them as food? This sort of thing is not commonly termed "corruption," which is most of all the name for a vice. We can easily observe in other cases that often a stronger nature corrupts a lesser one (*d*) without using it to satisfy any need. On the one hand, this happens in the order of justice when the stronger nature redresses some fault. From this rule comes the remark of the Apostle Paul: "If anyone corrupts the temple of God, God will corrupt him" [1 Cor. 3:17]. On the other hand, this happens in the order of changeable things, which give way to one another in accordance with the entirely suitable laws that were laid down for the flourishing of every part of the universe. For instance, if the brightness of the Sun damages someone's eyes, which are weak in tolerating the light in accordance with the measure of their nature, the Sun should not be thought to change them to satisfy a need of its own light. Nor does the Sun do this by any vice of its own. Nor, finally, should the eyes themselves be blamed because they submitted to their owner and so were opened into the light, or because they submitted to the light and so were damaged. Hence the only one of all these types of corruption [3*a*]–[3*d*] that is rightly blamed is the one that involves vice, [3*a*]. The others either should not be called cases of

3.14.39.136

3.14.39.137

3.14.40.138

3.14.40.139

3.14.40.140

3.14.40.141

corruption at all, or, in any event, cannot be worthy of blame since they do not involve vice. Indeed, the word "blame" (*uituperatio*) is etymologically derived and so called from "made ready for, *i.e.* apt for or owing to, vice alone" (*uitium + paratum*).[100]

3.14.41.142   Vice, as I had begun to say, is evil simply because it is opposed to the nature of the thing of which it is the vice. Accordingly, it is clear that the selfsame thing whose vice is blamed is a nature that is worthy of praise. We must admit in consequence that to blame the vices is itself entirely to praise the natures whose vices are being blamed. Because the vice is opposed to the nature, exactly as much is added to the evil of the vices as

3.14.41.143   is taken away from the completeness of the nature. Therefore, when you blame the vice you are really praising something whose completeness you desire. And the completeness of what, but the nature? For a nature that is perfect of its kind not only does not deserve any blame but even merits praise. Therefore, you call what you recognize is missing from the perfection of the nature a vice – thereby demonstrating that you are pleased with the nature and, in blaming its imperfection, you would that it be perfect.

3.15.42.144   Hence if blaming vices commends the worth and loveliness even of the very natures of which they are the vices, how much more should God the Maker of all natures be praised even in their vices! For they have it from Him that they *are* natures. They are riddled with vice to precisely the extent that they fall away from His design, in accordance with which they were made. And they are blamed to precisely the extent that the one who blames them sees the design in accordance with which they were made, so that he blames them for what he does not see of the design in them.

3.15.42.145   If the design in accordance with which all things were made, that is, the supreme and unchangeable wisdom of God, truly and supremely *is* – as in fact it is – consider where anything that falls away from that design is heading!

Yet that defect would not be worthy of blame unless it were voluntary. Please consider whether you blame rightly what is exactly as it was supposed to be. I do not think so. Instead, you blame rightly what is *not* exactly as it was supposed to be. But no one is indebted[101] for something

---

[100]  Augustine's etymology is correct though his interpretation is not: *uituperatio* is derived from the verb *uituperare = uitium + paro*, to find fault.

[101]  "Indebted": *debet*, the same word rendered 'supposed [to be]' before. Augustine is trying to explain what ought to be the case as a kind of debt.

he has not received. And to whom is anyone indebted but the one from whom he received what makes him indebted? Even debts that are repaid 3.15.42.146 through a bequest are repaid to him who made the bequest, and a debt repaid to the legitimate successors of creditors is surely repaid to the creditors of whom they are the rightful successors. Otherwise it should not be called a "repayment," but a "surrendering" or "loss" or something of the sort.

It follows that all temporal things have been positioned in this order of things in such a way that future things could not succeed past ones unless they were to cease to exist, so that the whole beauty of the ages is fully accomplished in their kind. It is quite ridiculous for us to say that they are not supposed to cease to exist. They act to precisely the extent that 3.15.42.147 they have received, and they repay just as much to Him to Whom they are indebted for their being, to whatever extent they exist. Anyone who laments that these things cease to exist should pay attention to whether he thinks that his own words, giving voice to his complaint, are just and proceed from prudence. If someone were to value one part of this speech insofar as its mere sound is concerned, and were to wish that it not cease and give way to the rest, we would judge him to be completely mad, since his entire speech is itself put together out of such instances of ceasing to exist and succession. Hence in the case of things that cease to exist pre- 3.15.43.148 cisely because they do not receive further being, so that all things may be accomplished in their own times, no one can rightly blame them for ceasing to exist. For no one can say: "It was supposed to have lasted," since it could not overstep the boundaries it received.

Now in the case of rational creatures, with whom the beauty of the 3.15.43.149 universe reaches the boundaries most appropriate to it, whether they sin or not, either: (*a*) there are no sins, which is an absurd claim, since at least the person who condemns what are not sins as though they were sins himself is sinning. Or (*b*) sins should not be blamed, which is no less absurd, for then we shall begin to praise deeds that are not rightly done; the whole orientation of the human mind will be thrown off and turn life upside down. Or (*c*) a deed will be blamed which was done as it was supposed to be done, and this will give rise to horrible madness, or, to speak more mildly, a dreadful mistake. Or (*d*) if the most true reasoning 3.14.43.150 compels us to conclude that sins should be blamed (as indeed it does), and that whatever is blamed rightly is blamed precisely because it is not as it was supposed to be, then ask what debt the sinful nature owes. You will find that it owes right deeds. Ask to whom it owes the debt. You will find that it is to God – for it received from God the power to act rightly when it willed to do so, and it received from God also that it be unhappy if it did not so act and happy if it did so act.

3.15.44.151 Since no one overcomes the laws of the Almighty Creator, it is not permitted for the soul not to repay its debt. Now the soul repays it either by using well what it received, or by losing what it was unwilling to use well. Thus if the soul does not repay it by doing justice, it will repay it by suffering unhappiness, since in each case the word "debt" applies. We could put the point like this: "If the soul does not repay its debt by doing what it ought, it will repay its debt by suffering what it ought."

3.15.44.152 No temporal interval separates these two things, as though at one time someone does not do what he ought and at another time he suffers what he ought. Consequently, the beauty of the universe is not marred for even a moment, [as would happen if] the ugliness of sin were in it without the loveliness of redressing it. But whatever is redressed now (in a completely hidden fashion) is kept for its disclosure and for its bitter sense of unhap-

3.15.44.153 piness in the Judgment that is to come.[102] Just as someone who is not awake is asleep, so too whoever does not do what he ought suffers what he ought, without delay, since the happiness of justice is so great that nobody can fall away from it except into unhappiness.

Therefore, in all defects, either the defective things did not receive further being, and there is no fault – just as even while they exist there is nonetheless no fault because they did not receive more being than they are – or they were unwilling to be what, if they had been willing, they would have received as their being, and, since [what they would have received] is good, it is an offense if they are unwilling.

3.16.45.154 God, however, does not owe anything to anyone, since He provides everything for free. Suppose that someone claims that God owes him something on account of his deserts. Surely the fact that he exists was not owed to him, for there was no one to whom it was owed. And what deserts are there in being turned to Him from Whom you exist, so that you also have a better existence from Him from Whom you have your existence? What then do you pay Him beforehand, which you demand as though it were a debt? If you were unwilling to be turned to Him, He would not be missing anything. But you are missing Him, without

---

[102] "The Judgment that is to come": the Last Judgment.

Whom you would be nothing, and from Whom you are something in such a way that, unless you repay Him from Whom you are by turning yourself to Him, you will not indeed be nothing but you will nevertheless be unhappy.

Therefore, all things owe to God (*a*) anything they are *qua* natures; (*b*) anything better they can be if they will whatever they have received, insofar as they will it; (*c*) anything they are bound to be. Hence no one is an offender for what he did not receive, but he is, in justice, an offender for not doing what he ought. As he ought to, if he has received free will and has abilities more than up to the task. 3.16.45.155

When anyone does not do what he ought, no fault attaches to his Maker, to the point that it is praise, since he suffers what he ought; and He to Whom the debt is owed is praised precisely in virtue of the fact that [the offender] is blamed for not doing what he ought. For if you receive praise for seeing what you ought to do, even though you see it only in Him Who is unchangeable Truth, how much more praise does God receive, Who prescribes what you will, Who provides you with the power, and Who does not allow you to be unwilling with impunity! 3.16.46.156

If everyone owes what he has received, and human beings are made in such a way that they necessarily sin, then they ought to sin. Therefore, when someone sins, he does what he ought. But if this is a wicked claim, then no one is compelled to sin by his own nature. Nor is he compelled to sin by the nature of another; nobody sins in suffering that which he does not will. On the one hand, if he suffers justly, he does not sin in suffering unwillingly; rather, he sinned in having acted willingly in such a way that he rightly suffers what he is unwilling to suffer. On the other hand, if he suffers unjustly, in what way does he sin? It is not a sin to *suffer* something unjustly, but to *do* something unjustly. Yet if no one is compelled to sin, either by his own nature or by the nature of another, it follows that sinning occurs through our will. 3.16.46.157

3.16.46.158

Now if you want to assign the sinning to the Creator instead, you will exonerate the sinner. The sinner has then done nothing beyond the precepts of his Creator. If he is defended justly, he did not sin, and so there is nothing to assign to the Creator. Therefore, let us praise the Creator if the sinner can be defended; let us praise the Creator if he cannot. For if he is defended rightly, he is not a sinner; therefore praise the Creator! But if the sinner cannot be defended, he is a sinner precisely to the extent that he turns himself away from the Creator; therefore praise the Creator! 3.16.46.159

3.16.46.160    Hence I find no way in which our sins are assigned to our Creator – and I declare that no way can be found, since there is none at all – when I find Him praiseworthy even in our sins, not only because He punishes them, but also because they occur precisely at the time when there is a withdrawal from His truth.

EVODIUS: I gladly accept these points and give them my approval. I agree that it is completely true that it cannot happen in any way that our sins are assigned rightly to our Creator.

3.17.47.161    But, if possible, I would still like to know why *this* nature, which God foreknew would not sin, does not sin, and why *that* nature, which He foresaw would sin, does sin. I no longer think it due to God's foreknowledge that the former does not sin and that the latter is compelled to sin.

3.17.47.162    Yet nevertheless, if there were no cause, rational creatures would not be divided into (*a*) those who never sin; (*b*) those who persevere in their sinning; and (*c*) those who sometimes sin and sometimes are turned to acting rightly, the group "intermediate" between (*a*) and (*b*). What is the cause dividing rational creatures into these three groups?

3.17.47.163    Now I do not want you to reply: "the will." I am looking for the cause of the will itself. It is not without cause that the first group never wills to sin, the second group always wills to sin, and the third sometimes wills to sin and sometimes does not, despite the fact that they are all of the same kind. This alone seems clear to me: The threefold will of rational creatures is not without cause. But what the cause is I do not know.

3.17.48.164    AUGUSTINE: The will is the cause of sin, but you are searching for the cause of the will itself. If I were able to find this cause, are you not also going to ask about the cause of this cause that has been found? What will limit our investigation? What will be the end of our discussion and examination?

3.17.48.165    You should not search for anything beyond the root of the matter. Be careful that you not think anything more true than the dictum that the root of all evils is greed [1 Tim. 6:10], that is, to will to have more than is enough. Now 'enough' is exactly as much as is required for a nature

3.17.48.166    of a given kind to preserve itself. 'Greed' (or φιλαργυρία in Greek) should not be understood only with respect to silver, or rather coins,[103] from which the Greek name is derived – coins happened to be made of

---

[103] The Greek term for "greed," namely φιλαργυρία, is compounded out of the words for "love" and "silver."

silver, or a silver alloy, more commonly in the past – but in all cases of immoderate desire, wherever it may be that anyone wills to have more than is enough. This greed is desire. Desire, moreover, is a wanton will. Therefore, a wanton will is the cause of all evils. If the will were in accordance with nature, surely it would maintain the nature and not be destructive of it; hence it would not be wanton. Accordingly, we may conclude that the root of all evils is *not being in accordance with nature*, which is a sufficient rejoinder to all those who want to lay the blame on natures. But if you ask again about the cause of this root, how will it be the *root* of all evils? The root will be that which is its cause! And when you find this one, you are also going to ask about *its* cause, as I declared, and our investigation will have no limit. 3.17.48.167

But what, in the end, could be the cause of the will *before* the will? Either it is the will itself, in which case there is no getting around this root of the will, or it is not the will, in which case it has no sin. Hence either the will is the first cause of sinning, or no sin is the first cause of sinning. No sin is rightly assigned to anyone but the sinner. Therefore, it is rightly assigned only to someone who wills it. I do not know why you want to look any further. 3.17.49.168<br>3.17.49.169

Finally, whatever the cause of the will is, surely it is either just or unjust. If it is just, anyone who obeys it will not sin; if unjust, let him not obey it, and he will not sin.

EVODIUS: What if it is violent and compels someone against his will?[104] 3.18.50.170

AUGUSTINE: How many times are we going to repeat the same things? Remember the many things we said earlier about sin and free will! But if it is too much effort to commit them all to memory, keep the following brief summary in mind: Whatever the cause of the will is, if it cannot be resisted there is no sin in yielding to it; but if it can be resisted, let someone not yield to it, and there will be no sin.

EVODIUS: What if it tricks him, catching him off his guard? 3.18.50.171

AUGUSTINE: Then let him guard against being tricked.

EVODIUS: What if the trickery is so great that he could not guard against it in any way?

AUGUSTINE: If so, there are no sins, for who sins in the case of what one cannot guard against in any way? But there is sin. Hence one can guard against it.

---

[104] I follow some manuscripts in attributing this and the next two questions to Evodius.

3.18.51.172 However, even some things done in ignorance are censured, and they are judged to deserve correction, as we read in our divine authorities. The Apostle Paul says: "I obtained mercy since I did it in ignorance" [1 Tim. 1:13]. The Prophet says: "Remember not the sins of my youth and my ignorance" [Ps. 24:7 (25:7 RSV)]. Even things done by necessity

3.18.51.173 are censured, as when a person wills to act rightly but cannot. That is why there are these words: "For I do not do the good that I will; but the evil I hate, that I do" [Rom. 7:19]. Also this passage: "To will the good is present with me, but how to accomplish it I find not" [Rom. 7:18]. And this: "The flesh has lusts against the spirit, and the spirit against the flesh; they are contrary to one another, so that you do not do the things you will" [Gal. 5:17].

Yet all these things have afflicted human beings since their damnation to death. For if this is not a penalty but human nature instead, they

3.18.51.174 are not sins. If there is no getting around the way human beings were naturally made, so that they could not be better, then they do what they should when they do these things. Of course, if human beings were good, matters would be otherwise. But as matters stand now, human beings are not good, and they do not have it in their power to be good – either because they do not see how they should be, or because they see it but they are not able to be such as they see that they should be.

3.18.51.175 Who could doubt that this is a penalty? But every just penalty is a penalty for sin, and is called a "punishment." If, however, it is an unjust penalty (and no one questions that it *is* a penalty), then it was imposed on human beings by someone ruling over them unjustly. What is more, since it is the mark of madness to doubt the omnipotence and the justice of

3.18.51.176 God, this penalty is just, and it is meted out for some sin. For no unjust ruler could either steal human beings away from God as though unbeknownst to Him, or wrestle them away by fear or force against His will as though He were weaker, so as to torture the human race with an unjust penalty. We must conclude, therefore, that this penalty is just, and that it comes from the damnation of human beings.

3.18.52.177 Nor should it be a surprise that we do not have free choice of the will to elect what we do rightly, due to ignorance; or we see what ought to be done rightly and will it, but we cannot accomplish it due to the resistance of carnal habits, which the vehemence of our mortal inheritance

3.18.52.178 has somehow naturally grown into. This penalty for sin is completely just: Someone loses what he was unwilling to use well, although he could have used it well without trouble had he been willing. That is, anyone who knowingly does not act rightly thereby loses the knowledge of what is right; and anyone who was unwilling to act rightly when he could thereby loses the ability when he is willing. For there really are two penalties for each sinful soul: ignorance and trouble. Through ignorance the soul is dishonored by error; through trouble it is afflicted with torments. But to approve falsehoods as truths so that one errs against one's will, and to not be able to hold oneself back from lustful actions due to the relentless and tortuous affliction of carnal bondage, is *not* human nature as originally established, but the penalty after being damned. When we speak of free will to act rightly, obviously we are speaking of it as human beings were originally made. 3.18.52.179

Here there arises a disparaging question that people who are ready to lay the blame on anything but themselves for sinning often mutter to one another: "Suppose Adam and Eve sinned. What did *we* unhappy people do, on our part, to be born with the blindness of ignorance and the torments of trouble? First, not knowing what we should do, we fall into error – and then, once the precepts of justice begin to be revealed to us, we will to do these things but we cannot, held back by some sort of necessity belonging to carnal lust!" 3.19.53.180

My reply to them is brief: Let them stop muttering against God and be quiet! Perhaps they would have a legitimate complaint if there had existed no one among human beings who triumphed over error and lust. But there *is* one, present everywhere throughout the Creation that serves Him as Lord, who calls out in many ways to the person who has turned away; who instructs the person who believes; who comforts the person who hopes; who encourages the person who persists; who helps the person who strives; who gives heed to the person who prays for forgiveness. Accordingly, it is not counted as a fault of yours that you act in ignorance against your will, but rather that you do not search for what you do not know; nor that you do not bind up your wounded members, but rather that you reject the one willing to heal you – *these* are properly your sins. No human being has been deprived of knowing how to investigate advantageously matters of which it is disadvantageous to be ignorant, or the need to confess humbly his weakness, so that He Whose support is unerring and effortless support the person who investigates and confesses. 3.19.53.181

3.19.53.182

What anyone ignorant does not do rightly and what anyone rightly willing cannot do are called "sins" precisely because they take their origin 3.19.54.183

3.19.54.184  from that sin of free will;[105] the one that came first deserved those that followed upon it. For just as we call 'tongue' not only the bodily part we move in our mouth when we speak, but also what follows upon its movement – that is, the formation and the intonation of words, so that we speak of "the Greek tongue" and "the Latin tongue" – so too "sin" is not only what is strictly so called (namely what is committed knowingly and through free will), but also what necessarily follows now upon its punishment.

3.19.54.185  Likewise, we say "nature" in one way when we are speaking strictly about the nature of human beings in which they were first made, faultless in their kind. We say it in another way when we are speaking about that nature in which we are born as mortal, ignorant, and slaves to the flesh, due to the penalty from damnation. The latter is the sense in which the Apostle Paul says: "We were by nature the children of wrath, even as others" [Eph. 2:3].

3.20.55.186  With complete justice it pleased God, Who regulates all things, that we be born of that first union[106] with ignorance and trouble and mortality, since when they sinned they fell headlong into error and distress and death, in order that His justice in punishing us would be apparent at the origination of the human race, and later on His mercy in setting us free. When the First Man was damned, his happiness was not revoked so far as to deprive him of his ability to have children. From his descendants, despite being carnal and mortal, a lovely adornment to the world of this kind was able to come about. Yet it was not fair that he beget offspring

3.20.55.187  better than he was himself. However, anyone willing to turn back to God so as to overcome the punishment that his origin deserved in turning away must not only not be hindered but even be helped. Thus did the Creator of things show how easily Adam could have remained as he was made, if he had willed to, since his offspring were able to overcome even what they were born with.

3.20.56.188  [1] First of all, if a single soul was made from which the souls of all those born were derived, who can say that he did not sin when the First Man sinned?[107]

[2] If souls come about individually for each one born, it is not perverse, but instead seems completely in order and appropriate, that (*a*)

---

[105] "That sin of free will": Original Sin.
[106] "That first union": Adam and Eve.
[107] This is the first of four theories about the soul, summed up in 3.21.59.200.

the deserved evil of the earlier belongs by nature to the later, and (*b*) the deserved good of the later belongs by nature to the earlier. What is [3.20.56.189] unworthy if the Creator also wanted to show that the worth of the soul so far exceeds the worth of material Creation, to the point that one soul takes its starting-point from the level to which another had fallen? For it is rightly called a penalty when the sinful soul arrives at ignorance and trouble, since it was better before this penalty. Thus suppose that one [3.20.56.190] soul, not only before sin but before its entire life, began to be exactly as another soul was made after its fault-filled life. It has no small good for which to give thanks to its Maker! Its starting-point and beginning is better than the most perfect material object. These are not mediocre goods: that the soul by its very nature takes precedence over any material body; that the soul has the ability, with the help of its Creator, to cultivate itself and by religious efforts it can acquire and possess all the virtues through which it may be freed from the torments of trouble and the blindness of ignorance. But if this is so, ignorance and trouble will [3.20.56.191] not be a punishment for sin in newborn souls, but rather a reminder to make progress and the beginning of their perfection.

It is no small matter that, before deserving anything due to good works, the soul has implanted in it the natural judgment by which it puts wisdom ahead of error and peace ahead of trouble, so that it might attain these things not by being born to them but by pursuing them. If it is unwilling to do so, it will rightly be held guilty of sin, as a soul which has not used well the ability it received. Although it was born in ignorance [3.20.56.192] and trouble, it is nevertheless not pressed by any necessity to remain in the condition in which it was born. Nor could anyone but God the Almighty be the creator of such souls. Not being loved He made them, and being loved He perfects them; to those not existing He provides their being, and to those loving Him from Whom they are He provides their happiness.

[3] Now if souls already exist in some hidden place belonging to God [3.20.57.193] and are sent forth to breathe life into and rule over the bodies of each individual who is born, surely they are sent forth for this purpose: (*a*) to look properly after the body that is born of the penalty of sin (namely the mortality incurred by the First Man) – that is, to correct it by the virtues – and (*b*) to subject it to a well-ordered and legitimate servitude, even preparing for it, at the right time in due order, a place of heavenly incorruption. When these souls enter into this life and find their way inside the [3.20.57.194]

mortal limbs they are to bear, they must submit to forgetfulness of their previous life and to the labor of their present one. From this there results ignorance and trouble. In the First Man this was the penalty of mortality, meant to mete out unhappiness to the mind. In those who came later, this is the beginning of their task of restoring the incorruptedness of the body.

3.20.57.195    In this [third] way, too, "sins" are so called only because the flesh that comes from the stock of a sinner produces this ignorance and trouble for the souls that come to it. This is attributed neither to them nor to their 3.20.57.196 Creator, as though they were at fault. For God gave them the ability to act well in burdensome tasks; the road of faith in the blindness of their forgetfulness; and, most important of all, that [natural] judgment[108] by which every soul grants that it should investigate what to its disadvantage it does not know, exert itself with perseverance in burdensome duties to overcome trouble in acting rightly, and entreat its Creator for the support that He help in its struggle. For God prescribed that there should be a struggle, whether outwardly by the law or by His address in the inmost places of the heart. He is making ready the glory of the Blessed City for those who triumph over the one[109] who brought the First Man, conquered by his thoroughly evil persuasion, to this unhappiness. They[110] take on 3.20.57.197 this unhappiness so as to conquer him through the greatest faith. It is a war of no small glory to conquer the Devil by taking on the same punishment by which he glories to have made captive the human race. But anyone who neglects this because he is captivated by his love of this life will not justly attribute his dishonorable desertion in any way to the command of his Ruler! Instead, he will be set under the Lord of all things,[111] on his side, whose shameful stipend he loved so deeply that he deserted his own camp.

3.20.58.198    [4] However, if souls constituted elsewhere are not sent by the Lord God but come to inhabit bodies of their own accord, then it is easy to see that any ignorance and trouble that followed on their will should not thereby in any way be blamed on their Creator. For even if He had sent them forth Himself, even in their ignorance and trouble He did not take away their free will to ask and inquire and strive: He will give to those

---

[108]  See 3.20.56.191.    [109]  "The one": the Devil.
[110]  Those who triumph over the Devil. Augustine has in mind martyrs who embrace death (the "unhappiness" he mentions here).
[111]  "The Lord of all things": the Devil, who is "prince of this world" (3.10.29.106).

who ask, He will show to those who inquire, He will open to those who knock, completely beyond fault. He furnishes the diligent and the well- 3.20.58.199 disposed with the ability to overcome such ignorance and trouble, to gain the "crown of glory."[112] He does not reproach the neglectful, who want to defend their sins on the grounds of weakness, with ignorance and trouble as a crime, but since they remain in that state rather than will to arrive at truth and ease through the effort of inquiry and learning, and the humility of confession and prayer, He pays them back with a just punishment.

There are [therefore] four theories about souls: [1] Souls come from 3.21.59.200 a stock. [2] Souls come about anew in each individual born. [3] Souls already exist somewhere and they are sent by God into the bodies of those who are born. [4] Souls already exist somewhere and they descend of their own accord into the bodies of those who are born. No one should affirm any of these theories rashly. Catholic commentators on Scripture have not yet untangled and clarified this question, due to its perplexing obscurity. Or at least, if they have, such texts have not yet come into my hands. Let us just have faith, thinking nothing false or unworthy of the 3.21.59.201 substance of the Creator! We are making our way to Him along the path of religiousness. Therefore, if we think of Him otherwise than He is, our aim drives us into futility rather than happiness. On the other hand, if we think anything about Creation otherwise than it is, there is no danger as long as we do not take it as something perceived and known. For we are 3.21.59.202 not bidden to make our way to Creation in order to be made happy, but instead to make our way to the Creator. If we are persuaded that God is otherwise than is the case, or than is fitting, we are deceived by an error that is extremely pernicious, for no one can attain a happy life while on course to what is not, or, if it is, does not make people happy.

Now as regards contemplating the eternity of Truth, in order that we 3.21.60.203 be able to hold fast to it and enjoy it, a road has been made for us, one leading away from temporal things. (*a*) Let us have belief in past and future things, inasmuch as this is enough for the path of those making their way to eternal things. The teaching of faith [about past and future things] is governed by divine mercy, and so has superior authority. (*b*) Present things, though, are sensed (inasmuch as the created universe is concerned) as though they were ephemeral, in the changeability and

---

[112] The "crown of glory" is referred to in 1 Cor. 9:25, 2 Tim. 4:8, and 1 Pet. 5:4.

the movability of mind and body. In the case of these things, whatever we do not experience we cannot grasp in any kind of cognition.

3.21.60.204    Therefore, whatever we are told about any creatures, whether past or future, should be believed on divine authority. Even though some became past before we could sense them, and others will come to our senses, they should nevertheless be believed without any doubt. For they greatly assist in strengthening our hope and encouraging our love while commending to us, through the well-ordered course of the ages, our deliverance, which God does not neglect.

3.21.60.205    Now any error that masquerades as divine authority is best refuted by the following line of reasoning. It is proven to believe or maintain that there is (*a*) some changeable species apart from God's Creation, or (*b*) some changeable species in God's substance; or it contends that (*c*) God's substance is either more or less than a trinity. Every watchful Christian is on the alert to understand the Trinity in a sober and religious fashion,

3.21.60.206    an understanding to which all his progress is directed. This is not the place to discuss the unity and equality and the distinctive features of each one of the Persons of the Trinity. For it is quite easy – many people have already done so over and over again – to call to mind some points about the Lord God, the Author of all things, Who shapes them and puts them in order; points relevant to the most wholesome faith. Nourished by these points, our goal of beginning to raise ourselves up from the Earth to the

3.21.60.207    heavens is supported to good advantage. But to debate and examine the entire question thoroughly, so that any intelligent human being will give in to our perspicuous argument, as far as is granted in this life, cannot seem an easy undertaking to accomplish not merely for the eloquence but even for the thinking of any person at all, or at least certainly too much for me.

3.21.60.208    Therefore, as far as we are allowed and given assistance, let us now deal with the question we set out to answer.[113] We should believe without a doubt (inasmuch as it is relevant to creatures) whatever past things we are told or whatever future things are pre-announced to us, things which are capable of commending upright religion by arousing us to the most

3.21.60.209    sincere love of God and neighbor.[114] Against unbelievers these things should be defended to the point that either their lack of faith is crushed

---

[113]  See 3.21.60.203–3.21.60.204.
[114]  See for example Gal. 5:14: "The whole of the Law is fulfilled in these words: *You shall love your neighbor as yourself* [Lv. 19:18]."

by the weight of authority, or they are shown, as far as possible, first how it is not foolish to believe such things, and thereafter how it is foolish not to believe such things. But in any event, we must refute false teachings about present things, and especially about unchangeable things, more than about past or future things – and to disprove them by clear argument, as far as this has been granted to us.

To be sure, in the course of the ages the expectation of future things should be preferred to the investigation of past things, seeing that even in Scripture things we are told about the past serve to prefigure or promise or bear witness to future things in advance. In fact, even in matters pertaining to this life, be they favorable or unfavorable, what anyone *was* is of no concern. All the turmoil of our cares piles itself onto hope for the future. Once things that have happened to us are over and done with, by some unknown natural sense within us their influence on our happiness or unhappiness is as though they never had happened. What hindrance is it to me if I do not know when I began to exist? I know that I do exist and I do not despair of existing in the future. I do not direct my attention to myself in past things, so that I am afraid of thinking them otherwise than they had been, as though it were a most pernicious error to do so. Instead, I direct my course towards what I am going to be, with the mercy of my Maker as my guide. 3.21.61.211

Hence I should be extremely watchful for error so that my thoughts and beliefs about what I am going to be, and about Him with Whom I am going to be, are not otherwise than the truth is, so that I do not fail to make the necessary preparations or am unable to reach my intended goal because one thing seemed to me to be another. It would not be a hindrance to me in buying a coat if I have forgotten last winter, whereas it would be if I did not believe that cold weather is coming in the future. Likewise, it will be no hindrance to my soul if it perhaps forgets what it has done, if it just is careful now to pay attention and hold on to how it has been advised to prepare itself for what is to come. For example, no harm is done to anyone sailing to Rome should it slip his mind from which shore the boat cast off, as long as he still knew how to steer his course from the place where he was. Yet it would not do him any good to remember the shores from which he set out on his journey if he runs onto the rocks, thinking something false about the Roman port. Likewise, it will be no hindrance to me if I do not remember the beginning of my life, as long as I know the end in which I shall find peace. Nor would memory 3.21.61.213

3.21.61.210

3.21.61.212

or conjecture about the start of my life do me any good if I held unworthy views about God Himself, the one goal of all the soul's efforts, and crashed onto the shoals of error.

3.21.62.214     This discussion does not mean that we prohibit anyone who has the ability from investigating, in accordance with divinely inspired Scripture, whether [1] soul is propagated from soul; [2] souls come about in each thing they animate; [3] God sends them from somewhere into bodies to rule over and animate them; [4] they make their way in by their own will. If reason demands the consideration of these matters for some necessary question to be straightened out, that is, or we are granted leisure from

3.21.62.215     more pressing business to look into and examine them. Rather, I made these remarks so that (a) nobody would be quick to anger with another person who did not give way to his own opinion, perhaps because of his all-too-human doubts about the subject; and (b) even if someone were to have a certain and lucid view of it, he would not thereby think that another person had lost hope of future things because he does not recall his past origins.

3.22.63.216     However things may be on this score – whether we should omit the problem [of the origin of souls] entirely or defer it now to be considered at another time – it is no hindrance to the present question.[115] It is quite clear that souls suffer punishments for their sins by the most upright and supremely just and unshaken and unchangeable majesty and substance of the Creator. These sins, as we have been discussing for a long time, should be attributed to their own will. Nor should any further cause of sins be looked for.

3.22.64.217     But ignorance and trouble, if natural, are the point of departure for the soul to begin to make progress, advancing towards knowledge and peace until the happy life is realized within it. If of its own will the soul neglects this progress in the best studies and in religiousness, the ability for which has not been denied to it, then it is justly cast into more serious ignorance and trouble (which is already a penalty). It is placed among

3.22.64.218     inferior things by the most fitting and suitable governance. The soul is not held guilty because it is naturally ignorant and naturally incapable, but rather because it did not make an effort to know, and because it did not work enough to acquire the ability to act rightly.

---

[115] "The present question": whether God is responsible for sins.

Not knowing how and not being able to speak is natural for an infant. This ignorance and trouble relative to speaking is not only faultless under the rules of the grammarians, it is even sweet and endearing to human affections. The infant did not "neglect" to acquire the ability because of any vice, or lose what he had acquired because of any vice. Thus, if our happiness consisted in eloquence, and so "sinning" in language were held a crime the way sinning in the actions of life is, surely no one would be blamed from his infancy because he had set out from that point to pursue eloquence. He would clearly deserve damnation, however, if he had either remained in that condition or returned to it, due to the perversity of his will. 3.22.64.219

Thus even now, if ignorance of the truth and trouble in doing right is natural to human beings, from which they begin to rise towards the happiness of wisdom and peace, no one rightly condemns this happiness for its natural beginning. But if someone is unwilling to make progress, or is willing to backslide from his progress, he will rightly and deservedly pay the penalties. 3.22.64.220

Yet the Creator of the soul is praised on all sides for implanting the capacity for the highest good from these beginnings; assisting our progress; perfecting and satisfying those who make progress; ordaining the most just damnation for the sinner – that is, for someone refusing to lift himself up to perfection from his beginnings or now relapsing from some progress – according to his deserts. God did not create the soul as evil just because it is not yet as great as it received the power to become by making progress, since all the perfections of physical objects are far inferior to it even at its beginning, even though anyone of sound judgment will judge these perfections to be praiseworthy in their kind. 3.22.65.221<br>3.22.65.222

Therefore, the soul is ignorant of what it ought to do, precisely because it has not yet received it. But it will receive this, too, if it uses well what it *has* received: the power to search diligently and religiously, if it is willing. As for the fact that it cannot always accomplish what it recognizes it ought to do – well, the soul has also not yet received this. The more exalted part of it has moved ahead to perceive the good of what has been done rightly. The slower and carnal part, however, is not thereby brought to the same view. As a result, on account of that very trouble the soul is given a warning to call upon Him Who helps in its perfection, the one Whom it perceives is the author of its inception. The upshot is that the soul becomes more dear to God, seeing that it is raised up to be happy 3.22.65.223

not through its own powers but instead through the mercy of Him from Whose goodness it has its being. The soul is more dear to Him from Whom it exists precisely to the extent that it finds secure peace in Him, and to the extent that it more richly enjoys His eternity.

3.22.65.224 We do not rightly call the young and immature shoot of a tree "barren," despite the fact that it goes through several summers without bearing fruit until, at the proper time, it brings out its fruitfulness. Why, then, should we not praise the Creator of the soul with all due religiousness for having supplied the soul with the sort of beginning that by exerting itself and making progress it may reach the fruit of wisdom and justice, and for having furnished the soul with so much dignity that He also put it in its power, if it is willing, to make its way to happiness?

3.23.66.225 At this point in the debate, unsophisticated people usually raise some nasty objection about the deaths of young children and the physical torments with which we often see them afflicted:[116] "What need was there for someone to be born who departed from life before doing anything in life that *deserved* anything? Furthermore, how will he be treated in the Judgment that is to come? His place is not among the just, since he never acted rightly, nor among the evil, since he never sinned."

3.23.66.226 I reply: It is not possible that a human being of any kind is created who is superfluous with respect to the surrounding universe and the well-ordered interconnection of Creation as a whole throughout time and space, where not a leaf on a tree is created superfluously. But it is certainly superfluous to ask about the deserts of one who did not do anything to deserve anything. Have no fear that there could not be some life intermediate between right action and sin, and that the sentence of the Judge could not likewise be intermediate between reward and punishment.[117]

3.23.67.227 At this point people typically examine the following issue: "What benefit does the sacrament of the baptism of Christ have for young children, when after receiving it they often die before they have been able to understand anything about it?"

On this issue, it is believed quite rightly and religiously that the benefit to the young child comes from the faith of those who offered the child up to be consecrated. The most wholesome authority of the Church sup-
3.23.67.228 ports this view. As a result, anyone may perceive what benefit his own

---

[116] This "nasty objection" is discussed extensively in *On the Gift of Perseverance* 8.16–13.33 (pp. 229–245).

[117] This passage is one of the grounds for the later Christian doctrine of Limbo.

faith has for himself, when you can lend it to help out others who do not yet have their own faith. What benefit did the widow's son get from his faith, which he certainly did not have while he was dead? Yet his mother's faith was so beneficial to him that he was restored to life.[118] How much more, therefore, can the faith of another succor a young child, to whom no faithlessness can be ascribed?

A more serious objection – and a compassionate one, it might be said – is usually raised about the physical torments that afflict children who, due to their age, have not committed any sins (if the souls by which they are animated did not begin to exist before the human beings themselves did): "What evil have they done so as to suffer these things?"[119] $\quad$ 3.23.68.229

As though there could be any merit of innocence before someone was able to do any harm! Since God accomplishes some good in correcting adults when they are scourged by the sufferings and death of their young children, who are dear to them, why should those things not happen? Once their sufferings have ended, it will be as if they did not happen to those to whom they happened, whereas the adults on whose account they happened will either be better, if they have been corrected by these temporary adversities and elect to live more rightly; or they have no excuse to avoid punishment in the Judgment that is to come, if they are unwilling to turn their desire from the worries of this life to eternal life. $\quad$ 3.23.68.230

Furthermore, who knows what is in store for these young children, whose torments grind down the hardness of their parents and vex their faith and try their compassion? Who knows what compensatory good God has in store for these young children in the hidden depth of His judgments? For, although they did not act rightly, they endured these things without committing any sins. Not for nothing does the Church commend to us those infants who were killed at the time when Herod was seeking the Lord Jesus Christ to slay Him;[120] they have been received with honor among the martyrs. $\quad$ 3.23.68.231

---

[118] See Lk. 7:12–15: "Now when [Jesus] came near to the gate of the city [of Nain], behold, there was a dead man carried out, the only son of his mother, and she was a widow: And many people of the city were with her. And when the Lord saw her, He had compassion on her. He said to her: Do not weep. And He came and touched the bier; the men who carried him stood still. And He said: Young man, I say to you, arise! And he who was dead sat up, and began to speak. And He delivered him to his mother."

[119] See 3.23.66.225 for this objection.

[120] The Slaughter of the Innocents is recounted in Mt. 2:16: "Then Herod, when he saw that he had been deceived by the wise men, raged in fury, and he sent forth and killed all the children that were in and around Bethlehem that were two years old and under."

3.23.69.232    Although these slanderous critics are not serious investigators of such questions (they are instead full of hot air), they often shake up the faith of the less educated with even the sufferings and travails of animals: "What evil have animals done to deserve to suffer such great distress? What good do they hope for, since they are vexed with such great distress?"

3.23.69.233    Well, those who speak or think this way have an unbalanced assessment of things. Since they cannot recognize what the highest good is, nor how great it is, they want everything to be the way they *think* the highest good is. For they are not able to think of a highest good apart from the highest physical objects, which are the heavenly bodies and are less subject to corruption. Hence they demand, quite out of order, that the bodies of animals suffer neither death nor any corruption – as though they were not mortal, despite being at the lowest level [of living creatures], or as though they were bad precisely because the heavenly bodies are better.

3.23.69.234    Now the pain that beasts feel reveals a certain wondrous power in their souls, praiseworthy of its kind. It is quite clear from this [power] how in governing and animating their bodies they pursue unity. What else is pain but a sense of division and intolerance of corruption?

3.23.69.235    Accordingly, it is as plain as day how eager and dogged the soul is in pursuing unity throughout the whole of its body. The soul confronts the physical suffering that threatens to destroy its unity and integrity not with pleasure or indifference, but instead with reluctance and resistance. It would not be apparent, then, how great the drive for unity

3.23.69.236    is in the lower animals of the Creation, if not for the pain of beasts. And if it were not apparent, we would be less aware than we need to be that they were all fashioned by the supreme and sublime and inexpressible unity of their Creator.

3.23.70.237    In point of fact, if you pay attention carefully and religiously, every movement and kind of creature that enters into the consideration of the human mind speaks to our instruction. On all sides, their diverse movements and states, as though in various languages, cry out in reproach that we should know their Creator. Every thing among those that feel neither pain nor pleasure acquires loveliness of its kind, or at least a sort

3.23.70.238    of stability for its nature, from some unity. Again, each and every thing among those that do feel the distress of pain and the allure of pleasure, by the very fact that it *does* avoid pain and pursue pleasure, confesses that it avoids its fragmentation and pursues unity. And in the case of the rational mind, the entire pursuit of knowledge, which delights its nature, traces everything it perceives back to unity, and in error it avoids only being confounded by incomprehensible ambiguity. On what grounds is any ambiguity a problem except because it has no definite unity? From this fact, it is apparent that all things, either when they inflict harm or suffer it, or when they are pleasing or are pleased, suggest and proclaim the unity of the Creator.   3.23.70.239

In any event, if the ignorance and trouble with which we must begin our life are not natural to minds, it remains that they were taken on as a duty or imposed as a punishment. And now, I think, we have had enough discussion of these matters.

Accordingly, we should investigate how the First Man himself was made, rather than the way in which his posterity was propagated. People who put forward this question think themselves quite clever: "If the First Man was created wise, why was he led astray? But if he was created foolish, how is God not the author of vices, since foolishness is the ultimate vice?"   3.24.71.240

As though human nature did not admit any state intermediate between foolishness and wisdom! Now this intermediate state cannot be called either foolishness or wisdom. For a human being begins to be wise or foolish at the time when he could have wisdom, were he not to neglect it so that his will is guilty of the vice of foolishness; he must then be called one or the other. No one is so silly as to call an infant foolish, although it would be more ridiculous if he wanted to call the infant wise. Therefore, an infant cannot be called either foolish or wise, despite already being human. From this it is apparent that human nature admits an intermediate state that cannot rightly be termed foolishness or wisdom.   3.24.71.241   3.24.71.242

Thus even if someone were endowed with a soul in the same state as those who lack wisdom through their neglect, no one who saw that he was in that state through nature, rather than through vice, would rightly call him a fool. Foolishness is not any ignorance at all about things to be pursued and avoided, but only ignorance stemming from vice. Accordingly, we do not call an irrational animal "foolish," since it did not receive the ability to be wise. Yet often we apply terms to things by some likeness rather than strictly. Although blindness is the worst vice in the eyes, in newborn animals it is not a vice, and cannot be called "blindness" strictly speaking.   3.24.71.243

3.24.72.244 Therefore, suppose that the First Man was so made that, although he was not yet wise, he could in any event receive a precept, which he surely ought to have obeyed. It is then not surprising that he was able to be led astray. Nor is it unjust that he paid the penalty for not obeying the precept. Nor is his Creator the author of vices, since not having wisdom was

3.24.72.245 not yet a human vice if he had not yet received the ability to have it. But he *did* have something by which, if he had willed to use it well, he would have risen up to what he did not have.

It is one thing to be rational, another to be wise. By reason one becomes capable of apprehending a precept, to which one ought to be faithful, so that one does what is prescribed. Just as the nature of reason takes in the precept, so observance of the precept takes in wisdom; what nature is

3.24.72.246 prescribed to take in is the will for observance. And just as the rational nature deserves to receive the precept, so to speak, so too does the observance of the precept deserve to receive wisdom.

Now that by which humans begin to be capable of apprehending a precept is the very thing by which they begin to be able to sin. There are two ways for someone to sin before becoming wise: (*a*) he does not accommodate himself to receiving a precept; (*b*) he does not observe it

3.24.72.247 once received. The wise person, however, sins if (*c*) he turns away from wisdom. Just as the precept does not come from the one who receives it but from Him Who issues it, so too wisdom does not come from the one who is illuminated but from Him Who illuminates.

Therefore, what are the grounds on which the Creator of human

3.24.72.248 beings should *not* be praised? A human being is something good, and better than an animal in virtue of the fact that he is capable of apprehending a precept. He is better still when he has taken in the precept, and better yet again when he complies with the precept; and better than all these when he is happy in the eternal light of wisdom. Sin, however, is evil in neglecting either to receive the precept, or to observe it, or to continue in the contemplation of wisdom.

3.24.72.249 On this basis, we understand how the First Man was still able to be led astray even if he was made as wise. And since his sin was in his free choice, by divine law there followed a just penalty. Hence the Apostle Paul says: "Professing themselves to be wise they became fools" [Rom. 1:22]. Pride turns away from wisdom, and foolishness is the result of this turning away. Indeed, foolishness is a kind of blindness, as the

Apostle Paul also says: "And their foolish heart was darkened" [Rom. 1:21]. How does this darkness come about, if not by turning away from the light of wisdom? How does this turning away come about, if not that he whose good is God wills to be his own good for himself, as if his own god? Thus: "My soul is cast down within me" [Ps. 41:7 (42:6 RSV)] and: "Eat and you shall be as gods" [Gen. 3:5].    3.24.72.250

This question disturbs those who reflect upon it: "Did the First Man draw away from God due to foolishness, or did he become a fool by drawing away?"    3.24.73.251

On the one hand, if you reply that he drew away from wisdom due to foolishness, he will seem to have been a fool before he drew away from wisdom, so that foolishness was the reason for his drawing away.

On the other hand, if you reply that he became a fool by drawing away, they ask whether he acted foolishly or wisely in drawing away. "If he acted wisely, he acted rightly and committed no sin; if foolishly, then the foolishness was already in him, through which it came about that he drew away – for he could not have acted foolishly without foolishness."

From this dilemma, it is apparent that there is some intermediate state through which one passes from wisdom to foolishness, which cannot be said to be done either wisely or foolishly. Human beings in this life only understand this state through its contraries. For no mortal becomes wise unless he passes from foolishness into wisdom. This passage, if it comes about foolishly, surely does not come about well, which is complete madness to say; yet if it comes about wisely there already was wisdom in the person before he passed to wisdom, which is no less ridiculous. Consequently, we understand that there is an intermediate state which can be called neither. Likewise, the First Man left the stronghold of wisdom if he passed into foolishness, and his passage was neither wise nor foolish. For example, in the case of being asleep and being awake, falling asleep is not being asleep, nor is waking up being awake; there is a passage from one state into the other. But there is this difference. These passages [between being awake and being asleep] often come about without the will, whereas the former passages, [namely between foolishness and wisdom], only ever happen by the will. This is why the retributions that follow are completely just.    3.24.73.252 · 3.24.73.253 · 3.24.73.254

3.25.74.255 But since the only thing that influences the will to do anything is some impression,[121] and since what anyone accepts or rejects is in his power, but there is no power over which impression he is affected by, then it must be granted that the mind is affected by impressions derived from higher things and derived from lower things. As a rational substance, it accepts what it wants from each source, and, on the basis of 3.25.74.256 what it accepts, there follows its deserved happiness or unhappiness. For example, in the Garden of Eden, God's precept is an impression deriving from higher things, the serpent's suggestion an impression deriving from lower things. For neither what the precept given to Adam by the Lord was, nor what the suggestion given to him by the serpent was, 3.25.74.257 lay in his control. But just how free and unconstrained by any chains of trouble in the established soundness of wisdom he was *not* to give in to the impression of a lower enticement can readily be understood from the fact that even fools overcome them as they proceed towards wisdom, despite the challenge of giving up the deadly delight of their ruinous habits.

3.25.75.258 At this point a question can be raised. "If Adam was provided with impressions on each side, one from God's precept and the other from the serpent's suggestion, where did the judgment that was suggested to the Devil come from – the judgment that irreligiousness should be pursued, the judgment by which he fell from the heights of heaven?"

If the Devil were not affected by any impression, he would not have elected to do what he did. For if nothing had entered his mind he would 3.25.75.259 not have turned his attention to wickedness at all. So from where did it enter his mind – whatever it is that entered his mind – to undertake those deeds by which he turned from a good angel into the Devil?

Whoever wills surely wills *something*. But he cannot will unless this "something" is either suggested externally through the bodily senses or enters into the mind in hidden ways. Hence we should distinguish two kinds of impressions: (*a*) impressions arising from the will of someone trying to persuade, like the Devil's suggestion to which Adam consented when he sinned; (*b*) impressions derived from things that come to the 3.25.75.260 mind's attention or to the bodily senses. Coming to the mind's attention – apart from the unchangeability of the Trinity, which does not come to the

---

[121] "Some impression": *aliquod uisum*. Augustine is using "impression" in a technical sense adopted from Stoicism, as likewise are the terms "accept," "reject," "control," and "be affected (by)."

mind but rather surpasses it – coming to the mind's attention, therefore, is first of all the mind itself, whereby we also perceive that we live; and next the body that it oversees, by which it moves to any given task the bodily member needed when it is needed. Coming to the bodily senses are any given physical objects.

In contemplating the highest wisdom – which is surely not the mind, for the highest wisdom is unchangeable – the mind looks upon itself, which is changeable, and in some way enters into its own mind.[122] This happens only in virtue of the difference by which the mind is not what God is, and yet it is something that can please, next to God. However, it is better if it forgets itself before the love of the unchangeable God, or sets itself completely at naught in comparison with Him.   3.25.76.261   3.25.76.262

If instead [the mind] gets in its own way, so to speak, and it pleases it to imitate God perversely so that it wills to enjoy its own power, it becomes lesser to precisely the extent that it desires itself to be greater. And this is: "Pride is the beginning of all sin" [Sir. 10:15 (10:13 RSV)] and "The beginning of pride is when one departs from God" [Sir. 10:14 (10:12 RSV)]. Now to the pride of the Devil was added his most malevolent envy, so that he persuaded man to this very pride through which he knew he was damned.[123] On these grounds did it come to pass that humans were subject to a corrective penalty rather than a deadly one: to the human race the Devil had offered himself as an example of pride, but the Lord offered Himself as an example of humility, through Whom we are promised eternal life.[124] Consequently, since Christ paid for us with His blood after His indescribable trials and miseries, let us hold fast with great love to our liberator! And let us be so taken into Him by His great radiance that no impressions derived from lower things wrench us away from the higher vision! However, even if something were suggested to our attention by them, the everlasting damnation and torment of the Devil would call us back from the pursuit of lower things.   3.25.76.263   3.25.76.264

So great is the beauty of justice, so great is the delightfulness of eternal light, that is, of unchangeable truth and wisdom, that even if we were allowed no more than the span of a single day to dwell in it, for this alone would we rightly and deservedly set at naught countless years of this life that were filled with delights and an overflowing abundance of temporal   3.25.77.265

---

[122] The mind (*animus*) enters into its own mind (*mens*).
[123] See 3.10.29.105–3.10.29.107.    [124] See 3.10.30.108–3.10.31.110.

3.25.77.266    goods. As the Psalmist said with genuine feeling: "One day in Your courts is better than a thousand!" [Ps. 83:11 (84:10 RSV)]. This could, however, be understood another way, namely "a thousand days" refers to the changeability of time, whereas "one day" expresses the unchangeability of eternity.

3.25.77.267    I do not know whether I have left anything out of my reply while answering your questions as well as the Lord has granted me. However, even if some point occurs to you, the compass of this book compels us now to put an end to it and rest from this discussion for a bit.

# Reconsiderations, 1.9

While we were still delayed at Rome [due to bad weather],[1] we wanted 1
to inquire through argument into the origin of evil. We conducted our
discussion in such a way that, if we could, our considered and detailed
reasoning would lead us to understand what we believed about this topic
by divine authority – to the extent that we could do so by examination,
with God's assistance. And since we agreed after careful reasoning that
the sole origin of evil is the free choice of the will, the three books which
our discussion produced were called *On the Free Choice of the Will*. After
I was ordained a priest at Hippo Regius, I finished off the second and
third books as well as I could at the time.[2]

So many issues were examined in these books that I postponed 2
some incidental questions – which either I could not untangle or which
demanded a lengthy discussion – so that when it was not clear what came
closer to the truth, our reasoning then would nonetheless draw the conclusion from each side (or from all the sides) of these selfsame incidental
questions, in order that whichever of them may be true, we could believe,
or even prove, that God ought to be praised.

The discussion was undertaken on account of those who deny that the
origin of evil lies in the free choice of the will, and who contend that, if this
is so, God as the Creator of all natures ought to be blamed; as a result, they
want to introduce some unchangeable nature of evil that is co-eternal with
God in accordance with their irreligious error (for they are Manichaeans).

---

[1] After the death of his mother Monica at Ostia, Augustine and Evodius were delayed in their
return to Africa by bad weather that made sea-travel impossible.
[2] See *On the Gift of Perseverance* 12.30: "I began *On the Free Choice of the Will* as a layman and
finished it up as a priest."

Now since this was the question at hand, there was no examination of grace in these books, by which God so predestines the people He elects that He Himself even prepares the wills of those among them who are already making use of free choice. Whenever an opportunity to mention this grace came up, it was mentioned only in passing and not defended by detailed reasoning as though it were the subject being dealt with. For it is one matter to look into the origin of evil, another to look into how we may return to our former good or reach a greater good.

3      Consequently, the new Pelagian heretics – who maintain that the choice of the will is so free that they leave no place for God's grace when they declare that it is given in accordance with our deserts – should not congratulate themselves, as though I had been pleading their case, on the grounds that I said many things in *On the Free Choice of the Will* on behalf of free choice which were required for the sake of the discussion.

I said: "Evildoings are redressed by God's justice," and added: "It would not be just to redress them unless they come about through the will."[3]

Again, when I showed that the good will is itself so great a good that it is deservedly more important than all bodily and external goods, I said: "Then I think you see now that it lies in our will to enjoy or to lack such a great and genuine good. For what is so much in the power of the will as the will itself?"[4]

In another passage: "Therefore, is there any reason for us to hesitate in thinking that even if we have never been wise before, nevertheless it is by our will that we have and deserve either a happy and praiseworthy life, or an unhappy and disgraceful one?"[5]

Again, in another passage: "The upshot is that anyone who wills to live rightly and honourably, if he wills himself to will this instead of transient goods, acquires so great a possession with such ease that having what he willed is nothing other for him than willing it."[6]

Again, elsewhere I said: "The eternal law – it is now time for us to consider it again – established firmly with unchangeable stability that deserts are in the will, whereas reward and punishment are in happiness and unhappiness."[7]

---

[3] *On the Free Choice of the Will* 1.1.1.3.      [4] *On the Free Choice of the Will* 1.12.26.86.
[5] *On the Free Choice of the Will* 1.13.28.96.      [6] *On the Free Choice of the Will* 1.13.29.97.
[7] *On the Free Choice of the Will* 1.14.30.101.

In another passage: "We have established that what each person elects to pursue and embrace is located in the will."[8]

In Book 2, I said: "For a human being *qua* human being is something good, since he can live rightly when he wills to."[9]

In another passage: "One cannot act rightly except by this selfsame free choice of the will."[10]

In Book 3, I said: "What need is there to investigate where the movement of the will comes from, the movement by which it is turned from the unchangeable good to the changeable good? We admit that it is a movement of the mind and that it is voluntary, and therefore blameworthy. All useful teaching that deals with this subject amounts to this: Once we have restrained and condemned that movement, let us turn our will away from its lapse into temporal goods and turn it to the enjoyment of the everlasting good."[11]

In another passage: "How well the truth cries out from within you! You could not perceive anything to be in our power except what we do when we will. Accordingly, nothing is so much in our power as the will itself. Surely it is at hand with no delay as soon as we will."[12]

Again in another passage: "For if you receive praise for seeing what you ought to do, even though you see it only in Him Who is unchangeable Truth, how much more praise does God receive, Who prescribes what you will, Who provides you with the power, and Who does not allow you to be unwilling with impunity!"[13]

Once more: "What, in the end, could be the cause of the will *before* the will? Either it is the will itself, in which case there is no getting around this root of the will, or it is not the will, in which case it has no sin. Hence either the will is the first cause of sinning, or no sin is the first cause of sinning. No sin is rightly assigned to anyone but the sinner. Therefore, it is rightly assigned only to someone who wills it."[14]

Shortly afterwards: "Who sins in the case of what one cannot guard against in any way? But there is sin. Hence one can guard against it."[15] Pelagius used this statement of mine in his book [*Nature*]; when I replied to it, I chose the title of my book to be *Nature and Grace*.

---

[8]  *On the Free Choice of the Will* 1.16.34.114.   [9]  *On the Free Choice of the Will* 2.1.2.4.
[10]  *On the Free Choice of the Will* 2.18.47.179.   [11]  *On the Free Choice of the Will* 3.1.2.11.
[12]  *On the Free Choice of the Will* 3.3.7.27.   [13]  *On the Free Choice of the Will* 3.16.46.156.
[14]  *On the Free Choice of the Will* 3.17.49.168–3.17.49.169.
[15]  *On the Free Choice of the Will* 3.18.50.171.

4    Since God's grace was not mentioned in these words of mine (and others like them) – it was not the subject being dealt with at the time – the Pelagians think, or are able to think, that I held their view. But they think this in vain. The will is indeed that by which we sin and that by which we live rightly, which we were dealing with in these statements. Therefore, unless the will itself is set free by God's grace from the servitude in which it was made the slave of sin, and is helped to overcome its vices, mortals cannot live rightly and religiously. And unless this divine kindness by which the will is set free came first, grace would then be given in accordance with deserts, and it would not be grace, which is of course given gratuitously.[16] I have dealt with this sufficiently in other short works of mine,[17] in which I refute the newfangled heretics who are enemies of this grace. Even in *On the Free Choice of the Will*, however, which was written not against them (since they did not yet exist) but against the Manichaeans, I was not entirely silent about this grace of God which the Pelagians are trying to get rid of altogether.

In Book 2, I said: "Not only great but even small goods are able to exist from Him alone from Whom all good things are, namely God."[18] And shortly afterwards: "The virtues by which we live rightly are great goods. The beauties of any given physical objects, without which we can live rightly, are small goods, whereas the powers of the mind, without which we cannot live rightly, are intermediate goods. No one uses the virtues for evil, but the other goods – namely, the intermediate and small goods – can be used not only for good but also for evil. Hence no one uses virtue for evil, because the task of virtue is the good use of things that we can also fail to use for good. But no one uses [something] for evil in using it for good. Accordingly, the abundance and the greatness of God's goodness has furnished not only great goods but also intermediate and small goods. His goodness is more to be praised in great goods than in intermediate goods, and more in intermediate goods than in small goods, but more in all of them than if He had not bestowed them all."[19]

---

[16] An allusion to Rom. 11:6: "But if [election] is through grace, then it is not through works; otherwise grace then is not grace – but if it is through works, then it is not through grace; otherwise grace is not then grace."

[17] For example *Nature and Grace, The Grace of Christ and Original Sin, Against Two Letters of the Pelagians*.

[18] *On the Free Choice of the Will* 2.19.50.191.

[19] *On the Free Choice of the Will* 2.19.50.191–192.

In another passage: "Hold firm with resolute religiousness that you will not encounter, by sensing or understanding or whatever kind of thinking, any good thing which is not from God."[20]

And again in another passage I said: "But since we cannot rise of our own accord as we fell of it, let us hold on with firm faith to the right hand of God stretched out to us from above, namely our Lord Jesus Christ."[21]

And in Book 3, after I had made the remark which, as I have men-   5
tioned, Pelagius used from my works – namely: "Who sins in the case of what one cannot guard against in any way? But there is sin. Hence one can guard against it"[22] – I straightaway added:

> Even some things done in ignorance are censured, and they are judged to deserve correction, as we read in our divine authorities. The Apostle Paul says: "I obtained mercy since I did it in ignorance" [1 Tim. 1:13]. The Prophet says: "Remember not the sins of my youth and my ignorance" [Ps. 24:7 (25:7 RSV)]. Even things done by necessity are censured, as when a person wills to act rightly but cannot. That is why there are these words: "For I do not do the good that I will; but the evil I hate, that I do" [Rom. 7:19]. Also this passage: "To will the good is present with me, but how to accomplish it I find not" [Rom. 7:18]. And this: "The flesh has lusts against the spirit, and the spirit against the flesh; they are contrary to one another, so that you do not do the things you will" [Gal. 5:17].

> Yet all these things have afflicted human beings since their damnation to death. For if this is not a penalty but human nature instead, they are not sins. If there is no getting around the way human beings were naturally made, so that they could not be better, then they do what they should when they do these things. Of course, if human beings were good, matters would be otherwise. But as matters stand now, human beings are not good, and they do not have it in their power to be good – either because they do not see how they should be, or because they see it but they are not able to be such as they see that they should be.

> Who could doubt that this is a penalty? But every just penalty is a penalty for sin, and is called a 'punishment.' If, however, it is an unjust penalty (and no one questions that it *is* a penalty), then it was imposed on human beings by someone ruling over them

---

[20] *On the Free Choice of the Will* 2.20.54.202.    [21] *On the Free Choice of the Will* 2.20.54.205.
[22] *On the Free Choice of the Will* 3.18.50.171.

unjustly. What is more, since it is the mark of madness to doubt the omnipotence and the justice of God, this penalty is just, and it is meted out for some sin. For no unjust ruler could either steal human beings away from God as though unbeknownst to Him, or wrestle them away by fear or force against His will as though He were weaker, so as to torture the human race with an unjust penalty. We must conclude, therefore, that this penalty is just, and that it comes from the damnation of human beings.[23]

In another passage I say: "To approve falsehoods as truths so that one errs against one's will, and to not be able to hold oneself back from lustful actions due to the relentless and tortuous affliction of carnal bondage, is *not* human nature as originally established, but the penalty after being damned. When we speak of free will to act rightly, obviously we are speaking of it as human beings were originally made."[24]

6    You see how, long before the Pelagian heresy had existed, I was already arguing as if against them. For when all good things – great, intermediate, and small – are said to come from God,[25] free choice of the will is found among the intermediate goods for the reason that we can use it badly, although it is such that we cannot live rightly without it.[26] Now the good use of free choice is virtue, which has its place among the great goods which no one can use badly. And since all goods – great, intermediate, and small – come from God, as noted, it follows that the good use of free will, which is virtue and is counted among the great goods, also comes from God.

Then I said that the grace of God sets sinners free from the misery that is most justly inflicted upon them.[27] For of our own accord we were able to fall, namely by free choice, but not also to rise up.[28] And this misery of our just damnation includes ignorance and trouble, which every human being suffers from the first moment of his birth.[29] No one is set free from this evil except by God's grace. The Pelagians are not willing for this misery to stem from a just damnation, since they deny Original Sin. However, as I argued in Book 3, even if ignorance and trouble were

---

[23] *On the Free Choice of the Will* 3.18.51.172–3.18.51.176.
[24] *On the Free Choice of the Will* 3.18.52.179.    [25] *On the Free Choice of the Will* 2.19.50.191.
[26] *On the Free Choice of the Will* 2.19.50.192.
[27] See Rom. 7:24–25: "How unhappy I am! Who shall set me free from this body of death? The grace of God, through Jesus Christ our Lord."
[28] *On the Free Choice of the Will* 2.20.54.205.
[29] Introduced in 3.18.52.177; see also 3.20.57.194 and 3.23.70.238.

primordial features of the nature of human beings, God still ought to be praised rather than blamed.[30]

This discussion was directed against the Manichaeans, who do not accept the Old Testament, in which Original Sin is described, as Scripture, and who contend with despicable shamelessness that whatever is read about it in the New Testament was inserted by people who corrupted the text of Scripture, as if these things had not been said by the apostles at all.[31] Against the Pelagians, by contrast, we need to defend what both the Old Testament and the New Testament say, since they claim to accept each of them.

---

[30] *On the Free Choice of the Will* 3.22.64.217–3.22.65.221.

[31] See *Confessions* 5.11.21: "The Manichaeans ... held that the Scripture of the New Testament had been corrupted by someone unknown who wanted to weave the Jewish Law into the Christian faith."

# Confessions, 8.8.19–8.10.24

Augustine, with Alypius, has just heard several conversion-stories from Ponticianus, which moved him greatly and made him despair of his own irresolution; he describes before God the "grand struggle in his heart" as follows.

At our lodging there was a small garden. We had the run of it, as we did of the whole house, since our host (the owner of the house) was not liv-ing there. My inner turmoil took me to the garden, where nobody would impede the burning struggle I had ventured upon with myself until it was settled. You knew the outcome, but I did not: only that I was becoming sick with health and dying with life, aware how evil I was and unaware how good I was shortly going to be. So off I went into the garden with Alypius close behind. My solitude was not impaired by his presence, and how could he leave me in such a state? We sat down as far as possible from the buildings. I was raging in spirit, indignant with tempestuous indignation that I was not entering into a pact and covenant with You, my God, for which all my bones were crying out,[1] singing its praises to the heavens. We do not reach that destination by traveling in ships, or chariots, or on foot,[2] not even as far as I had gone from the house to the place where we were sitting. For not only the going but also the arrival was nothing other than willing to go – but willing resolutely and whole-heartedly, not thrashing and turning a half-wounded will this way and that, wrestling with one part rising while another part was sinking.

---

[1] See Ps. 34:10 (35:10 RSV): "All my bones shall cry out: Lord, who is like You?"
[2] Plotinus, *Enneads* 1.6.8.21: "We do not reach that destination with our feet, for they carry us only from one land to another; nor need you get ready a chariot or a ship."

8.8.20    Finally, in the very waverings of my hesitation, I did many things with my body that people sometimes will but are unable to do, if they do not have the limbs, or if their limbs are fettered with chains, or weakened by illness, or are somehow prevented. If I tore my hair, struck my forehead, and clasped my knee with interlaced fingers, I did so because I so willed. However, I was able to will and yet not to do [these things] if the ability to move my limbs were not to comply. Therefore, I did many things where *willing* was not the same as *being able*. But I did not do what I was longing to do with an incomparably greater yearning and which I would be able to do as soon as I willed to, since as soon as I willed I would indeed will. In this case the faculty is the will, and the willing itself already *is* the doing. Yet it did not happen. My body more easily obeyed my soul's slightest will to move its limbs at its pleasure, than the soul obeyed itself to accomplish in the will alone [and not the body] its own great will.

8.9.21    Where does this monstrosity come from? What is the explanation? Let Your mercy shine forth as I ask whether the darkest hidden sorrows of human punishments that belong to the sons of Adam can perhaps furnish me with an answer. Where does this monstrosity come from? What is the explanation? The mind commands the body and is obeyed immediately; the mind commands itself and meets resistance. The mind commands that the hand be moved, and its facility is so great that the command can hardly be told apart from its execution: And the mind is the mind, whereas the hand is the body. The mind commands that the mind will, and [the mind] is not something else; yet it does not do so. Whence this monstrosity? What is the reason? It commands that it will, I say, and it would not command unless it willed. Yet it does not do what it commands.

However, it does not will as a whole. Therefore, it does not command as a whole. For it commands to the extent that it wills, and what it commands does not happen to the extent that it does not will, since the will commands that there be a will, which is not another [will] but itself. Thus it does not command as complete; hence what it commands does not exist. If it were complete, it would not command that it be, since it would already be. Hence this monstrosity is not partly to be willing and partly to be unwilling. Instead, it is a sickness of the mind, since it does not rise up as a whole by the truth, but is weighted down by custom. Hence there are two wills. Neither one of them is the whole; each has what the other lacks.

"Let them perish from Your presence" [Ps. 67:3 (68:2 RSV)], God, 8.10.22
as perish those "empty talkers and deceivers" [Tit. 1:10] of the mind,
namely the Manichaeans. Once they notice two wills in the process of
deliberation, they maintain that there are two natures belonging to two
minds: one good, the other evil. They are themselves truly evil, since they
hold these as evils. Yet they will be themselves good, if they were to hold
truths and agree to truths, so that your apostle might say to them: "At
one time you were darkness, but now you are light in the Lord" [Eph.
5:8]. For while they will to be light not in the Lord but in themselves,
thinking that the nature of the soul is what God is, they are thus made
even thicker darknesses, since they withdraw farther away from You due
to their horrendous arrogance – from You, "the true light illuminating
every man that comes into this world" [Jn. 1:9]. They should pay attention to what they say, and blush; "Look unto Him and be illuminated,
and your faces will not blush" [Ps. 33:6 (34:6 RSV)]. For my part, while I
was deliberating that I might now serve the Lord my God, as I had long
before resolved, it was *I* who was willing, *I* who was unwilling: It was I.
I was neither completely willing nor completely unwilling. So I strug-
gled with myself and was put to flight by myself. This flight indeed took
place while I was unwilling, yet it did not point to a nature belonging to
an outside mind, but rather to a penalty belonging to my own. And so I
myself was not doing this at the time; it was instead "the sin that dwelt
in me" [Rom. 7:17], sin due to punishment for a more free sin, because I
was a son of Adam.

If there are as many contrary natures as there are wills offering 8.10.23
resistance to one another, there will be not just two, but many. If someone
were to deliberate about whether to go to the [Manichaean] meeting or to
the theatre, they exclaim: "Look! Two natures! One good which leads to
the former, the other evil which leads back to the latter! For where does
the very hesitation of wills opposed to one another come from?" Well, I
call them both evil, the one which leads to them and the one which leads
back to the theatre. But they believe only the one by which a person goes
to them is good. What then if one of our [Catholic Christians] were to
deliberate, vacillating between two wills fighting it out, about whether
to go to the theatre or to our church? Are not *they* the ones who would
vacillate over what answer to give? For either (*a*) they admit what they
are not willing to admit, namely that he heads over to our church by a
good will (as in the case of those heading over who are filled with its

sacraments and are kept there); (*b*) they think that two evil natures and two evil minds conflict in a single person, in which case what they usually maintain – that one is good and the other evil – will not be true; or (*c*) they will be converted to the truth and will not deny that, when someone deliberates, a single soul is wavering between diverse wills.

8.10.24    Therefore, when the Manichaeans perceive that two wills in a single person are opposed to one another, let them not say that two contrary minds derived from two contrary substances and derived from two contrary principles are in contention, one good and the other evil. For You, God the Truthful, disprove them and refute and confound them. For instance, each will is evil when someone deliberates over whether to kill a man with poison or with a knife; whether to encroach upon the grounds of one of his neighbors or of another, when he cannot do both; whether to buy his pleasure due to lechery or to hold on to his money due to avarice; whether to go to the circus or to the theatre, if both have a show on the same day, or (to add a third) to steal from someone else's house if the occasion arises, or (to add a fourth) whether to commit adultery if the opportunity presents itself then. Suppose all these happen at one and the same stretch of time and are equally desired, though they cannot all take place at once. The [Manichaeans] tear apart the mind with four wills opposed to one another, or even more in the vast range of things that are pursued, yet they typically do not say that there is such a multitude of diverse substances. So too in the case of good wills. For I ask them whether it is good to take delight in a reading of the Apostle Paul, whether it is good to take delight in a sober psalm, whether it is good to discourse upon the gospels. They will answer each question: "It is good." Then what if they all equally offer delight at one and the same time? Will not these diverse wills pull asunder the human heart while we deliberate over which is the most important one to take up? All are good, and they struggle with one another, until the election is made of one to which is borne the whole and single will that was divided into many. So too, when eternity offers delight above and the pleasure of temporal good keeps us below, it is the same soul willing the one and the other, though not with a whole will. And so it is torn apart by this weighty vexation as long as it prefers the former on account of truth but does not discard the latter on account of its familiarity.

# Confessions, 7.3.5

Augustine earlier described his knowledge of the will as follows.

I made an effort to comprehend what I was hearing, namely that the free 7.3.5
choice of the will is the cause that we do evil and that we suffer Your
right judgment. But I was not able to comprehend it clearly. So, I tried to
raise my mind's eye up from the abyss, but I sank back in again. I tried
repeatedly, but I sank back in again and again. What lifted me up towards
Your light was that I knew myself to have a will as much as I knew myself
to be alive. Thus whenever I was willing or unwilling with regard to
something, I was completely certain that none but myself was willing or
unwilling. And more and more did I recognize that there lay the cause of
my sin. I saw that what I did unwillingly I *suffered* rather than *did*, and
I judged it not a fault but a penalty; and recognizing that You are just,
I admitted immediately that I was not punished unjustly...

# On Grace and Free Choice

To Valentine and his monks:

On account of those who preach and defend human free choice in such 1.1 a way that they dare to deny and try to get rid of the grace of God – the grace by which we are called to Him and are set free from our evil deserts, and through which we acquire good deserts by which we might attain eternal life – I have already examined a number of points and written about them, as far as the Lord found worthwhile to grant to me. But since there are some people who defend the grace of God in such a way that they deny human free choice, or who hold that free choice is denied when grace is defended, I have for this reason been inspired by our mutual charity to take the trouble to write something on this issue to Your Charity, brother Valentine, and to the others who serve God with you. Word about you has reached me, brothers, from some members of your community who came to me (and by whom I have sent along this work), that there are disagreements among you on these matters.

Therefore, dearly beloved, I advise you first to thank God for what you do understand, so that the obscurity of the question not disturb you. As for anything still beyond the reach of your mind's effort, pray for understanding from the Lord while maintaining peace and charity among yourselves. Until He brings you to those matters you do not yet understand, walk along the path you have been able to reach. This is the advice of the Apostle Paul who, shortly after declaring he was not yet perfect,[1] says: "Let us therefore, as many as are perfect, be thus minded"

---

[1] Phl. 3:12: "Not as though I had already attained [the goal] or were already perfect, but I follow after."

[Phl. 3:15]. That is: we are "perfect" to the extent that we have not yet come to the perfection that is enough for us. He immediately adds: "If in any thing you be otherwise minded, God shall reveal this to you as well; nevertheless, let us walk along the path we have reached" [Phl. 3:15–16]. In fact, by walking "along the path we have reached" we shall be able to reach what we have not yet reached – with God revealing it to us, if we are of another mind about anything, as long as we do not abandon what He has already revealed.

2.2     Now God has revealed to us through His own Scripture that human beings have free choice of the will. I shall remind you how He revealed this, not with my human words but rather with His divine eloquence. First of all, the divine precepts would themselves be pointless for human beings unless we had free choice of the will, by which we might reach the promised rewards through carrying them out. For the precepts were given to human beings in order that they not have an excuse on the grounds of ignorance, as the Lord says of the Jews in the gospel: "Had I not come and spoken to them, they would have no sin; but now they have no excuse for their sin" [Jn. 15:22]. Of what sin is He speaking if not the great one He foreknew would be theirs when He said these things, that is, the sin in which they were going to put Him to death? For they had no sin before Christ came in the flesh to them.

Again, the Apostle Paul says [Rom. 1:18–20]:

> The wrath of God is revealed from heaven against all the irreligiousness and injustice of those people who in their iniquity hold back the truth; for what is known of God is evident to them, since God has made it evident to them. Indeed, from the world's creation His invisible features are clearly seen and understood through the things that are made, even His everlasting power and divinity, so that they are without excuse.

What does he mean by "without excuse" other than the excuse that human pride typically offers: "If I had known I would have done it; hence because I did not know, I did not do it" or "If I knew I would do it; hence because I do not know, I am not doing it"? This excuse is taken away from them once a precept is given, or the knowledge how not to sin is made evident.

2.3     Yet there are people who try to use God Himself to excuse themselves. To them the Apostle James says [Jas. 1:13–15]:

Let no one say when he is tempted, "I have been tempted by God"; for God is not tempted by evils, nor does He tempt anyone. But each person is tempted when he is drawn away and enticed by his own lust. Then when lust has conceived, it brings forth sin; and sin, when it is accomplished, brings forth death.

Again, Solomon's book of Proverbs gives an answer to those who wish to excuse themselves on the basis of God Himself: "The folly of a man perverts his ways, and in his heart he holds God to blame" [Prv. 19:3]. The book of Ecclesiasticus declares [Sir. 15:12–18 (15:11–17 RSV)]:

Say not: "It is through the Lord that I fell away," for you should not do the things He hates. Say not: "He Himself has caused me to err," for He has no need of the sinner. The Lord hates all abomination, and those who fear God love it not. It was He Who made human beings from the beginning, and left them in the hand of their own counsel. If you are willing, you shall keep the commandments and keep good faith with His pleasure. He sets fire and water before you: stretch forth your hand to whichever you will. Before us is life and death, and whichever you please shall be given you.

We see expressed here most clearly the free choice of the human will.

What of the fact that in so many passages God bids that all His 2.4 commandments be kept and fulfilled? How can this be bidden if there is no free choice? Consider that happy man of whom the Psalmist says "His will was in accord with the Law of the Lord" [Ps. 1:2]. Surely he makes it clear that a person takes his stand in God's Law by his will.

Next, there are so many commandments that in some way address the will itself by name.[2] For example: "Be unwilling to be overcome by evil" [Rom. 12:21]. There are other similar examples, such as: "Be unwilling to become as the horse or the mule, which have no understanding" [Ps. 31:9 (32:9 RSV)]; "Be unwilling to forsake the counsels of your mother" [Prv. 1:8]; "Be unwilling to be wise in your own eyes" [Prv. 3:7]; "Be unwilling to fall away from the teaching of the Lord" [Prv. 3:11]; "Be unwilling to neglect the Law" [Prv. 3:1]; "Be unwilling to withhold doing well for those in need" [Prv. 3:27]; "Be unwilling to devise evils

---

[2] Augustine's examples in this paragraph are formulated using *nolle*, lit. "to be unwilling (to)." These cases are artefacts of rendering negative imperatives into Latin: The Hebrew and Greek originals make no mention of the will, even indirectly. I have translated them "Be unwilling to" rather than the more familiar "Do not" (or "Thou shalt not") to preserve Augustine's point.

against your friend" [Prv. 3:29]; "Be unwilling to attend to the deceits of a woman" [Prv. 5:3]; "He was unwilling to understand that he should act well" [Ps. 35:4 (36:3 RSV)]; "They were unwilling to receive teaching" [Prv. 1:29]. There are countless such passages in the Old Testament. What do they show but the free choice of human will?

In the New Testament, the same thing is shown when it says: "Be unwilling to lay up for yourselves treasures upon Earth" [Mt. 6:19]; "Be unwilling to fear those who kill the body" [Mt. 10:28]; "Whoever is willing to follow after me, let him deny himself" [Mt. 16:24]; "Peace on Earth to men of good will" [Lk. 2:14]. The Apostle Paul says: "Let him do what he will, he does not sin if he marries; nevertheless he does well who stands steadfast in his heart, having no necessity, but, having power over his own will, decrees in his heart to keep [his wife] a virgin" [1 Cor. 7:36–37]. Again, he says: "If I do this willingly, I have a reward" [1 Cor. 9:17]. In another passage: "Be sober, just, and unwilling to sin" [1 Cor. 15:34]. Once more: "As there was a readiness to will, so too let there be a readiness to act accordingly" [2 Cor. 8:11]. To Timothy he says: "Younger widows are willing to marry once they have begun to grow wanton in disregard of Christ" [1 Tim. 5:11]. And elsewhere: "All who are willing to live religiously in Jesus Christ are going to suffer persecution" [2 Tim. 3:12]. To Timothy himself he says: "Be unwilling to neglect the grace that is in you" [1 Tim. 4:14]. To Philemon: "Your good should not be of necessity, as it were, but willing" [Phm. 14]. He even admonishes slaves to serve their masters "from the heart with good will" [Eph. 6:6–7]. Again, James: "Be unwilling to err, my brothers" [Jas. 1:16]; "My brothers, be unwilling to discriminate among persons who have faith in our Lord Jesus Christ" [Jas. 2:1]; "Be unwilling to speak evil one of another" [Jas. 4:11]. Again, John in his Epistle: "Be unwilling to delight in the world" [1 Jn. 2:15]. There are other passages of the same kind.

Surely wherever Scripture says "be unwilling" to do this or that, and wherever the will's work is required to do or not to do something in the divine admonitions, that is sufficient proof of free choice. Therefore, let no one "hold God to blame in his heart" [Prv. 19:3], but let him instead hold himself to blame when he sins. Nor does the fact that something is done in accordance with God take it away from one's own will. When a person acts willingly, then should his deed be called good; then a reward for his good deed should be hoped for from Him of Whom it is said: "He shall

144

render to each one in accordance with his deeds" [Ps. 61:13 (62:12 RSV), Mt. 16:27, Rom. 2:6].

Therefore, those who know the divine commandments are deprived 35 of the excuse of ignorance that people usually offer. But even those who do not know God's Law will not be free of penalty: "For as many as have sinned without the Law shall also perish without the Law: and as many as have sinned under the Law shall be judged by the Law" [Rom. 2:12]. I do not think the Apostle Paul meant that those who do not know the Law were going to suffer something worse in their sins than those who do know it. Perishing seems worse than being judged. Yet he was speaking about the Gentiles and the Jews; since the former are without the Law but the latter received the Law, who would dare to say that the Jews who sin under the Law are not going to perish? For they have not believed in Christ, and indeed the apostle says of them that they "shall be judged by the Law." Without faith in Christ nobody can be delivered. For this reason, they will be judged and perish.

Now if the condition of those who do not know God's Law is worse than the condition of those who know it, how will what the Lord says in the gospel be true? He says: "The slave who knows not his master's will and does things worthy of lashes shall be whipped with few lashes; but the slave who knows his master's will and does things worthy of lashes shall be whipped with many lashes" [Lk. 12:47–48]. See where he shows that sinning is more serious for someone who knows than for someone who does not know! Yet we should not therefore take refuge in the shadows of ignorance, where each of us looks for an excuse. Indeed, *not knowing* differs from *being unwilling to know*. The will is at fault in the man of whom it is said: "He was unwilling to understand that he should act well" [Ps. 35:4 (36:3 RSV)].

Yet even the ignorance found in people not unwilling to know, but rather who simply (so to speak) do not know, is not such as to excuse anyone from burning in the everlasting fire, if he did not believe precisely because he did not hear anything at all to believe – though perhaps he will burn more gently. Not without reason did the Psalmist say: "Pour out Your anger upon the peoples who know You not" [Ps. 78:6 (79:6 RSV)]. Likewise the Apostle Paul: "He shall come in flames of fire to take vengeance upon those who do not know God" [1 Ths. 1:7–8]. Even so, the human will is addressed in order that we have this very knowledge, and so that when it is said "Be *unwilling* to become as the horse or the mule, which have no understanding" [Ps. 31:9 (32:9 RSV)], none of us may say "I did not know," "I did not hear," "I did not understand." However, clearly worse is the person of whom it is said: "A stubborn slave will not be corrected by words; for though he understands he will not obey" [Prv. 29:19].

When someone objects: "I cannot do what is prescribed because I am overcome by my lust," then indeed he has no excuse in virtue of ignorance. Nor does he hold God to blame in his heart. Instead, he knows his own evil in himself, and laments. The Apostle Paul says to him: "Be unwilling to be overcome by evil, but overcome evil with good" [Rom. 12:21]. Surely in the case of someone to whom it is said "be *unwilling* to be overcome" the choice of his will is undoubtedly involved, for *to be willing* and *to be unwilling* are proper to the will.

4.6  Now you should be careful that all these divine testimonies in defense of free choice, and whatever other passages there are (doubtless there are many), not be understood in such a way that no place is left for the assistance and the grace of God in the conduct of a good and religious life deserving an eternal reward. And be careful that when miserable human beings live well and act well – or rather when they seem to themselves to live and act well – they dare to glory in themselves rather than in the Lord, and to put their hope of living rightly in themselves, so that they call on themselves the curse of the prophet Jeremiah [Jer. 17:5]:

> Cursed is the man who has his hope in man, and makes strong the flesh of his arm, and whose heart abandons the Lord.

You must understand, my brothers, the testimony of this prophet. Because he did not say 'Cursed is the man who has his hope in *himself*,' it could then seem to someone that he said "Cursed is the man who has his hope in man," so that no one has hope in anyone but himself. Therefore, to show that he was warning each man not to have his hope even in himself, when he had said "Cursed is the man who has his hope in man" he immediately added "and makes strong the flesh of his arm." Here 'arm' is used to mean the power of acting, while in the term "flesh" we should understand human weakness. Accordingly, someone who thinks that weak and inadequate power (*i.e.* human power) is sufficient by itself for acting well "makes strong the flesh of his arm." Nor does he hope for assistance from the Lord, and so Jeremiah added: "and whose heart abandons the Lord."

Such is the Pelagian heresy. It is not an old heresy but one that sprang up a little while ago. After arguments against this heresy had been made for a long time, it was necessary in the end for it to come before the episcopal councils.[3] I sent you not all but at least some of the proceedings from them to read.[4] Let us, therefore, not have our hope of acting well in man, making the flesh of our arm strong; nor let our heart abandon the Lord, but let it say to Him: "Be my helper; do not forsake me or leave me, God my Saviour" [Ps. 26:9 (27:9 RSV)].

Accordingly, my dear brothers, just as we showed above[5] by testimony    47 from Scripture that there is free choice of the will in human beings for the sake of living well and acting rightly, let us also see what divine testimonies there are about God's grace, without which we can do nothing well.

First, I shall say something about your [monastic] profession. This community in which you lead lives of continence would not gather you together if you did not condemn marital pleasure. But while the Lord was speaking about this [Mt. 19:10–11]:[6]

> His disciples said to Him: "If such is the case of a man with his wife, it is not good to marry." He replied to them: "Not all accept this saying, but those to whom it is given."

Did not the Apostle Paul encourage free choice for Timothy when he said: "Keep yourself continent" [1 Tim. 5:22]? And on this score he pointed out the power of the will when he says: "having no necessity, but having power over his own will, to keep [his wife] a virgin" [1 Cor. 7:37]. Yet "not all accept this saying, but those to whom it is given" [Mt. 19:10]. Those to whom it is *not* given either are unwilling or do not carry out what they will. "Those to whom it is given," however, will in such a way that they carry out what they will. Therefore, "this saying," which is not accepted by all, is accepted by some; it is both God's gift *and* free choice.

With regard to marital chastity, the apostle of course says: "Let him do    48 what he will, he does not sin if he marries" [1 Cor. 7:36]. Yet even this is

---

[3] Augustine presumably has in mind the Councils of Carthage and Milevis (416), upheld by papal pronouncement in 418–419.
[4] In *Letters* 215.2, Augustine lists all the material he sent to the monks of Hadrumetum, including excerpts from the trial proceedings.
[5] See 2.2–3.5.
[6] In discussing marriage, Jesus has just said, "And I say to you: Whoever shall put aside his wife, except for fornication, and marry another, is committing adultery" (Mt. 19:9).

God's gift. For Scripture says: "A woman is joined to a man by the Lord" [Prv. 19:14]. And so the Teacher of the Nations[7] commends in his words (*a*) marital chastity, through which adultery does not come about; and (*b*) more perfect continence, through which no sexual intercourse is sought. He showed that each is God's gift when he wrote to the Corinthians and advised spouses not to deprive one another of their marital rights. For once he had advised them he added: "I would that all men be even as I myself" [1 Cor. 7:7]. For he surely restrained himself from any sexual intercourse. Continuing, he remarked: "But every person has his own gift from God – one person this one, but another that one" [1 Cor. 7:7].

Do the many things that are prescribed in God's Law against committing fornication and adultery point to anything but free choice? They would not be prescribed unless a human being had a will of his own by which he might obey the divine precepts. Yet it is God's gift, without which the precepts about chastity cannot be kept. Accordingly, the writer of the book of Wisdom says: "For I knew that no one can be continent unless God gives this – and it was itself an indication of wisdom to know Whose gift this was" [Wis. 8:21]. However, "each person is tempted when he is drawn away and enticed by his own lust" [Jas. 1:14] from keeping the holy commandments regarding chastity.

If someone were to object: "I am willing to keep [these commandments] but I am overcome by my lust," Scripture will reply to his free choice what I said above: "Be unwilling to be overcome by evil, but overcome evil with good" [Rom. 12:21]. Yet it is grace that helps this to happen. And unless grace helps, the Law will be nothing but the power of sin. Lust is increased and strengthened by the prohibition of the Law, unless the spirit of grace helps us. This is what the Teacher of the Nations himself tells us: "The sting of death is sin; and the power of sin is the Law" [1 Cor. 15:56]. Now you see *why* someone says "I am willing to keep the commandment of the Law but I am overcome by the power of my lust." When his will is addressed and he is told "Be unwilling to be overcome by evil" [Rom. 12:21], what use to him is all this, unless with the succor of grace it comes to pass?

The Apostle Paul himself made this point. After he had said "the power of sin is the Law," he immediately added: "But thanks be to God

---

[7] Paul describes himself as "Teacher of the Nations" (*doctor gentium*) in 1 Tim. 2:7 and 2 Tim. 1:11.

who gives us victory through our Lord Jesus Christ" [1 Cor. 15:57]. Therefore, even the "victory" in which sin is overcome is nothing but God's gift, helping out free choice in this struggle.

This is why the heavenly Teacher says: "Be watchful and pray that you not enter into temptation" [Mt. 26:41]. Therefore, let each who is fighting against his own lust pray that he "not enter into temptation," that is, that he not be "drawn away and enticed" by it. For he does not 'enter into temptation' if he overcomes evil lust with his good will. Yet the choice of the human will is not sufficient unless God grants victory to the one who prays that he not enter into temptation. What is more evident than God's grace in the case where what is prayed for is received? If our Saviour had said "Be watchful that you not enter into temptation," He would appear to have addressed only human will. But when he added "and pray," He showed that God provides help that we not enter into temptation. He addressed free will as follows: "My son, be unwilling to fall away from the teaching of the Lord" [Prv. 3:11]. And the Lord said: "I have prayed for you, Peter, that your faith may not fail" [Lk. 22:32]. Human beings are therefore assisted by grace, so that their wills are not bidden to no purpose.

When God says: "Turn to me and I shall turn to you" [Zch. 1:3], one of these actions seems to pertain to our will, namely that we turn to Him, whereas the other pertains to His grace, namely that He also turns to us. The Pelagians may think that this passage confirms their theory, in which they claim that God's grace is given in accordance with our deserts. Pelagius himself did not dare to affirm this when his case was being heard by the bishops in the East, that is, in Palestine where Jerusalem is located.[8] For among the other accusations that were made against him, he was also accused of claiming that God's grace is given in accordance with our deserts. This view is so alien to Catholic doctrine and inimical to the grace of Christ that, unless he had declared this accusation to be anathema, he himself would have left under anathema. But his later books,[9] in which he defends absolutely nothing but [the view]

---

[8] At the end of 415 the Primate of Palestine, Eulogius, convened the Council of Diospolis, at which some thirteen bishops examined Pelagius on his views about grace, in response to charges brought against him. His views were found not to be contrary to Catholic doctrine. Augustine held that Pelagius avoided condemnation only by skillful evasion and legal technicalities, being less than forthright about his views.

[9] Pelagius wrote two major treatises after the Council of Diospolis, his *On Nature* and *Defense of Free Will*. Neither is extant.

that God's grace is given in accordance with our deserts, show that his declaration of anathema was fraudulent.

Thus the Pelagians gather from Scripture such passages as the one I mentioned just a little while ago: "Turn to me and I shall turn to you" [Zch. 1:3]. They do this so that God's grace, in which He turns Himself to us, is given in accordance with our deserts in turning to Him.

Those who think this are not paying attention. Unless our turning to God were itself also God's gift, we would not say to Him: "God of hosts, turn us to You!" [Ps. 79:8 (80:7 RSV)]; "God, You shall give us life in turning us to You!" [Ps. 84:7 (85:6 RSV)]; "Turn us, God our Saviour!" [Ps. 84:5 (85:4 RSV)]. And there are other such passages that would take too long to mention. For what else is *coming to Christ* but *being turned to Him through belief*? And yet He says: "No one comes to me unless it be given to him by my Father" [Jn. 6:66].

5.11 Again, this passage makes the will's choice clear: "The Lord is with you when you are with Him, and if you seek Him you shall find Him; but if you foresake Him, He shall forsake you" [2 Chr. 15:2]. But those who claim that God's grace is given in accordance with our deserts construe these passages in such a way as to claim that (*a*) our deserts consist in the fact that we are with God; (*b*) His grace is given in accordance with these deserts; (*c*) as a result, He is with us. Again, our deserts consist in the fact that we are seeking Him. His grace is given in accordance with these deserts, so that we find Him. And this passage proclaims the will's choice [1 Chr. 28:9]:

> Know God and serve Him with a perfect heart and a willing soul, Solomon my son, for the Lord searches every heart, and knows every thought of your mind; if you seek Him, you shall find Him; and if you forsake Him, He shall cast you off for ever.

The Pelagians, however, postulate human deserts in the words "if you seek Him" and hold that grace is given in accordance with these deserts in the words "you shall find Him." They labor as hard as they can to show that God's grace is given in accordance with our deserts, that is, to show that grace is not grace.[10] For if it is rendered to people in accordance

---

[10] An allusion to Rom. 11:6: "But if [election] is through grace, then it is not through works; otherwise grace then is not grace – but if it is through works, then it is not through grace; otherwise grace is not then grace."

with their deserts, "the reward is not paid as a matter of grace, but of debt" [Rom. 4:4], as the Apostle Paul says quite clearly.

There were deserts in the Apostle Paul, but evil deserts, when he per- 5.12 secuted the Church. Accordingly, he says: "I am not fit to be called an apostle, for I persecuted the Church of God" [1 Cor. 15:9]. Therefore, although he had these evil deserts, good was rendered to him for evil. Hence he immediately added: "But by the grace of God I am what I am" [1 Cor. 15:10]. And to show free choice, he quickly added: "His grace in me was not fruitless, but I labored more abundantly than all of them" [1 Cor. 15:10]. Human free choice is encouraged in other passages, too, in which Paul says: "We beseech you not to receive the grace of God in vain" [2 Cor. 6:1]. How could he beseech them if they were to receive grace in such a way that they lost their own will? Nevertheless, so that the will itself not be thought capable of doing anything good without God's grace, after "His grace in me was not fruitless, but I labored more abundantly than all of them," he immediately added: "Not I, but the grace of God which was with me" [1 Cor. 15:10]. That is: I was not alone, but God's grace was with me. Accordingly, it was neither the grace of God alone, nor the apostle himself alone, but the grace of God *with* him. However, it was the grace of God alone that the apostle be called upon from heaven and converted by so great and efficacious a calling, for his deserts were great but evil.

Finally, the apostle says elsewhere to Timothy: "Work with me for the gospel according to the power of God, Who saves us and calls us with His holy calling, not in accordance with our works but in accordance with His own plan and grace, which was given to us in Jesus Christ" [2 Tim. 1:8–9].[11] Again, recalling his own evil deserts, he says: "For we ourselves also were sometimes foolish, unbelievers, in error, enslaved to various desires and pleasures, acting with malice and envy, hateful, and hating one another" [Tit. 3:3]. What indeed is owed to these deserts that are so evil, other than penalties? Yet with God rendering good for evil through grace, which is not given in accordance with our deserts, there took place what the apostle then describes in these words [Tit. 3:4–7]:

> But when the kindness and humanity of God our Saviour shone
> forth, not by works of righteousness which we have done, but

---

[11] The latter part of the passage is cited in *On Reprimand and Grace* 7.14.

according to His mercy, He saved us through the washing of rebirth and the renewal of the Holy Spirit, which He poured forth on us most abundantly through Jesus Christ our Saviour, so that, become just through His grace, we are made heirs according to the hope of eternal life.

6.13 These and other such testimonies prove that God's grace is not given in accordance with our deserts, since we see that it is given, and given daily, not only where there are no previous good deserts but even where there are many previous evil deserts. Yet clearly, once grace has been given, our deserts begin to be good, though only by means of it. For if grace were to withdraw itself, human beings would fall, no longer raised up but cast down by free choice. Accordingly, even when someone begins to have good deserts he ought not attribute them to himself, but rather to God, to Whom it was said: "Be my helper; do not forsake me" [Ps. 26:9 (27:9 RSV)]. In saying "do not forsake me" the Psalmist shows that if he were forsaken he would not be capable of any good of his own accord. This is why he also says: "I said in my fullness, 'I shall never be moved'" [Ps. 29:7 (30:6 RSV)]. He thought that the good, which he had in such fullness that he would not be moved, was his own. But to show him Whose good it was, the good in which he had begun to glory as though it were his own, he was chastised with a brief departure of grace. He says: "Lord, in Your will You have furnished strength to my glory; but You turned Your face from me, and I was confounded" [Ps. 29:8 (30:7 RSV)]. Hence it is necessary for human beings that the grace of God not only makes the irreligious just – that is, when good is rendered to an irreligious person in place of evil, he becomes just – but also, once they have already become just through faith, that they walk along with that grace and lean upon it so as not to fall. For this reason it is written of the Church in the Song of Songs [Sol. 8:5]:

> Who is the one coming up who has been made white,[12] leaning upon her kinsman?

She has been "made white" who could not be white of her own accord. And by whom was she made white if not by Him Who says through the prophet: "If your sins be as scarlet, I shall make them white as snow"

---

[12] "Been made white": *dealbata* Augustine; *innixa* Vulgate, there usually interpreted as "[dressed in] white."

[Is. 1:18]? Thus at the time when she was made white, she deserved nothing good. Now, however, she has been made white and walks well, but only if she perseveres in "leaning upon" Him by Whom she was made white. Accordingly, Jesus himself – upon Whom she who was made white is leaning – said to his disciples: "Without me you can do nothing" [Jn. 15:5].

Therefore, let us return to the Apostle Paul, whom we found to have 6.14 gained the grace of God (Who renders good for evil) surely without any good deserts, but rather with many evil deserts. Let us see what he says in writing to Timothy at the time his final suffering drew near: "Now it is I who am being offered as a sacrifice, and the time of my departure is approaching; I have fought the good fight, I have run the race, I have kept the faith" [2 Tim. 4:6–7]. He calls these things to mind as his good deserts now, so that he who gained grace after his evil deserts might now gain a crown after his good deserts. Finally, note what comes next: "There remains for me the crown of justice, which the Lord, the just Judge, shall award me at that day" [2 Tim. 4:8]. To whom would the just Judge award a crown if the merciful Father had not given him grace? How would this be a "crown of justice" unless grace, which makes the irreligious just, had come first? How would the crown be awarded as something due, unless grace were first given gratuitously?

However, the Pelagians claim that the only grace that is not given in 6.15 accordance with our deserts is that by which human sins are forgiven, whereas the grace which is given at the end, namely eternal life, *is* rendered in accordance with our previous deserts.

They should be answered as follows. If they understood our deserts in such a way as to acknowledge that they too are gifts of God, their view would not have to be rejected. But since they preach human deserts by claiming that human beings have their deserts of themselves, quite rightly does the apostle reply: "Who singles you out? What do you have that you have not received? But if you have received it, why do you glory as though you had not received it?" [1 Cor. 4:7]. To someone thinking such things, we say in all truth that God crowns His gifts and not your deserts, if your deserts are from yourself and not from Him. For if they are such, they are evil, and God does not crown them. But if they are good, they are the gifts of God, since, as the Apostle James says: "Anything excellent that is given [to us], and every perfect gift, is from above and comes down from the Father of lights" [Jas. 1:17]. On this basis John the Baptist, the precursor of the Lord, says: "No one can receive anything unless it be given to him from Heaven" [Jn. 3:27]. "From Heaven," to be sure, from which the Holy Spirit came when Jesus "ascended on high, took captivity captive, and gave gifts to human beings" [Eph. 4:8].[13] Therefore, if your good deserts are the gifts of God, God does not crown your deserts *qua* your deserts but rather *qua* His own gifts.

7.16     Next, let us consider the deserts of the Apostle Paul, for which he said the just Judge was going to award the "crown of justice" [2 Tim. 4:8]. Let us see whether his deserts *qua* his – that is, *qua* acquired of his own accord – are God's gifts.

Paul says [2 Tim. 4:7]:

> I have fought the good fight, I have run the race, I have kept the faith.

First of all, there would not be these good works unless good thoughts had preceded them. Take note, then, of what he says about these thoughts when writing to the Corinthians: "Not that we are sufficient of our own selves to think anything; our sufficiency is rather from God" [2 Cor. 3:5]. Second, let us examine these works one by one.

Paul says, "I have fought the good fight." I ask: By what power did he fight? Was it something that came from himself, or was it given "from above"? Surely so great a teacher was not ignorant of God's Law, which declares [Dt. 8:17–18]:

> Do not say in your heart: My strength and the might of my hand has made this great power for me. Instead, remember the Lord your God, for it is He Who gives you the strength to achieve such power.

Furthermore, what is gained by "the good fight" unless it is followed by victory? And He gives victory of Whom Paul says: "Thanks be to God Who gives us victory through our Lord Jesus Christ" [1 Cor. 15:57]. In another passage, after calling to mind the psalm: "For your sake are we put to death all the day long; we are reckoned as sheep for the slaughter" [Ps. 43:22 (44:22 RSV)], Paul then adds: "Yet in all these things we more than conquer through Him Who loved us" [Rom. 8:36–37]. Not through ourselves, but "through Him Who loved us."

---

[13] An echo of Ps. 67:19 (68:18 RSV): "You have ascended on high, taken captivity captive, and received gifts for human beings."

Paul next says "I have run the race." But the one who said this says in another passage, "Thus it does not depend on the one who is willing or on the one who is running, but on God, Who shows mercy" [Rom. 9:16]. There is no way to turn this sentence around so that it says 'It does not depend on the mercy of God but on the one willing and the one running.' Anyone venturing to say this clearly shows that he is contradicting the apostle.

Finally, Paul says "I have kept the faith." But the man who said this 7.17 says elsewhere: "I have obtained mercy that I might be faithful" [1 Cor. 7:25]. He did not say "I have obtained mercy *because I was* faithful" but rather "*that I might be* faithful": showing from this that even faith itself can only be had through God's mercy, and that it is God's gift. He teaches this lesson explicitly when he says: "By grace have you been saved through faith; and this is not from yourselves but is the gift of God" [Eph. 2:8]. For [the Pelagians] could make the claim: "We have received grace *because* we believed" – as though attributing faith to themselves and grace to God. For this reason, when the apostle said "through faith," he adds "and this is not from yourselves but is the gift of God." Again, to prevent [the Pelagians] from claiming to have deserved such a gift by their works, he goes on to add: "It is not from works, lest anyone be filled with pride" [Eph. 2:9]. It is not that he denied good works or made them pointless, since he says: "God renders to each one in accordance with his deeds" [Ps. 61:13 (62:12 RSV), Mt. 16:27, Rom. 2:6]. Rather, works are from faith, not faith from works, and for this reason we have works of justice from Him from Whom there is faith itself. On this score it is written: "The just man lives by faith" [Hab. 2:4, Rom. 1:17, Hbr. 10:38].

Yet people not understanding that the selfsame apostle says "We hold 7.18 that a person is made just through faith without the works of the Law" [Rom. 3:28] thought he said that faith is enough for a person, even if he lives an evil life and does not have good works. By no means does the Vessel of Election[14] think this! After he had said in a certain passage, "In Jesus Christ neither circumcision nor its absence mean anything" he straightaway added: "but faith which works through love" [Gal. 5:6]. This is the faith that separates those faithful to God from unclean demons. For even they, as the Apostle James says, "believe and tremble"

---

[14] "The Vessel of Election": the Apostle Paul. See Acts 9:15: "The Lord said to [Ananias]: Go your way, for he [=Paul] is my Vessel of Election, to bear my name before the nations, and kings, and the children of Israel."

[Jas. 2:19], but they do not do their works well. Therefore, they do not have the faith by which the just person lives, that is, the faith "which works through love," so that God renders to him eternal life in accordance with his works. But since we have those good works from God too, from Whom we also have faith and love, Paul, the Teacher of the Nations, also named eternal life itself a grace.[15]

8.19     And from this there arises no small question, to which God must give a solution. If eternal life is rendered for good works, as Scripture explicitly says (since God "shall render to each one in accordance with his works" [Ps. 61:13 (62:12 RSV), Mt. 16:27, Rom. 2:6], how is eternal life a grace? For grace is not rendered for works but is given gratuitously, as the apostle says: "The reward for him who works is not paid as a matter of grace, but of debt" [Rom. 4:4]. Again, he says: "There is a remnant saved through the election of grace" [Rom. 11:5], and he immediately adds: "But if [election] is through grace, then it is not through works; otherwise grace then is not grace" [Rom. 11:6]. How then is eternal life, which is obtained from works, a grace?

Did the apostle perhaps *not* say that eternal life is a grace? Hardly! He declared it in such a way that it cannot be denied at all. He does not require someone shrewd to understand it, merely someone attentive to hear it. For after he had said, "The wages of sin is death" [Rom. 6:23], he immediately added: "Eternal life in Jesus Christ our Lord is a grace of God."

8.20     Therefore, it seems to me that the only way this question can be resolved is for us to understand that our good works, for which eternal life is rendered, themselves belong to God's grace, in line with what the Lord Jesus says: "Without me you can do nothing" [Jn. 15:5]. After the apostle himself had said: "By grace have you been saved through faith; and this is not from yourselves but is the gift of God: It is not from works, lest anyone be filled with pride" [Eph. 2:8–9], he saw (*a*) that people certainly could think he said this as though good works were not necessary for believers but faith alone would be sufficient for them; and again (*b*) that people could be filled with pride over these good works as if they were of themselves sufficient for doing them. Thus he quickly added: "For we are His workmanship, created in Jesus Christ in good works, which God has made ready that we may walk in them" [Eph. 2:10]. Why is it that,

---

[15] See Rom. 6:23: "Eternal life in Jesus Christ our Lord is a grace of God."

while commending the grace of God, he had said "It is not from works, lest anyone be filled with pride"? He explains this in saying "we are His workmanship, created in Jesus Christ in good works." Why did he explain this by saying "not from works, lest anyone be filled with pride"? Well, hear and understand: He said "not from works" as if they existed for you as yours from yourself, but rather as these things for which God fashioned[16] you – that is, for which he created and formed you. Paul says "we are His workmanship, created in Jesus Christ in good works," not with respect to the creation in which human beings were made, but with respect to the creation of which he who was already a human being did say: "God, create in me a clean heart" [Ps. 50:12 (51:12 RSV)] and of which the apostle says: "Hence if anything new is created in Christ, the former things have passed away; behold, they are made new: But all things are from God" [2 Cor. 5:17–18]. Thus we are fashioned – that is, created and formed – "in good works," which we have not made ready but "which God has made ready that we may walk in them." Hence, my dear brothers, if our good life is nothing but a grace of God, doubtless so too eternal life, by which a good life is rewarded, is a grace of God. For eternal life is given gratuitously, since a good life, for which it is given, was given gratuitously. But a good life, for which it is given, is simply a grace; eternal life, which is given for it, since it is the prize for it, is a grace for a grace, as though it were the reward for justice. In such a way is it true – for it *is* true – that God "shall render to each one in accordance with his works" [Ps. 61:13 (62:12 RSV), Mt. 16:27, Rom. 2:6].

Perhaps you will ask whether we read in Scripture 'a grace for a grace.' <sub>9.21</sub>

Well, you have the clearest case in the Gospel according to John, where John the Baptist says of Christ the Lord: "Yet of His fullness have we received even a grace for a grace" [Jn. 1:16]. Thus to the extent that we are capable, "we have received" our small portions (so to speak) "of His fullness" so that we may live well, "as God has apportioned to each the measure of his faith" [Rom. 12:3]. For "every person has his own gift from God – one person this one, but another that one" [1 Cor. 7:7], and this is grace. But over and above this we shall receive "even a grace for a grace" when eternal life will be rendered to us. And on this score the apostle said: "Eternal life in Jesus Christ our Lord is a grace of God"

---

[16] "Fashioned": *finxit*, etymologically linked to "workmanship" (*figmentum*).

[Rom. 6:23]. He had earlier said: "The wages of sin is death" [Rom. 6:23]. "The wages" deservedly, since eternal death is rendered *qua* debt for service to the Devil. Although he could (rightly) have said "The wages of justice is eternal life," he preferred to say "The grace of God is eternal life" so that we might thereby understand that God does not bring us to eternal life on account of our deserts, but on account of His mercy. It is of Him the Psalmist speaks, addressing his soul: "Who crowns you in compassion and mercy?" [Ps. 102:4 (103:4 RSV)]. Is not a crown awarded for good works? But He works these selfsame good works in good people. On this score it is written: "God is the one Who works in you both willing and doing works in conformity with good will" [Phl. 2:13]. Hence the Psalmist said "He crowns you in compassion and mercy," since it is through His compassion that we do the good works for which a crown is awarded.

Now one should *not* think that free choice has been taken away because the apostle said: "God is the one Who works in you both willing and doing works in conformity with good will" [Phl. 2:13]. If this were so, he would not have said immediately before that: "Work out your own salvation with fear and trembling" [Phl. 2:12]. When He bids them to work, this is addressed to their free choice – but then "with fear and trembling," so that they not become filled with pride over their good works, attributing their working well to themselves, as if their good works were their own. Thus as though he were asked the question: "Why did you say 'with fear and trembling'?" the apostle explains the reason for these words, saying "God is the one Who works in you." If you fear and tremble, you are not filled with pride over your good works as though they were yours, since "God is the one Who works in you."

10.22    So, my brothers, you should not do evil things through free choice, but good things. God's Law prescribes this for us in Scripture, in both the Old and New Testaments. But let us read and, with the Lord's help, understand the apostle when he says: "No flesh shall be made just before Him on the basis of the Law; for the knowledge of sin is through the Law" [Rom. 3:20]. He said "the knowledge," not "the extinction," [of sin].[17] Furthermore, when a person knows sin, if grace does not help him to guard against what he knows, undoubtedly the Law works wrath. The

---

[17] Augustine's point is that (knowledge of) the Law does not extinguish sin; grace is required for that.

apostle himself says this in another passage. His words are: "The Law works wrath" [Rom. 4:15]. He said this because God's wrath is greater in the case of the transgressor who knows sin through the Law and nevertheless does it. Such a person is indeed a transgressor of the Law, as the apostle declares in another passage:[18] "Where there is no Law, there is no transgression" [Rom. 4:15]. For this reason he says elsewhere: "That we may serve in the newness of spirit and not in the oldness of the letter" [Rom. 7:6]. He wants the Law to be understood by "the oldness of the letter" – and what is "the newness of spirit" if not grace?

The apostle, to avoid appearing to have accused or blamed the Law, immediately puts a question to himself: "What shall we say then? Is the Law sin? By no means!" [Rom. 7:7]. Then he adds: "Yet I knew sin only through the Law" [Rom. 7:7]. This is what he had said earlier: "The knowledge of sin is through the Law" [Rom. 3:20]. The apostle says [Rom. 7:7–13]:

> I knew lust only because the Law had said: *You shall not lust* [Ex. 20:17]. But sin, taking the commandment as an occasion, worked in me every lust. Indeed, without the Law, sin is dead. For once I was living without the Law, but when the commandment came, sin revived, and I died. And the commandment, which was meant for life, I found to be for death: Sin, taking the commandment as an occasion, deceived me, and through it slew me. Thus the Law is holy, and the commandment holy and just and good. Was then that which is good made death for me? By no means! But sin, that it might appear sin, worked death for me by that which is good, in order that the sinner or the sin come to pass beyond measure through the commandment.

The apostle also says [Gal. 2:16]:

> Knowing that a human being is not made just through the works of the Law except through faith in Jesus Christ, even we have believed in Jesus Christ, that we might be made just by faith in Christ and not through the works of the Law: Since no flesh shall be made just by works of the law.

Why then do these preening perverse people, the Pelagians, say that the [11.23] Law is the grace of God which helps us to not sin? Why do these wretches

---

[18] This immediately follows the verse just cited.

make this claim and beyond any doubt contradict so great an apostle? He says that sin gained its strength against human beings through the Law, and, through the commandment, although it is "holy and just and good," it slays him, and "through that which is good" it works death for him, from which he would not be set free unless the Spirit gave life to him whom the letter had killed, as he says in another passage: "The letter kills but the Spirit gives life" [2 Cor. 3:6]. These obstinate persons, blind to God's light and deaf to God's voice, claim that the death-dealing letter gives life, contradicting the life-giving Spirit.

Thus let me warn you with the words of the apostle himself: "Therefore, my brothers, we are debtors not to the flesh, to live according to the flesh; for if you live according to the flesh you shall die, but if through the Spirit you mortify the deeds of the flesh, you shall live" [Rom. 8:12–13]. I said these things so that with the words of the apostle I might deter your free choice from evil and encourage it towards something good. Yet you must not on this account glory in humanity – that is, in yourselves – rather than in the Lord, when you live not "according to the flesh" but "through the Spirit mortify the deeds of the flesh." In order that those to whom the apostle said these things not fill themselves with pride, by reckoning that they are able to perform these great good works through their own spirit rather than through [the Spirit] of God, after he had said "If you through the Spirit do mortify the deeds of the flesh, you shall live" he immediately added: "For as many as are driven by the Spirit of God, they are the children of God" [Rom. 8:14]. Therefore, when "through the Spirit you mortify the deeds of the flesh" in order to live, glorify Him, praise Him, give thanks to Him through Whose Spirit you are driven to be capable of these things, so that you show yourselves to be the children of God. For "as many as are driven by the Spirit of God, they are the children of God."

12.24    Therefore, those who are driven by their own spirit, trusting in their own strength without the assistance of grace, with the sole addition of the assistance of the Law, are *not* children of God. Such are those people of whom the same apostle says: "Being ignorant of God's justice and wanting to establish their own, they have not submitted to God's justice" [Rom. 10:3]. He says this about the Jews, who presumptuously rejected grace and, consequently, did not believe in Christ. He says that they wanted "to establish their own" justice, which is justice from the Law – not because they established the Law but rather because they established their justice in the Law, which is from God, when they believed themselves able to fulfill the selfsame Law through their own powers – "being ignorant of God's justice," not the justice by which God is just, but the justice human beings have from God.

So that you know that the apostle was talking about this justice of theirs which is from the Law, and about the justice of God which human beings have from God, listen to what he says in another passage while speaking of Christ [Phl. 3:8–9]:

> For His sake did I believe all things to be not only losses but I even reckoned them as trash, that I may enrich myself with Christ, and be found in Him not having my own justice from the Law but that which comes through faith in Christ, which is from God.

What does he mean by "not having my own justice from the Law"? The Law was not his but God's. Unless he called it his justice, despite being from the Law, because he thought himself able to fulfill the Law by his own will without the assistance of grace, which comes through faith in Christ. Hence when he said "not having my own justice which comes from the Law" he went on to add "but that which comes through faith in Christ, which is from God."

The Jews were ignorant of this. He said of them: "Being ignorant of God's justice," that is, the justice that is from God – after all, the death-dealing letter does not give this, but rather the life-giving spirit[19] – and "wanting to establish their own" (and the apostle declared this justice to be from the Law when he said "not having my own justice which is from the Law"), "they have not submitted to God's justice," that is, they have not submitted to God's grace. They were under the Law, to be sure, but not under grace, and so sin had dominion over them. Human beings do not become free of sin by the Law, but rather by grace. This is why he says elsewhere: "Sin shall not have dominion over you, for you are not under the Law but under grace" [Rom. 6:14]. It is not because the Law is evil, but because under it are those whom He makes guilty by giving His bidding without giving His assistance. Grace in fact assists someone to be a doer of the Law, and someone who is put under the Law without this grace will be merely a hearer of the Law. To such people the apostle

---

[19] See the citation of 2 Cor. 3:6 in 11.23.

thus says: "You who are made just in the Law have fallen from grace" [Gal. 5:4].

13.25 Who is so deaf to the words of the apostle, who is so foolish, or rather insanely ignorant of what he is saying, that he dares to claim that the Law is grace?[20] For the apostle, who *did* know what he was saying, proclaimed: "You who are made just in the Law have fallen from grace" [Gal. 5:4]. However, the Law is not grace, for the simple reason that in order for the Law to come to pass, the Law itself cannot be of assistance, whereas grace can. Will nature not then be grace? For the Pelagians have even dared to make the claim that grace is the nature in which we were created such that we have a rational mind, by means of which we, who were made in God's image, are capable of understanding that we "have dominion over the fish of the sea, and over the birds of the air, and over all the beasts that move upon the Earth" [Gen. 1:28].

Yet this is *not* the grace which the apostle commends through faith in Jesus Christ. For it is certain that this nature is common to us and to unbelievers and the irreligious, whereas grace through faith in Jesus Christ belongs exclusively to those who have this faith: "For not all have faith" [2 Ths. 3:2].

Finally, to those who, wanting to be made just in the Law, "have fallen from grace" the apostle says in perfect truth: "If justice is from the Law, then Christ died gratuitously"[21] [Gal. 2:21]. Likewise is it said in perfect truth to those who think nature to be the grace which faith in Christ recognizes and commends: "If justice is from the Law, then Christ died gratuitously." The Law existed at that time and it did not make anyone just. Nature also existed at that time, and it did not make anyone just. Hence it is gratuitous that Christ died so that (*a*) the Law be fulfilled through Him, Who declared "I am come not to destroy the Law but to fulfill it" [Mt. 5:17]; and (*b*) the nature that was lost through Adam would be recovered through Him, Who said that He came "to seek and to save what had been lost" [Lk. 19:10; Mt. 18:11]. Even the Fathers of old, who loved God, believed in Him Who was to come.

13.26 The Pelagians also claim that God's grace, which is given through faith in Jesus Christ, which is neither Law nor nature, can only bring it

---

[20] This, according to Augustine, is what the Pelagians hold: see the beginning of 11.23.
[21] "Gratuitously": *gratis*, the same word Augustine uses to describe the essential feature of grace, as in 8.19–8.20. The traditional rendering here, "Christ died in vain," does not capture this connection.

about that past sins are forgiven, not that future ones be avoided or that obstacles be overcome.

Well, if this were true, then when we say: "Forgive us our trespasses, as we forgive those who trespass against us" [Mt. 6:12] in the Lord's Prayer, we surely would not add "and lead us not into temptation" [Mt. 6:13]. We say the former in order for our sins to be forgiven, the latter to guard against or to overcome them. But there would be no reason for asking for this from "our Father Who is in Heaven" if we could bring it about through the strength of human will.

I advise and strongly encourage Your Charity to read carefully the book that St. Cyprian wrote about the Lord's Prayer.[22] Understand it, as far as the Lord gives His assistance, and commit it to memory. You will see there how he addresses the free choice of those whom he instructs by writing his treatise, so as to show them that they must still petition in prayer for those things they are bidden to fulfill in the Law. But this would be completely pointless if human will were sufficient to do these things without divine assistance.

14.27 The Pelagians, however, were shown not to defend free choice, but rather to overstate and overthrow it. For the grace given through Jesus Christ our Lord is neither the knowledge of divine law, nor nature, nor simply the remission of sins. Rather, it brings it about that the Law is fulfilled and our nature is freed, preventing sin from having dominion. Therefore, since the Pelagians were shown to be wrong on these matters, they turned themselves to trying to show (in any way they could) that God's grace is given in accordance with our deserts. They say: "Even if grace is not given in accordance with our deserts for our good works, since we do our works well through it, it is still given in accordance with the deserts of our good will: For the good will of the person praying comes first, and this is preceded by the will to believe, so that the grace of God Who hears our prayers follows in accordance with these deserts."

14.28 I have already examined faith above[23] – that is, the will to believe – to the point of showing that it is a matter of grace. As a result, the apostle did not say 'I have obtained mercy because I was faithful' but instead said: "I have obtained mercy that I might be faithful" [1 Cor. 7:25].

[22] Cyprian, *The Lord's Prayer*. Augustine cites §12 of this work in *On Reprimand and Grace* 6.10.
[23] See 7.17–7.18.

There are other passages in which this point is well attested. The apostle says: "Think moderately, as God has apportioned to each the measure of his faith" [Rom. 12:3]. I have already cited this passage: "By grace have you been saved through faith; and this is not from yourselves but is the gift of God" [Eph. 2:8]. He also wrote: "Peace and charity to my brothers, along with faith from God the Father and the Lord Jesus Christ" [Eph. 6:23]. And the passage where he says: "For it is given to you on behalf of Christ, not only to believe in Him but also to suffer for His sake" [Phl. 1:29]. Each therefore is a matter of the grace of God: (*a*) the faith of those who believe; (*b*) the patience of those who suffer. For he declares each to be a gift. Above all there is the passage where the apostle says: "We who have the same spirit of faith" [2 Cor. 4:13]. He did not say '*knowledge* of faith' but instead "*spirit* of faith," which he said so that we understand that faith is granted unasked for, in order for other things to be granted to the one asking for them. He says: "How then shall they call upon Him in Whom they have not believed?" [Rom. 10:14]. Therefore, the spirit of grace brings it about that we have faith, so that through our faith we may achieve by prayer the ability to do what we are bidden to do. Hence the apostle himself constantly put faith ahead of the Law, since we are not capable of doing what the Law bids unless, through our faith, we achieve by entreaty the capacity to do it.

14.29    If faith is due solely to free choice and is not given by God, why do we pray for those who are unwilling to believe that they might believe? This would be completely pointless were we not to believe, quite rightly, that Almighty God is able to turn to belief even perverse wills hostile to the faith. Human free choice is touched upon when the Psalmist says: "If today you shall hear His voice, be unwilling to harden your hearts" [Ps. 94:8 (95:7–8 RSV)]. Yet if God were not able to take away even that hardness of heart, He would not declare through the Prophet: "I shall take away from them their heart of stone and I shall give them a heart of flesh" [Ez. 11:19]. The apostle fully showed that this had been predicted with regard to the New Testament when he says: "You are our epistle … written not with ink but with the Spirit of the living God; not in tablets of stone but in the fleshy tablets of the heart" [2 Cor. 3:2–3]. We should not think that he said this so that those who ought to live spiritually would lead lives of the flesh! Instead, since a stone, to which he compared a hard heart, is without feeling, to what should he have compared an understanding heart, if not flesh with feeling?

The point was put this way by the prophet Ezekiel [Ez. 11:19–20]:

> The Lord says: I shall give them another heart and I shall give them
> a new spirit; I shall take out of their flesh their heart of stone and
> I shall give them a heart of flesh, so that they may walk in my pre-
> cepts and observe my decrees and carry them out; and they shall be
> my people, and I will be their God.

Therefore, how can we say without complete absurdity that the good
deserts of a good will came first in a human being,[24] so that this heart
of stone might be taken away? After all, "heart of stone" itself signifies
precisely a will that is inflexible and completely hardened against God.
Where a good will comes first, there is of course no longer a "heart of
stone."

In another passage, God shows most evidently through the selfsame    14.30
prophet that He does these things not because of any good deserts of
theirs, but because of His own name [Ez. 36:22–27]:

> I do this, house of Israel, but for the sake of my holy name, which
> you have profaned among the Nations whither you have gone; and
> I shall make my great name holy, which was profaned among the
> Nations, which you have profaned in the midst of them; and the
> peoples shall know that I am the Lord, said the Lord God, when
> I shall be made holy in you before their eyes. And I will take you
> from the Nations and gather you from all the lands, and I will bring
> you into your own land. Then will I sprinkle clean water upon you,
> and you shall be cleansed of all your filthiness, and from all your
> idols will I cleanse you. A new heart also will I give you, and a new
> spirit will I put within you; and I will take your heart of stone away
> from your flesh, and I will give you a heart of flesh. I will put my
> Spirit within you, and bring it about that you walk in my justifica-
> tions, and you shall keep my judgments and carry them out.

Who is so blind that he does not see, who is so made of stone that he does
not feel, that grace is not given in accordance with the deserts of a good
will, since the Lord declares and attests "I do this, house of Israel, but for
the sake of my holy name"? Why did He say "I do it but for the sake of
my holy name" if not to prevent them from thinking that it happens on
account of their good deserts, as the Pelagians do not blush to claim?

---

[24] See the Pelagian claim at the end of 14.27.

Furthermore, He proves not only that their good deserts are nothing but also that evil deserts had come first, when He says "but for the sake of my holy name, which you have profaned among the Nations." Who does not see that it is a terrible evil to profane the holy name of the Lord? Yet for the sake of my very name, He says, which you have profaned, I will make you good people – not for your sakes. He says: "And I shall make my great name holy, which was profaned among the Nations, which you have profaned in the midst of them." He says He makes his own name holy, which He previously had called 'holy.' This is therefore what we pray for in the Lord's Prayer, when we say "may Your name be made holy" [Mt. 6:9],[25] namely, that what is without doubt always holy in itself be made holy among people. Then there follows: "and all the peoples shall know that I am the Lord, said the Lord God, when I shall be made holy in you." Thus, although He is always holy, He is nevertheless made holy in those upon whom He bestows His grace, taking away their "heart of stone" through which they profaned the name of the Lord.

15.31 So that we not think that human beings themselves do nothing in this case through free choice, the Psalmist says: "Be unwilling to harden your heart" [Ps. 94:8 (95:7–8 RSV)]. And through Ezekiel himself the Lord says [Ez. 18:31–32]:

> Cast away from yourselves all your irreligious doings which you have done irreligiously against me; make for yourselves a new heart and a new spirit; and follow all my commandments. For why will you die, house of Israel? I do not want the death of him who dies, says the Lord God; turn yourselves [to me] and you shall live.

Let us keep in mind that He Who says here "turn yourselves [to me] and you shall live" is the one to Whom we say: "Turn us, God!" [Ps. 79:4 (80:3 RSV); Ps. 84:5 (85:4 RSV)]. Let us keep in mind that He says "Cast away from yourselves all your irreligious doings," although He Himself makes the irreligious just. Let us keep in mind that He Who says here "Make for yourselves a new heart and a new spirit" also says: "A new heart also will I give you, and a new spirit will I put within you" [Ez. 36:26].

How then does He Who says "Make yourselves" also say "I will give you"? Why does He bid it, if He is going to give it? Why does He give it, if a man is going to do it?

---

[25] More familiarly: "Hallowed be Thy name."

The reason must be that He gives what He bids when he helps the one He bids to do it. The will is always free in us, but it is not always good. For it is either (*a*) free from justice, when it is the servant of sin, and then it is evil; or (*b*) free from sin, when it is the servant of justice, and then it is good. But God's grace is always good. Through grace it happens that a human being who previously had an evil will has a good will. Through grace it also happens that this good will, which has now begun to exist, increases, and becomes so great that it can fulfill the divine commandments, which it shall will to do, since it shall will firmly and completely. Now "If you are willing, you shall keep the commandments" [Sir. 15:16 (15:15 RSV)] means that those who are willing but unable [to keep the commandments] should recognize that they do not yet fully will [to do so], and should pray to have a will that is great enough to fulfill the commandments. Thus are they helped to do as they are commanded. Willing is useful when we have the ability; having the ability is useful when we will. For what good is it if we will what we cannot do, or are unwilling to do what we can?

The Pelagians think that they know some great truth when they declare: "God would not bid what He knew human beings could not do." 16.32

Who does not know this? But He has bidden some things we cannot do, so that we know what we should ask of Him. For it is faith itself which achieves by prayer what the Law commands. Then indeed, the one who said "If you are willing, you shall keep the commandments" [Sir. 15:16 (15:15 RSV)] says a little bit later in the same book: "Who shall set a guard my mouth and a seal of wisdom upon my lips, lest perhaps it cause me to fall and my tongue destroy me?" [Sir. 22:33 (22:27 RSV)]. Without a doubt he had already received the commandment: "Keep your tongue from evil, and your lips from speaking guile" [Ps. 33:14 (34:13 RSV)]. Since what he says is true, namely "If you are willing, you shall keep the commandments" [Sir. 15:16 (15:15 RSV)], why then does he seek for a guard to be set upon his mouth? Similarly, the Psalmist says: "Set a guard, Lord, upon my mouth" [Ps. 140:3 (141:3 RSV)]. Why are God's commandments and his own will not sufficient for him? Especially seeing that if he is willing, he shall keep the commandments! He already knows how many of God's commandments are directed against pride. If he is willing, he shall keep them. Why then does he say shortly afterwards: "Lord, the Father and God of my life, do not give me a prideful air" [Sir. 23:4–5 (23:4 RSV)]? The Law had already said to him: "You shall not lust!" [Ex. 20:17]. Thus let him will and do what he is bidden; for if he is willing, he shall keep the commandments. Why does he go on to say: "Turn lust away from me" [Sir. 23:5]? How many things has God commanded against the dissolute life! Let him do the [things God has commanded], for, if he is willing, he shall keep the commandments. Why is it that he cries out to God: "Let not the greediness of the belly nor of sexual intercourse take hold of me!" [Sir. 23:6]? If we were to put these questions to him in person, he would reply to us with complete accuracy, saying: "On the basis of this prayer of mine, in which I ask for these things from God, understand how I meant 'If you are willing, you shall keep the commandments'" [Sir. 15:16 (15:15 RSV)]. For it is certain that we keep the commandments if we will to do so – but since "the will is made ready by the Lord" [Prv. 8:35 LXX], we should ask of Him that we will as much as is enough for us to do through our willing.

It is certain that *we* will, when we will. But God brings it about that we will something good. On this score, Scripture says what I cited a moment ago: "The will is made ready by the Lord" [Prv. 8:35]. It also says: "The steps of a man shall be directed by the Lord, and he shall will His road" [Ps. 36:23 (37:23 RSV)]. It also says: "It is God Who works in you the willing" [Phl. 2:13].

It is certain that *we* act, when we act. But God brings it about that we act by furnishing our will with efficacious strength. He said: "I shall bring it about that you walk in my justifications, and you shall keep my judgments and carry them out" [Ez. 36:27]. When He says "I shall bring it about that ... you shall ... carry them out," what else is He saying but: "I will take away from you the heart of stone" due to which you were not carrying them out, "and I will give you a heart of flesh" due to which you shall carry them out [Ez. 36:26]? And what is this but: I will take away your hard heart (due to which you were not carrying them out), and I will give you an obedient heart (due to which you shall carry them out)? God brings it about that we act. The Psalmist says to Him: "Set a guard, Lord, upon my mouth" [Ps. 140:3 (141:3 RSV)]. This is to say: Bring it about that *I* set a guard upon my mouth. The one who said "I have set a guard upon my mouth" [Ps. 38:2 (39:1 RSV)] had already obtained that benefit from God.

17.33　　Thus anyone who wills to carry out God's commandment, and is not able to do so, does indeed already have a good will, but one that is as yet slight and weak. But he will be able to do so once he has a will that is great and strong.

When the martyrs carried out those great commandments, surely they did so with a great will, that is, with great charity. Of this charity the Lord Himself says: "No one has greater charity than this, that he should lay down his life for his friends" [Jn. 15:13]. Accordingly, the apostle too says [Rom. 13:8–10]:

> He who loves his neighbor has fulfilled the Law. For *You shall not commit adultery* [Ex. 20:14], *You shall not commit murder* [Ex. 20:13], *You shall not steal* [Ex. 20:15], *You shall not lust* [Ex. 20:17], and whatever other commandment there is, is summed up in these words: *You shall love your neighbor as yourself* [Lv. 19:18]. The love of one's neighbor works no evil: The fullness of the Law, therefore, is love.

The Apostle Peter did not yet possess that charity when he denied the Lord three times out of fear.[26] As John the Evangelist says: "There is no fear in charity; instead, perfect charity casts out fear" [1 Jn. 4:18]. Yet even though it was slight and imperfect, charity was not absent from Peter when he said to the Lord: "I shall lay down my life for You" [Jn. 13:37]. For he thought that he was able to do what he felt himself willing to do. Who had begun to give this charity, albeit "slight," but He Who makes the will ready? By working along [with us] He perfects what He began by working [in us].[27] For He begins by working that we will, which He perfects by working along with our willing. Accordingly, the apostle says: "I am confident that He Who is working His good work in you will continue perfecting it up to the day of Jesus Christ" [Phl. 1:6].[28] In order that we will, then, God works without us; but when we will, and we will in such a way that we act, He works along with us. Yet without

---

[26] After Jesus was arrested at Gethsemane, Peter three times denied knowing Him, as had been foretold. For Peter's denial, see Mt. 26:71–75, Mk. 14:66–68, Lk. 22:57–59, Jn. 18:15–18.

[27] That is: *cooperando perficit quod operando incipit*, literally "by co-working He completes what by working [alone] He started" (a famous formulation that is the origin of the doctrine of "cooperative grace").

[28] Augustine reads Phl. 1:6 with God as the subject, parallel to Phl. 2:13 (and more distantly to 1 Cor. 1:6–8). His reading is possible even according to the original Greek text, as well as the later Vulgate. The traditional interpretation takes the subject to be any member of the community addressed by Paul: "I am confident that any one among you who is performing good work will bring it to completion on the day of Jesus Christ." The "day of Jesus Christ" is usually read as the Second Coming. Augustine cites this passage in context in *On Reprimand and Grace* 6.10.

Him either (*a*) working that we will, or (*b*) working along when we will, we are powerless to accomplish good religious works.

As regards (*a*), working that we will, it is written: "It is God Who works in you the willing" [Phl. 2:13].

As regards (*b*), working along when we already will, and by willing we act, the apostle says: "We know that God, along with those who love Him, works everything for the good" [Rom. 8:28].[29] What is "everything" here, if not those cruel and terrible sufferings?[30] The burden of Christ, which is heavy for our weakness, is made light for charity. For the Lord declared that his burden was light [Mt. 11:30] for such people as Peter was when he suffered for Christ, not as Peter was when he denied Christ.

17.34     The Apostle Paul, commending this charity (namely a will set completely on fire with divine love), says [Rom. 8:35–39]:

> Who shall separate us from Christ's charity? Shall tribulation, distress, persecution, famine, nakedness, peril, the sword? As it is written: *For your sake are we put to death all the day long; we are reckoned as sheep for the slaughter* [Ps. 43:22 (44:22 RSV)]. Yet in all these things we more than conquer through Him Who loved us. For I am certain that neither death, nor life, nor angels, nor principalities, nor things present, nor things to come, nor virtue, nor height, nor depth, nor any other creature shall be able to separate us from God's charity, which is in Jesus Christ our Lord.

In another passage he says [1 Cor. 12:31–13:8]:

> Yet I show you a more excellent way. If I speak with the tongues of human beings and of angels, but have not charity, I am become as sounding brass or a tinkling cymbal. And if I have the gift of prophecy and understand all mysteries, and if I have all faith, so that I could move mountains, but have not charity, I am nothing. And if I bestow all my goods on the poor and hand over my body to be burned, but have not charity, it profits me nothing. Charity is

---

[29] Augustine here, as well as in *On Reprimand and Grace* 7.14 and 9.23, reads *cooperatur* rather than *cooperantur* in this passage, the latter reading found in his earlier works and in the Vulgate. The original text reads: οἴδαμεν δὲ ὅτι τοῖς ἀγαπῶσι τὸν θεὸν πάντα συνεργεῖ [ὁ θεὸς] εἰς ἀγαθόν. Augustine's present reading is possible and well expresses his notion of "cooperative grace." The Vulgate reading takes πάντα (*omnia*) to be the subject: "We know that all things work together for good to them that love God" [RSV].

[30] The "cruel and terrible sufferings" of the martyrs, with which Augustine began 17.33.

generous, is kind; charity is not envious; it does not act wrongly, it is not filled with pride, is not unseemly, is not self-seeking, is not provoked, does not think evil; it does not rejoice in iniquity but instead rejoices along with truth; it endures all things, believes all things, hopes all things, suffers all things; charity never fails.

And shortly afterwards he says: "There remains faith, hope, charity, these three; but the greatest of these is charity: Aim at charity" [1 Cor. 13:13–14]. Again, the apostle says to the Galatians: "My brothers, you have been called to freedom; only use not freedom as an opportunity for the flesh, but serve one another through charity – for the whole of the Law is fulfilled in these words: *You shall love your neighbor as yourself* [Lv. 19:18]" [Gal. 5:13–14]. This is what he says to the Romans: "He who loves his neighbor has fulfilled the Law" [Rom. 13:8]. Again, he says to the Colossians: "Above all these things put on charity, which is the bond of perfection" [Col. 3:14]. To Timothy he says: "The point of the precept is charity" [1 Tim. 1:5], and he adds what kind of charity: "out of a pure heart, a good conscience, and faith unfeigned." He says to the Corinthians: "Let all your deeds be done with charity" [1 Cor. 16:14]. Here the apostle shows sufficiently that even reprimands, which are felt as sharp and biting by those who have been reprimanded, should be delivered with charity. Accordingly, once he had remarked in another passage: "Reprimand the unruly, succor the timid, support the weak; be patient towards all" [1 Ths. 5:14], he immediately added: "See that none renders evil for evil unto anyone" [1 Ths. 5:15]. Therefore, even when the unruly are reprimanded, evil is not rendered for evil, but good for evil. What but charity works all these things?

The Apostle Peter says: "Above all things have constant charity among yourselves, for charity covers a multitude of sins" [1 Pet. 4:8].[31] 17.35 The Apostle James also says: "If you keep the royal Law according to Scripture, *You shall love your neighbor as yourself* [Lv. 19:18], you do well" [Jas. 2:8]. Again, the Apostle John says: "He who loves his brother abides in the light" [1 Jn. 2:10]. And in another passage: "He who is not just is not from God, nor he who loves not his brother; for this is the message that we heard from the beginning, that we should love one another" [1 Jn. 3:10–11]. And again in another passage: "This is His commandment, that we believe in the name of His son Jesus Christ, and love one

---

[31]  Peter is alluding to Prv. 10:12: "Charity covers all sins."

another" [1 Jn. 3:23]. Later John says: "This commandment we have from Him, that he who loves God also love his brother" [1 Jn. 4:21]. Shortly afterwards he says: "In this we know that we love the children of God when we love God and follow His precepts; for this is the love of God, that we keep His precepts, and His precepts are not burdensome" [1 Jn. 5:2–3]. In the second letter he writes: "It is not as though I am writing to you a new precept, but that which we had from the beginning, that we love one another" [2 Jn. 5].

17.36    The Lord Jesus Himself also declares that the whole of the Law and the prophets rest upon the two precepts to love God and to love our neighbor.[32] In the Gospel according to Mark it is written of these two precepts [Mk. 12:28–31]:

> And one of the scribes came who had heard them reasoning together, and seeing that He answered him well, he asked Him what was the first commandment of all. But Jesus answered him, "The first commandment of all is: *Hear, O Israel! The Lord your God is one God, and you shall love the Lord your God with all your heart and with all your mind* [Dt. 6:4–5]: this is the first commandment. The second is similar to it: *You shall love your neighbor as yourself* [Lv. 19:18]. There is no other commandment greater than these.

In the Gospel according to John, He says: "A new commandment I give to you, that you love one another – that you love one another even as I have loved you; in this all will know that you are my disciples, if you have love for one another" [Jn. 13:34–35].

18.37    All these precepts concerning love – that is, concerning charity – are of such great importance that whatever anyone thinks himself to do well, if it be done without charity, it is not in any way done well. These precepts concerning charity, therefore, would have been pointless to give to human beings unless they had free choice of the will. Now since they are given by the Old Law and the New Law – though in the New Law there came the grace that was promised in the Old Law – and Law without grace is the letter that kills, whereas in grace the spirit gives life,[33]

---

[32]  When one of the Saducees asked Jesus which is the greatest commandment of the Law, "Jesus said to him, *You shall love the Lord your God with all your heart, with all your soul, and with all your mind* [Dt. 6:5]. This is the first great commandment. The second is similar to it: *You shall love your neighbor as yourself* [Lv. 19:18]. On these two commandments rest all the Law and the prophets" [Mt. 22:37–40].

[33]  See 2 Cor. 3:6: "The letter kills but the spirit gives life."

where then does charity towards God and one's neighbor come from in human beings, if not from God Himself? If it is not from God but from human beings, the Pelagians have prevailed. But if it is from God, we have prevailed over the Pelagians. Therefore, let the Apostle John sit in judgment between us, and let him say to us: "My dear friends, let us love one another" [1 Jn. 4:7]. When the Pelagians begin to fill themselves with pride at these words of John and say, "Why is this prescribed to us? Is it not because we have the ability of ourselves to love one another?" the selfsame John continues on, confounding them, by saying: "for love is from God" [1 Jn. 4:7].³⁴ Thus it is not from us but rather from God.

Why then does John say "Let us love one another, for love is from God"? Is it not because the precept counsels our free choice to ask for God's gift? This counsel would be completely fruitless had not [free choice] first received some love, so that it would then ask that it also be given whatever was required to fulfill what was bidden. When he says "Let us love one another" it is the Law; when he says "for love is from God" it is grace: "God's wisdom carries law and mercy on its tongue" [Prv. 3:16 LXX]. Accordingly, it is written: "He Who gave the Law shall also give His blessing" [Ps. 83:8 (84:67 Variant II RSV)].

Therefore, let no one deceive you, my brothers. For we would not love God unless He loved us first. The selfsame John shows this quite explicitly when he says: "Let us love, for our part, since He first loved us" [1 Jn. 4:19]. Grace makes us lovers of the Law, but the Law itself without grace makes us only transgressors. The Lord says to His disciples: "You have not elected me, but I have elected you" [Jn. 15:16]. This tells us nothing else. For if we first loved Him so we thereby deserve that He love us, then we first elected Him so that we would deserve to be elected by Him. But He Who is Truth says otherwise and explicitly contradicts this human vanity: "You have not elected me," He says. Therefore, if you have not elected Him, you have undoubtedly not loved Him. For how would they elect Him Whom they did not love? "But I," He says, "have elected you."

Did they not afterwards elect Him, and put Him before all the goods of this world? But it is because they were elected that they elected Him; it is not because they elected Him that they were elected. There would

18.38

---

³⁴ Cited in 19.40 and alluded to in *On Reprimand and Grace* 6.9, in each case with the Vulgate reading "charity" (*caritas*) in place of "love" (*dilectio*) as it is here.

be no deserts in human election unless there came first the grace of God, Who elects them. Accordingly, the Apostle Paul offers his blessing as follows: "May the Lord make you increase and abound in charity towards one another and towards all" [1 Ths. 3:12]. The one who had given the Law that we love one another gave this blessing so that we would love one another. Finally, in another passage to the same audience – since doubtless some of them already possessed what he wishes them to have – the apostle says: "We are bound to give thanks to God always for you, my brothers, as it is worthy, because your faith grows exceedingly, and the charity of every one of you towards each other is abundant" [2 Ths. 1:3]. He said this so that those who have so great a good from God would not perhaps be filled with pride, as though they had it from themselves. Because "your faith grows exceedingly," he says, "and the charity of every one of you towards each other is abundant"; therefore "we are bound to give thanks to God" concerning you, not to praise you as though you had this from yourselves.

18.39    The Apostle Paul says to Timothy: "For God has not given us the spirit of fear, but the spirit of virtue and charity and continence" [2 Tim. 1:7]. In this testimony of the apostle we ought well to beware of thinking that we have not received the spirit of the fear of God, which is doubtless a great gift of God. On this score, the prophet Isaiah says: "Upon him shall rest the spirit of wisdom and understanding, the spirit of counsel and might, the spirit of knowledge and religiousness, the spirit of the fear of the Lord" [Is. 11:2–3]. This is not the fear due to which Peter denied Christ.[35] Instead, we have received the fear of God, of which Christ Himself says "Fear Him who has the ability to destroy both soul and body in Hell" [Mt. 10:28] and "Yea, I say unto you, fear Him" [Lk. 12:5]. He said this to prevent us from denying Him out of the fear that had shaken Peter. He wanted this fear to be taken away from us, when he said earlier: "Be not afraid of them that kill the body, and after that have no more that they can do" [Lk. 12:4]. We have not received the spirit of this fear, but instead the spirit "of virtue and charity and continence" [2 Tim. 1:7].

The selfsame apostle says about this spirit: "We glory in tribulations, knowing that tribulation works in us patience, patience experience, experience hope; and hope does not disappoint, for the charity of God is shed

---

35 See the note to 17.33 for Peter's denial.

abroad in our hearts through the Holy Spirit, Who has been given to us" [Rom. 5:3–5]. Thus it happens, not through ourselves, but rather "through the Holy Spirit, Who has been given to us," by this charity (which he shows to be God's gift) "tribulation works in us patience" rather than taking it away. He also says: "Peace and charity to my brothers, along with faith." Great goods, but let him say where they come from: "from God the Father and the Lord Jesus Christ" [Eph. 6:23]. Therefore these great goods are nothing other than God's gifts.

Well, this is not surprising. "The light shines in the darkness, and the darkness grasps it not" [Jn. 1:5]. The Light says: "Behold what manner of love the Father has given to us, that we should be and be called God's children" [1 Jn. 3:1]. And the Darkness in the Pelagian writings says, "We have love from ourselves." If the Pelagians had genuine love – that is, Christian love – they would also know where it came from! The apostle knew when he said: "Now we have received not the spirit of the world, but the spirit which is from God, that we might know which things have been given to us by God" [1 Cor. 2:12]. John says: "God is love" [1 Jn. 4:16]. 19.40

The Pelagians also claim that they even have God Himself not from God, but from themselves. And while they admit that our knowledge of the Law is from God, they hold that charity is from ourselves.

They do not hear the apostle when he says: "Knowledge fills one with pride, whereas charity instructs one" [1 Cor. 8:1]. What is more idiotic – rather, what is greater madness – and more removed from the holiness of charity, than to admit that knowledge, which without charity fills one with pride, comes from God, whereas charity, which makes knowledge incapable of filling one with pride, comes from ourselves? Again, the apostle says: "Christ's charity far surpasses knowledge" [Eph. 3:19]. What greater madness than to think knowledge, which should be subordinated to charity, comes from God, whereas charity, which "far surpasses knowledge," comes from human beings? True faith and sound doctrine declare that both come from God, since it is written: "Out of His mouth comes knowledge and understanding" [Prv. 2:6]. It is written:[36] "Charity comes from God" [1 Jn. 4:7]. We read "the spirit of knowledge and religiousness" [Is. 11:2]; we read "the spirit of virtue and charity and

---

[36] Cited in 18.37, where Augustine has "love" (*dilectio*) in place of "charity" (*caritas*), and in *On Reprimand and Grace* 6.9.

continence" [2 Tim. 1:7]. But charity is a greater gift than knowledge, for when there is knowledge in a human being, charity is necessary so that he not be filled with pride; whereas "charity is not envious; it does not act wrongly, it is not filled with pride" [1 Cor. 13:4].

20.41    I think I have argued sufficiently against those who vehemently attack the grace of God, through which human will is (*a*) not taken away, but rather (*b*) changed from an evil to a good will, and (*c*) given assistance once it is good. I have argued in such a way that not I, but Scripture itself, has spoken to you, with the clearest attestations of the truth. And if Scripture is inspected carefully, it shows not only that good human wills are in God's power – that is, wills which He makes good from evil, and, once made good by Him, He directs to good acts and to eternal life – but also [human wills] which maintain their worldly condition[37] are in God's power, in such a way that He makes them inclined as He wills when He wills: either to rewards offered to some people, or to penalties inflicted on others, as He judges in His judgment which is completely hidden but undoubtedly completely just.

In fact, we find that some sins are even penalties for other sins. For instance, such are "the vessels of wrath" which the apostle says "are fitted for perdition" [Rom. 9:22]. Such is the hardening of Pharaoh, the reason for which is said to be to show God's power in him [Ex. 9:16]. Such is the flight of the Israelites from the city of Ai before the face of the enemy [Jsh. 7:12]: He put fear into their mind so that they fled. This was done so that their sin would be redressed in the way in which it ought to be redressed. Accordingly, the Lord says to Joshua the son of Nun: "The children of Israel could not stand before the face of their enemies" [Jsh. 7:12]. What does 'could not stand' mean? Why did they not stand through free choice, but rather flee when their will was shaken by fear, if it was not because God has dominance even over human wills and, when angered, turns those He wills to dread? Was it not of their own will that enemies of the Israelites fought against the people of God whom Joshua the son of Nun was leading? Yet Scripture says: "Their heart was much

---

[37] "Which maintain their worldly condition": *quae conseruant saeculi creaturam*, to contrast with the 'heavenly condition' (*noua creatio*) of the human wills God directs to eternal life. The expression is obscure. The editors of the *Bibliothèque augustinienne* mention Morel's conjecture of *exornant* for *conseruant*, parallel to Augustine's claim in *Against Julian* 5.4.14 that God made "vessels of wrath" deliberately and fashioned human nature in them so as "to adorn the order of the present world through them" (see the following paragraph).

strengthened by the Lord, that they should come against Israel in battle so that they be destroyed utterly" [Jsh. 11:20].

Was it not of his own will that the wicked Benjaminite cursed King David? Yet what did David, full of genuine and profound religious wisdom, say? What did he say to the man who wanted to strike down the one cursing him?[38] He said [2 Sam. 16:10]:

> What is it to me and to you, sons of Zeruiah? Leave him alone and let him curse, for the Lord told him to curse David. Who then shall say to him: "Why have you done this?"

Then Scripture gives its approval to the whole view of the king by repeating it as though from a different beginning [2 Sam. 16:11–12]:

> And David said to Abishai, and to all his servants: "Behold my son, who came forth from my loins, seeks my life; the more now this Benjaminite too. Let him alone, let him curse, for the Lord has told him to, in order that the Lord might look upon my humility and return me good things for his cursing this day."

Who is so wise as to understand how the Lord told this man to curse David? For He did not tell him by bidding him, in which case his obedience would be praised. Instead, in accordance with His own just and hidden judgment, He inclined his will that was evil from its very own vice to this sin.[39] Hence it is written, "The Lord told him." For if he had been complying with God's bidding, he ought to be praised rather than punished. As we know, he was punished afterwards for this sin. Nor is the reason left unspoken why the Lord told him to curse David in this way, that is, why He sent forth or released his evil heart for this sin: "in order that the Lord might look upon my humility and return me good things for his cursing this day" [2 Sam. 16:12].

See how it is proved that God uses the hearts even of evil people to praise and help good people! Thus did He use Judas to betray Christ; so too did He use the Jews to crucify Christ. And what great goods He provided from that to the peoples who would believe! He even uses the Devil himself, the worst of all, but in the best way: to test and prove the

---

[38] When David came to Behurim, a man of the family of Saul, Shimei son of Gera, threw stones at him and cursed him. David's follower Abishai son of Zeruiah wanted to kill him, but he was restrained by David: 2 Sam. 16:5–14.
[39] That is, God inclined Shimei's already evil will.

faith and religiousness of good people – not for His own sake, since He knows all things before they come to pass, but for our sake, since it was necessary that we be dealt with in this way.

Was it not of his own will that Absalom elected the counsel that was harmful to him? Yet he did it precisely because the Lord heard the prayer of his father to this effect.[40] Accordingly, Scripture says: "The Lord commanded the defeat of the good counsel of Ahithophel, so that the Lord might bring all evils upon Absalom" [2 Sam. 17:14]. Scripture called counsel "good" which served Absalom's cause for the moment, since it favored Absalom over his father against whom he had risen up in rebellion, so that he would be able to overthrow him had not the Lord defeated the counsel that Ahithophel had given, namely by acting in Absalom's heart so that he disdain such counsel and elect another which was not to his advantage.

21.42   Who would not tremble at these divine judgments in which God does whatever He wills even in the hearts of evil people, yet rendering to each one in accordance with his deserts? Rehoboam the son of Solomon rejected the salutary counsel the elders had given him not to deal harshly with the people, yielding instead to the words of his peers and replying with threats to those to whom he ought to have given a mild reply.[41] Where did this come from if not from his own will? But as a result the ten tribes of Israel fell away from him and set up another king for themselves, Jeroboam, so that the will of a wrathful God come to pass, as He had even foretold was going to be. What does Scripture say? "The king did not listen to the people, since his turning away was from the Lord, to carry out His word that He spoke by Ahijah the Shilonite about Jeroboam son of Nabat" [3 Kng. 12:15].[42] This was of course done through human will, in such a way that his turning away was nonetheless from God.

Read the Books of Chronicles and you will find it written [2 Chr. 21:16–17]:

---

[40]   See 2 Sam. 15:31: "A messenger told David, saying, 'Ahithophel is among the conspirators with Absalom.' And David said, 'Lord, I pray you turn the counsel of Ahithophel into foolishness.'" Ahithophel advised Absalom to press his attack against his father David. But Absalom elected to follow the advice of Hushai the Archite to delay and consolidate his position. Unknown to Absalom, Hushai was secretly a supporter of David, and his advice was designed to benefit David rather than Absalom: 2 Sam. 16:15–17:23.

[41]   See 3 Kng. 12:1–15.

[42]   Ahijah the Shilonite met Jeroboam, son of Nabat, on the road leading out of Jerusalem, and told him that God wanted to divide the kingdom of David and to make Jeroboam the king of Israel: 3 Kng. 11:29–39.

> And the Lord stirred up against Jehoram the spirit of the Philistines, and of the Arabs who were neighbors of the Ethiopians; and they came up into the land of Judah, and ravaged it, and carried away all the substance that was found in the house of the king.

Here it is shown that God stirs up enemies to devastate the lands He judges worthy of such a penalty. Yet did the Philistines and the Arabs come into the land of Judah to ravage it with no will of their own? Or did they come of their own will, in such a way that Scripture is lying when it says that the Lord stirred up their spirit to do this? No indeed. Each statement is true: they came of their own will, and yet God stirred up their spirit. The point can also be put this way: the Lord stirred up their spirit, and yet they came of their own will. The Almighty accomplishes in human hearts even the movement of their will, to accomplish through them what He wills to accomplish through them – He Who does not know at all how to will anything unjust.

What do the words of the "man of God" addressed to King Amaziah mean [2 Chr. 25:7–8]?

> Let not the army of Israel go with you; for the Lord is not with Israel, with all the children of Ephraim. For if you think you will prevail over your enemies, God will turn you to flight before them; for God has the power to help and to turn to flight.

How does the power of God help some in battle by imparting confidence, and turn others to flight by instilling fear, if not because He Who "did whatever He willed in heaven and on Earth" [Ps. 134:6 (135:6 RSV)] also works in human hearts?

Read what Joash, the king of Israel, said when he sent a messenger to King Amaziah, who wanted to fight with him. After some other matters he said: "Abide now at home; why call forth evil and fall, and Judah with you?" [2 Chr. 25:19]. Scripture then adds: "But Amaziah did not listen; for it was from God that he be delivered into their hands, for they[43] sought after the gods of Edom" [2 Chr. 25:20]. Look how God, wanting to redress the sin of idolatry, worked in the heart of him with whom He was justly angered that he not listen to the salutary warning but instead, holding it in contempt, that he go to war, where he fell along with his army.

---

[43] "They": Amaziah and his followers.

Through Ezekiel the prophet, God says: "If the prophet be deceived and has spoken, I the Lord have led that prophet astray, and I will stretch out my hand upon him, and I will destroy him utterly in the midst of my people Israel" [Ez. 14:9].

In the Book of Esther it is written that a woman of the people of Israel was made the wife of the foreign king Ahasuerus in the land of captivity. Thus, it is written in her book, when she needed to intervene on behalf of her people, whom the king had ordered to be slaughtered wherever they were found in his kingdom, she prayed to the Lord – for great necessity drove her to dare to enter into the presence of the king, contrary to his command and beyond her station. See what Scripture says [Est. 15:7–8 LXX]:

> He looked at her like a bull in the rush of his outrage. The queen was frightened; her color turned pale and faint, and she leaned for support on the head of her maid who went before her. Then God changed the outrage of the king and turned it into gentleness.

In the Proverbs of Solomon it is written: "The heart of the king is in the hand of God, as the flowing rush of the water; He shall turn it wherever He wills" [Prv. 21:1]. We read what God is said to have done to the Egyptians: "He turned their heart to hate His people, to practice guile on His servants" [Ps. 104:25 (105:25 RSV)].

See what is written even in the letters of the apostles. The Apostle Paul writes: "Wherefore God gave them up to the desires of their hearts, to uncleanness" [Rom. 1:24]. Again, shortly afterwards: "For this reason God gave them up to disgraceful passions" [Rom. 1:26]. Again, shortly afterwards: "Even as they did not like to have God in their thought, God gave them up to a reprobate mind, to do what is not proper" [Rom. 1:28]. He says of certain people [2 Ths. 2:10–11]:

> Because they received not the love of the truth, that they might be saved, for this cause God shall send them the working of error, that they should believe a lie: That they all might be judged who believed not the truth, but gave their consent to iniquity.

21.43 From these and such attestations of the divine words – recounting all of them takes far too long – it has been made sufficiently clear, I think, that God works in human hearts to incline their wills to whatever He wills, either to good due to His mercy or to evil due to their deserts. Of course,

this happens through His judgment, which is sometimes clear and sometimes hidden. Yet it is always just. It ought to be fixed immovably in your
heart that there is no iniquity in God.[44] Accordingly, when you read in
the texts of Truth that people are led astray by God, or that their hearts
are dulled or hardened, have no doubt that their evil deserts came first,
so that they suffered these things justly. Otherwise you run up against
the proverb of Solomon: "The folly of a man perverts his ways, and in his
heart he holds God to blame" [Prv. 19:3].

Grace, however, is not given in accordance with human deserts.
"Otherwise grace then is not grace" [Rom. 11:6], since it is called 'grace'
for precisely the reason that it is given gratuitously.[45] Now if God is able,
either through angels (good or evil) or in some other way, to work even
in the hearts of evil people in accordance with their deserts – and He did
not produce their evilness, but either it was originally drawn from Adam
or it was increased by their own will – what surprise is it if He works
good in the hearts of His elect through the Holy Spirit, He Who worked
it that their hearts became good from evil?

But let people suppose that there are good deserts that they think 22.44
come earlier, so that they are made just through the grace of God – not
understanding that, when they say this, they simply deny grace. Well, as
I said, let them suppose what they want, with regard to adults. In the case
of young children, though, the Pelagians certainly have no reply to make.
Young children do not have any will to receive grace, a will whose deserts
the Pelagians might claim had come earlier. Furthermore, we see infants
even cry and resist when they are baptized and feel the divine sacraments.
This would be chalked up against them as a grave sin of irreligion if they
already had the use of free choice. Yet grace is firmly attached even to
those resisting it, quite clearly without any earlier good deserts; "otherwise grace then is not grace" [Rom. 11:6].

Sometimes this grace is furnished to the children of unbelievers when,
in God's hidden providence, they somehow or other come into the hands
of religious people. Yet sometimes the children of believers do not obtain
it, when there is some obstacle so that it is not possible for it to come
to their support when endangered. These things happen by the hidden

---

[44] See Rom. 9:14: "What shall we say then – is there injustice in God? By no means!" The same
allusion occurs in *On Reprimand and Grace* 6.9, and *On the Gift of Perseverance* 8.16, 9.23, and
11.25.
[45] See 8.19–8.20.

providence of God, Whose "judgments are inscrutable and His ways past finding out" [Rom. 11:33]. To see why the apostle makes this statement, look at what he had said earlier. He was dealing with the Jews and the Gentiles while writing to the Romans – that is, to the Gentiles – and says [Rom. 11:30–32]:

> For as you at times have not believed God, yet have now obtained mercy in the face of their unbelief, even so have these also now not believed in the face of your mercy, so that they too may obtain mercy. For God has shut them all away in unbelief, that He might have mercy upon all.

Once he turned his attention to what he had said, marveling at the certain truth yet great profundity of his statement how "God has shut them all away in unbelief, that He might have mercy upon all," as if "doing evil that good might come" [Rom. 3:8], he immediately exclaimed: "The depth of the riches of God's wisdom and knowledge! His judgments are inscrutable and His ways past finding out!" [Rom. 11:33].

There are perverse human beings who do not think about these "inscrutable judgments" and "ways past finding out," people who are ready to find fault and are not well suited for understanding. They are full of hot air and suppose that the apostle is saying "Let us do evil that good may come" [Rom. 3:8]. By no means was the apostle saying this! But people who did not understand thought that he said this when they heard that the apostle said: "Moreover the Law entered, that the offence might be abundant; but where the offence was abundant, grace was all the more abundant" [Rom. 5:20]. Well, grace certainly produces the effect that good comes about from those who have done evil – not that they persevere in evil and reckon themselves to be repaid with good. Thus they ought not say "Let us do evil that good may come" but rather "We did evil and good came of it; now let us do good so that, in the world to come, we receive good for good, we who in this world have received good for evil."

Accordingly, it is written: "I shall sing of mercy and judgment to You, Lord" [Ps. 100:1 (101:1 RSV)]. Thus the Son of Man did not first come "into the world to judge the world, but that the world might be saved through Him" [Jn. 3:17]. This was due to mercy. But afterwards He shall come for judgment, to judge the living and the dead,[46] although even at

---

[46] "The living and the dead": cited from the Apostles' Creed.

this time salvation does not happen without judgment, albeit a hidden judgment. Hence He says: "For judgment I am come into this world, that those who are blind might see, and that those who see might be made blind" [Jn. 9:39].

Keep in mind the hidden judgments of God, therefore, when you look    23.45
at the one condition in which all young children certainly share: drawing hereditary evil from Adam. This infant is helped to receive baptism; that infant is not helped, so that he dies in his bondage [to sin]. One infant, whom God foreknew to have an irreligious future, is baptized and left to this life; another is baptized and snatched from this life "so that wickedness not change his understanding" [Wis. 4:11]. Do not in these cases attribute injustice or folly to God, Who is the font of justice and wisdom. Instead, as I have encouraged you from the beginning of this treatise, "walk along the path you have reached" and "God shall reveal this to you as well" [Phl. 3:15–16]; if not in this life, certainly in the next: "For there is nothing hidden that shall not be revealed" [Mt. 10:26].

Therefore, when you hear the Lord saying: "I the Lord have led that prophet astray" [Ez. 14:9], or what the apostle says, "He has mercy on whom He will, and He hardens whom He will" [Rom. 9:18], you are to believe that there are evil deserts in the one whom He permits to be led astray or to be hardened. However, you are to acknowledge with faith and without doubt that God's grace does not render evil for evil, but rather good for evil in the one on whom He has mercy. Nor should you take free choice away from Pharaoh just because in many passages God says "I have hardened Pharaoh" or "I have hardened the heart of Pharaoh" or "I shall harden the heart of Pharaoh."[47] It does not follow that Pharaoh himself did not harden his own heart. For when the plague of flies was lifted from the Egyptians, we read of him in Scripture: "Pharaoh hardened his heart at this time also, and he was unwilling to let the people go" [Ex. 8:32]. Consequently, God hardened [the heart of Pharaoh] by His just judgment, and Pharaoh himself did so by free choice.

Be certain, then, that your efforts will not be in vain if you make progress with your good resolution and persevere up to the end. God, Who at present does not render to those whom He sets free in accordance with their works, at that time "shall render to each one in accordance with his works" [Ps. 61:13 (62:12 RSV), Mt. 16:27, Rom. 2:6]. God will

---

47 See Ex. 4:21, 7:3, 9:12, 10:20, 10:27.

fully render evil for evil, since He is just; good for evil, since He is good; good for good, since He is good and just. However, He will not render evil for good, since He is not unjust. Therefore, He will render evil for evil as the penalty for injustice; He will render good for evil as grace for injustice; He will render good for good as "grace for grace" [Jn. 1:16].

24.46     Return to this treatise regularly. If you understand it, give thanks to God. Where you do not understand it, pray that you may understand it, for the Lord will give you understanding. Remember that Scripture says: "If any of you lack wisdom, let him ask it of God, Who gives liberally to all without reproach; and it shall be given to him" [Jas. 1:5]. As the Apostle James himself says, this is "the wisdom that comes down from above" [Jas. 3:17]. But cast away from yourselves the wisdom he despised, and pray that it not be in you. For he says [Jas. 3:14–17]:

> If you have bitter envy and strife in you, this wisdom does not come down from above, but is earthly, animal, devilish. For where there is envy and strife, there is changeableness and every wicked work. But the wisdom that comes down from above is first pure, then peaceable, gentle, open to persuasion, full of mercy and good fruits, priceless and without hypocrisy.

What good, then, will anyone lack who asks for and succeeds in obtaining this wisdom from the Lord? Understand grace from this. For if this wisdom were from us, it would not "come down from above," nor would it have to be asked for from God Who created us.

My brothers, pray for us: "We should live soberly, religiously, and justly in this present world, awaiting that blessed hope and the appearance of our Lord and Saviour, Jesus Christ" [Tit. 2:12–13]. To Christ belong honor and glory and kingdom, with the Father and the Holy Spirit, forever and ever. Amen.

# On Reprimand and Grace

To my dearest brother Valentine and those who serve God along with 1.1 him:

After reading the letters that Your Charity sent to me with Brother Florus and the others who came with him, I gave thanks to God when I learned from your reply to me of your peace in the Lord, your agreement in the truth, and your fervor in charity. The Enemy[1] has tried to undermine some among you. But God in His mercy and wonderful goodness turned the snares of the Enemy to the advantage of His servants, achieving instead the result that none of you was pulled down for the worse, while some were built up for the better.

Therefore, there is no need to re-examine over again all the matters that were sufficiently dealt with in the thorough book I sent to you.[2] Your response makes it clear how receptive you were. However, do not in any way think that a single reading was able to make it sufficiently well known to you. If you want it to be the most fruitful, then, do not be ashamed to re-read it so that it is thoroughly known. You will thereby know exactly which questions (and which kind of questions) should be resolved and put right there, by divine rather than human authority – authority from which we ought not draw away, if we want to reach the goal we are aiming at.

The Lord Himself not only has shown us what evil to turn away from 1.2 and what good to do – this alone the letter of the Law can do – but also assists us to turn away from evil and to do the good, which nobody can do without the spirit of grace. If grace is absent, the Law is there to make

---

[1] "The Enemy": the Devil.    [2] "The thorough book": *On Grace and Free Choice.*

people guilty and to kill them. Accordingly, the apostle says: "The letter kills but the Spirit gives life" [2 Cor. 3:6]. Therefore, anyone who lawfully uses the Law[3] learns in it good and evil; not trusting in his own strength, he takes refuge in grace, by means of which, when provided, he may turn away from evil and do good. Yet who takes refuge in grace, except when "the steps of a man shall be directed by the Lord and he shall will His road" [Ps. 36:23 (37:23 RSV)]? Accordingly, to desire the aid of grace is the beginning of grace. On this score the Psalmist says: "I said: Now have I begun; this change is due to the right hand of the Most High" [Ps. 76:11 (77:10 RSV)]. Thus we must admit that we have free choice for doing both evil and good. But in doing evil each person is free from justice and enslaved to sin,[4] whereas in doing good no one can be free unless he has been set free by Him Who said: "If the Son sets you free, then you shall truly be free" [Jn. 8:36]. But, although each person has been set free from the domination of sin, this does not happen in such a way that he no longer needs help from his liberator.[5] Rather, it happens in such a way that, upon hearing from Him Who says "Without me you can do nothing" [Jn. 15:5], one also says to Him: "Be my helper; do not forsake me!" [Ps. 26:9 (27:9 RSV)]. I rejoice that I have found this faith also in our brother Florus. It is without a doubt the genuine Catholic faith of the prophets and apostles. Accordingly, the brothers who did not understand him must instead be corrected. But I think that with God's favor they have already been corrected.

2.3   It is through Jesus Christ our Lord that we should understand God's grace. It alone sets human beings free from evil. Without it they do nothing good at all, whether in thinking, or in willing and loving, or in acting. And this is in order that human beings not only know what ought to be done, because grace shows them, but also in order that they do with love what they know [ought to be done], because grace provides it. The apostle called for this inspiration of a good will and a good deed for those to whom he said: "We pray to God that you not do anything evil, not so that we appear to have passed the test, but rather so that you do what is good" [2 Cor. 13:7]. Who could hear this and not wake up, admitting that it is by the Lord God that we turn away from evil and

---

[3]   See 1 Tim. 1:8: "We know that the Law is good, if one uses it lawfully (νομίμος)."
[4]   See Rom. 6:20: "When you were enslaved to sin, you were free from justice." Alluded to in 13.42.
[5]   "His Liberator": God, or more specifically Jesus.

do good? Indeed, the apostle did not say "We warn," "We teach," "We encourage," "We reproach," but rather: "We *pray to God* that you do no evil ... but rather that you do what is good." Yet he was also speaking to them and doing all the things I mentioned: warning, teaching, encouraging, reproaching. He knew that all these things he was doing in the open, by way of "planting" and "watering," would be of no avail unless He Who in secret "imparts growth" were to heed his prayers on their behalf. For just as the selfsame Teacher[6] says: "Neither the one who plants nor the one who waters is anything; rather, it is God who imparts growth" [1 Cor. 3:7].

Therefore, do not let those people deceive themselves when they say: "Why do they preach to us, prescribing that we 'turn away from evil and do good' [Ps. 36:27 (37:27 RSV)], if it is not *we* who do this, but rather God who works in us this willing and working?"[7] Rather, let them understand that if they are the children of God, then they are driven by the Spirit of God,[8] so that they (*a*) do what ought to be done, and (*b*) give thanks, once they have done it, to Him by Whom they are driven. For they are driven so that *they* do it – not so that they themselves do nothing. To this end, they are shown what they ought to do, in order that when they do it as it ought to be done, namely with love for (and delight in) justice, they may rejoice that they have received the sweetness which the Lord gave so that His land would give its bounty.[9] But when they do not act, whether by not doing it at all or by not doing it out of charity, let them pray that they may receive what they do not yet have. For what will they have that they do not receive? And what do they have that they did not receive?[10]

"Therefore," they say, "let our superiors merely prescribe what we ought to do, and pray on our behalf that we do it; but let them not reprimand or censure us if we do not do it."

On the contrary, let all these things be done! The apostles, the teachers of the churches, did them all. They prescribed what deeds should be done; they offered reprimands if they were not done; they

---

6 "Teacher": the Apostle Paul, usually 'Teacher of the Nations.'
7 See Phl. 2:13: "God is the one Who works in you both willing and doing works in conformity with good will."
8 See Rom. 8:14: "For as many as are driven by the Spirit of God, they are the children of God."
9 Ps. 84:13 (85:12 RSV): "God shall give his goodness and our land shall give its bounty."
10 See 1 Cor. 4:7: "What do you have that you did not receive?"

prayed that they be done. The apostle *prescribes* when he says, "Let all your deeds be done with charity" [1 Cor. 16:14]. He *reprimands* when he says [1 Cor. 6:7–9]:

> It is altogether a failing already that you bring lawsuits against one another. Why do you not rather suffer the wrong? Why not instead be cheated? Yet you yourselves are doing wrong and cheating, and this to your brothers. Do you not know that the unjust shall not inherit the kingdom of God?

Let us listen to him *praying* too: "May the Lord make you increase and abound in charity towards one another and towards all" [1 Ths. 3:12]. Paul prescribes charity to us; he reprimands us because we do not have charity; he prays that charity may abound. You people [who object]: Acknowledge in his prescription what you ought to have; acknowledge in his reprimand that it is your own fault that you do not have it; acknowledge in his prayer the source from which you receive what you want to have.

4.6    "How," the objector asks, "is it *my* fault that I do not have what I have not received from God? If He does not give it, there is no other source at all from which such a great gift might be had."

Permit me, my brothers, to put briefly a case on behalf of the truth of divine and heavenly grace. Not against you, whose "heart is right with God,"[11] but against those who savor things of this world, or, rather, against these human thoughts themselves. For this is what those who are unwilling to be reprimanded for their malign works by preachers of this grace say: "Prescribe to me what I should do, and, if I do it, give thanks on my behalf to God, Whose gift it was that I did it. However, if I do not do it, I ought not be reprimanded. Instead, God should be prayed to, that He may give what He has not given, namely faithful charity towards God and neighbor, the very charity through which what He prescribes is done. Pray for me, therefore, that I may receive this charity and through it do what He prescribes, from my heart and with a good will. Now it would be correct to reprimand me if it were through my own fault that I did not have charity – that is, either (*a*) if I could give it to myself or take it, and did not do so; or (*b*) if I were unwilling to receive it when God was giving it. But since "the will itself is made ready by the Lord" [Prv. 8:35 LXX], why do you reprimand *me* when you see that I am unwilling to do

---

11  See Ps. 77:37 (78:8 RSV) and Acts 8:21 for this turn of phrase.

what He prescribes? Why do you not instead ask *Him* to work in me the willing?"[12]

To these things we reply: You, whoever you are, who do not follow 5.7 God's precepts (which you already know) and who are not willing to be reprimanded – well, you should also be reprimanded for the very reason that you are not willing to be reprimanded! You are not willing to have your faults pointed out to you. You are not willing for them to be struck down, or to experience a useful pain that leads you to find a physician. You are not willing to be shown to yourself, so that when you see that you are deformed you will wish for someone to reform you, and plead with Him that you not remain in that ugliness. After all, it is *your* fault that you are evil, and being unwilling to be reprimanded because you are evil is a greater fault – as though faults were to be praised, or thought of indifferently, so that they are neither praised nor blamed. Either the fear (or the shame or the distress) of the person reprimanded does nothing, or it does nothing else but stir him in a healthful way, so that the good [Lord] is called upon; He makes good people who may be praised out of the evil ones who are reprimanded.

Someone who is not willing to be reprimanded and says "Pray for me instead" wants this to happen on his behalf. Hence he ought to be reprimanded so that he too does this on his own behalf. The distress that displeases him when he feels the sting of a reprimand puts him in the frame of mind for greater prayer. As a result, once he has been helped by an increase in charity through God's mercy, he no longer does deeds to be ashamed of and regret; he does deeds deserving of praise and congratulations. This is the usefulness of a reprimand which is administered healthfully, more or less severe according to the diversity of the sins. It is healthful precisely when the heavenly physician has regard for it. For it is beneficial only when it makes someone repent his sins. Who gives this but Him Who had regard for the Apostle Peter and made him weep for his denial?[13] Accordingly, after the Apostle Paul said that those who think otherwise should be reprimanded gently [2 Tim. 2:25], he immediately adds: "It may be that God gives them repentance to know the truth, and that they may recover themselves out of the snare of the Devil" [2 Tim. 2:25–26].

---

[12] See the beginning of 3.4.
[13] See Lk. 22:61–62. For Peter's denial see the note to *On Grace and Free Choice* 17.33.

5.8    Why do those people who are unwilling to be reprimanded say: "Just prescribe for me [what to do], and pray for me that I do what you prescribe"? Why do they not instead in their perversity reject these two things and say: "I want you neither to prescribe for me nor to pray for me!"? What person is presented to us [in Scripture] who prayed for Peter that God might give him the repentance by which Peter wept for his denial of the Lord?[14] Who instructed Paul in the precepts relevant to the Christian faith? Thus suppose that the Apostle Paul were heard while preaching the gospel, saying [Gal. 1:11–12]:

> My brothers, I make it known to you that the gospel I have preached
> is not merely human. For I have neither received nor learned it from
> any human being, but through a revelation of Jesus Christ.

He would be answered [by these objectors] as follows: "Why do you pester us to receive and learn from you what you 'neither received nor learned from any human being'? For He Who gave it to you is able to give it to us as He gave it to you."

If they do not dare to say this, however, but permit the gospel to be preached to them by a human being – even though it could be given to a human being in some other way than by a human being – let them also concede that they ought to be reprimanded by their superiors who preach Christian grace, without denying that God is able (*a*) to correct whomever He wills, even when no human being offers a reprimand, and (*b*) to bring him to the healthful regret that is repentance through the completely hidden and efficacious power of His medicine. There should be no cessation of prayer on behalf of those[15] whom we want to be corrected, despite the fact that the Lord had regard for Peter and made him weep for his sin even though no one was praying on his behalf. Likewise, reprimand should not be neglected, despite the fact that God corrects those whom He wills even if they were not reprimanded. Now someone benefits from a reprimand precisely when God – Who confers benefits upon whom He wishes, even without a reprimand – has mercy on him and gives His assistance. But as to why different people are called to

---

[14]  Christ petitioned the Lord on Peter's behalf (Lk. 22:32): see 6.10, 8.17, 12.38; *On Grace and Free Choice* 4.9.

[15]  See Rom. 9:20–21: "Who are human beings to answer back to God? Shall what has been formed say to Him Who has formed it: Why have you made me like this? Does not the potter have power over his clay, to make out of the same lump one vessel to honor and another to dishonor?"

reform themselves in such countless different ways, well, far be it from us to say that the judgment ought to belong to the clay rather than to the potter.

They object: "The apostle says 'Who singles you out? What do you 6.9 have that you did not receive? But if you received it, why do you glory as though you had not received it?' [1 Cor. 4:7]. Why, then, are we reprimanded, blamed, censured, accused? What have *we* done, we who 'have not received'?"

Those who say these things want to be seen as beyond blame in their disobedience to God. Their reason is that obedience itself is surely His gift; it must be present in anyone in whom there is charity, which is undoubtedly from God,[16] and the Father gives it to His children.

They retort, "We have not received this. Why then are we reprimanded as though we were able to give it to ourselves and, by our own choice, were unwilling to do so?"

They pay no heed, if they are not yet born again, to the primary reason why they ought to be displeased with themselves when they are upbraided with their disobedience to God. It is because "God made human beings upright" [Ecl. 7:30 (7:29 RSV)] at the beginning of human creation, and there is no iniquity in God.[17] Accordingly, the primary perverseness, where God is not obeyed, comes from humanity, since [Adam] was made perverse by his own evil will and fell from the uprightness in which God originally made him.

Or is this perverseness not to be reprimanded in human beings, precisely because it is not distinctive in the one who is reprimanded, but rather is common to all? Quite the contrary! Let what belongs to all be reprimanded in each. For it is *not* the case that something from which no one is exempt thereby does not belong to anyone. Indeed, these original sins are said to be the sins of others for the reason that people derive them from their parents. But not without cause are they also called ours, since, as the apostle says, "in that one all sinned" [Rom. 5:12].[18] Let

---

[16] See 1 Jn. 4:7: "Charity comes from God." Augustine cites this passage in *On Grace and Free Choice* 18.37, with 'love' (*dilectio*) in place of the Vulgate reading 'charity' (*caritas*) implied here, and again in *On Grace and Free Choice* 19.40.

[17] See Rom. 9:14: "What shall we say then – is there injustice in God? By no means!"

[18] Augustine's text of Rom. 5:12 is faulty. The earlier part is cited in *On the Gift of Perseverance* 12.30; like the Vulgate it reads *per unum hominem in hunc mundum peccatum intravit et per peccatum mors et ita in omnes homines mors pertransiit in quo omnes peccaverunt*. Augustine identifies the *in quo* as Adam (*Deserts and Forgiveness of Sins* 1.10–11), and understands the passage to

the source of damnation be reprimanded, then, so that the sting of the reprimand may give rise to the will to be born again; and if the one who is reprimanded is in fact a "child of the promise,"[19] while the blow of the reprimand stirs up a noisy commotion on the outside, God may work by His hidden inspiration the willing in him[20] on the inside. However, if after having been born again and made just, he falls back into an evil life by his own will, he certainly cannot say "I have not received." For he has lost the grace of God, which he had received, by his own free choice of evil. If, goaded by a reprimand, he suffers healthfully and returns to similar or even better good works, surely the usefulness of the reprimand is clearly apparent. Whether a reprimand from a human being stems from charity or not, nevertheless only God makes the one who has been reprimanded to benefit from it.

6.10   Now can the person who is unwilling to be reprimanded still say, "What did *I* do, I who did not receive?" It is evident that he did receive, and that he has lost what he received by his own fault.

He objects: "When you charge me with having fallen back from a good life into an evil life by my own will, I can *still* say: 'What did *I* do, I who did not receive?' For I received the 'faith which works through love' [Gal. 5:6], but I did not receive perseverance in it up to the end. Will anyone dare to claim that this perseverance is not a gift of God, and that this good of ours is so great that the apostle could not say to anyone who has it, 'What do you have that you have not received?' [1 Cor. 4:7], on the grounds that he has it in such a way that he did not receive it?"

In reply, we ourselves cannot deny that it is indeed a great gift from God to persevere in the good up to the very end. It comes only from Him of Whom it is written: "Anything excellent that is given [to us], and every perfect gift, is from above and comes down from the Father of lights" [Jas. 1:17]. But we should not on this score neglect to reprimand someone who has not persevered, just in case God might happen to give him repentance and he escape the snares of the Devil. As

assert our sinful condition via identity with Adam. The same is true here, where *in illo uno omnes peccauerunt* is meant to fill out the purported reference to Adam in *quo*. However, the Greek text reads ἐφ' ᾧ, to introduce an explanatory clause, and cannot bear Augustine's interpretation.

[19] Augustine takes this expression for God's elect from Rom. 9:8 and Gal. 4:28, where it appears in the plural.

[20] See Phl. 2:13: "God is the one Who works in you both willing and doing works in conformity with good will," a passage alluded to in 3.4, explicitly cited and discussed in 12.38 as well as in *On Grace and Free Choice* 9.21, 16.32, 17.33; cited in *On the Gift of Perseverance* 13.33.

I mentioned above, the apostle added this view about the usefulness of reprimand, saying: "Those who think otherwise should be reprimanded gently; it may be that God gives them repentance" [2 Tim. 2:25–26]. For if we say that perseverance, which is so praiseworthy and so fortunate, belongs to human beings in such a way that it is *not* from God, then we render meaningless what the Lord says to Peter: "I have prayed for you that your faith may not fail" [Lk. 12:32]. What else did He pray for on Peter's behalf but perseverance up to the end? Surely if one human being could get this from another, God would not need to be entreated for it. Next, when the apostle says: "We pray to God that you not do anything evil" [2 Cor. 13:7], he is undoubtedly praying to God for perseverance for them. After all, someone who does not persevere in the good does something evil when he forsakes the good and turns towards evil, from which he ought to turn away. So too in the passage where the apostle says [Phl. 1:3–6]:

> I thank my God upon every remembrance of you, always in every prayer of mine joyfully making an entreaty on behalf of all of you, for your fellowship in the gospel from the first day until now; I am confident that He Who is working His good work in you will continue perfecting it up to the day of Jesus Christ.[21]

What else is he promising them with regard to the divine mercy but perseverance in what is good up to the end?

Again, when the Apostle Paul says: "Epaphras, who is one of you – a servant of Jesus Christ – sends you greetings; he is always fighting on your behalf in his prayers that you may stand perfect and complete in all the will of God" [Col. 4:12], what does "that you may stand" mean if not 'that you may persevere'? Accordingly, it was said of the Devil, "He did not stand in the truth" [Jn. 8:44], because he was there but did not stay there. For surely the Colossians [whom the apostle was addressing] were already standing in the faith. When we pray that he who is standing may stand, we are praying for nothing other than his perseverance.

Again, when the Apostle Jude says: "Now to Him Who is able to preserve you faultless and set you unblemished before the presence of His glory with gladness" [Jud. 24], does he not explicitly show that persevering in the good up to the end is God's gift? When He preserves

---

[21] For the translation of the last part of this passage, see the note to *On Grace and Free Choice* 17.33.

them "faultless" so that He may set them "unblemished before the presence of His glory with gladness," what else is He giving them but perseverance in the good?

There is also what we read in the acts of the apostles: "And when the Gentiles heard this they were glad, and they accepted the word of the Lord: And as many who were destined for eternal life believed" [Acts 13:48]. Who could be destined for eternal life without the gift of perseverance, seeing that "he who perseveres up to the end shall be saved" [Mt. 10:22]? By what salvation, if not eternal salvation?

Now when in the Lord's Prayer we say to God the Father: "May Your name be made holy" [Mt. 6:9],[22] what are we saying but that His name should be made holy in us? Since this has already been accomplished by the bath of rebirth,[23] why do the faithful ask for it every day if not so that we may persevere in what has been done in us? For St. Cyprian also understands the matter in this way when he analyzes the same passage [The Lord's Prayer §12]:[24]

> We say "may Your name be made holy" not because we wish God to be made holy by our prayers, but because we are asking God to make His name holy in us. Furthermore, by whom is God made holy? God Himself makes things holy. But since He said: *You shall be holy, for I myself am holy* [Lv. 19:2], we ask and request this, so that we who have been made holy in baptism may persevere in what we have started to be.

Behold! This glorious martyr feels that in these words Christ's faithful ask every day that they may persevere in what they have started to be. But undoubtedly anyone who prays to God that he may persevere in the good admits that such perseverance is His gift.

7.11    Now since these things are so, we reprimand (and justly so) those who, although they have lived well, nevertheless did not persevere in it. They were changed by their own will from a good life to an evil one, and so are reprimanded. If the reprimand does them no good and they persevere in their abandoned life up to death, they are even worthy of divine damnation for eternity. Nor will they excuse themselves when, just as they now

---

22  More familiarly: "Hallowed be Thy name."
23  "The bath of rebirth": baptism, in which the person is "born again."
24  Augustine recommends Cyprian's account of the Lord's Prayer in *On Grace and Free Choice* 13.26.

say "Why are we reprimanded?," they then say: "Why are we damned? For we did not receive the perseverance by which we might remain in the good, and so fell from the good back into evil." They will not free themselves from their just damnation by this excuse! Truth declares that no one is freed from the damnation brought about by Adam except through faith in Jesus Christ.[25] Even those people who are able to say that they had not heard the gospel of Christ and that "faith comes from hearing" [Rom. 10:17] will nevertheless not free themselves from this damnation. How much less will those who are going to say "We did not receive perseverance" free themselves! The excuse of those saying "We did not receive a hearing [of the gospel]" seems more just than the excuse of those saying "We did not receive perseverance." For we can say to someone "Had you willed to, you would have persevered in what you heard and held"; but there is no way we can say "Had you willed to, you would have believed what you did not hear."

Consequently, (*a*) people who have not heard the gospel; (*b*) people 7.12 who have heard it, and were changed for the better, but did not receive perseverance; (*c*) people who have heard the gospel and were unwilling to come to Christ, that is, to believe in Him, for He said: "No one comes to me unless it be given to him by my Father" [Jn. 6:66]; (*d*) young children, who could not believe because of their age, but who could be released from the original wrongdoing[26] only by the bath of rebirth and yet perished in death without having received it – none of (*a*)–(*d*) were singled out from that lump[27] which, as we know, was damned, since all from one enter into damnation together.[28] They are singled out not by their deserts but through the grace of the Mediator. That is, they are gratuitously made just in the blood of the Second Adam.[29] Thus when we hear: "Who singles you out? What do you have that you did not receive? But if you received it, why do you glory as though you had not

---

[25] See Gal. 2:16.
[26] "The original wrongdoing": Original Sin.
[27] "Lump" (*consparsio*): postlapsarian human beings taken collectively; Augustine derives this usage from the text of Rom. 9:20–21 (φυράματος = *massa* [mass] Vulgate), cited in the note to 5.8 above.
[28] "From one": from Adam, whose Original Sin all humans have.
[29] "The Second Adam": Jesus, the "Mediator" between the human and the divine, through Whose sacrifice human beings are able to be saved. Which ones are actually saved is a matter left to unconstrained divine discretion – "gratuitously," as Augustine says here: *gratis*, etymologically linked to 'grace.' Augustine again calls Jesus the "Mediator" in 11.30, and the "Second Adam" in 12.35.

received it?" [1 Cor. 4:7], we should understand that no one can be singled out from that mass of perdition which was made by the First Adam except one who has this gift, and that anyone who has it has received it by the grace of the Savior. The testimony of the apostle is so important that St. Cyprian, writing to Quirinus, cites it under the heading 'We Should Glory in Nothing Since We Have Nothing of Our Own.'[30]

7.13     There is no doubt, then, that it was arranged for the gospel to be heard by whoever the people are who were singled out from that original damnation through the bestowal of divine grace. And when they hear it, they believe, and they persevere up to the end in the "faith which works through love" [Gal. 5:6]. If they wander off the path at some point, once reprimanded they are reformed. Some of them return to the life they abandoned even if they are not reprimanded by other people. A few, having received grace at whatever their age may be, are taken away from the dangers of this life by a swift death. He works all these things in them: He Who worked them to be "vessels of mercy" [Rom. 9:23], He Who elected them in His Son before the foundation of the world[31] "through the election of grace. But if [election] is through grace, then it is not through works; otherwise, grace then is not grace" [Rom. 11:5–6]. For they have not been called in such a way that they were not elected. On this score it was said: "Many are called, but few are elected" [Mt. 20:16 and 22:14].[32] But since they "are called in accordance with His plan" [Rom. 8:28], surely they are elected "through the election of grace" (as mentioned), not through the election of their own preceding deserts, since grace is for them the whole of deserts.

7.14     The Apostle Paul says of such people [Rom. 8:28–30]:[33]

> We know that God, along with those who love Him, works everything for the good; they are called in accordance with His plan. For those whom He foreknew beforehand He also predestined to conform to the image of His Son, that he might be the firstborn among many brethren. Moreover, those whom He has predestined He also called, and those whom He called He also made just, and those whom He made just He also glorified.

---

[30]  Cyprian, *Letters to Quirinus* 3.4. Augustine gives the title of the chapter in which 1 Cor. 4:7 is cited.
[31]  Eph. 1:4: "[God] has elected us in Him [=Christ] before the foundation of the world."
[32]  More familiarly: "Many are called but few chosen."
[33]  See the note to *On Grace and Free Choice* 17.33.

None among them perishes, since they have all been elected. Now they have been elected because "they are called in accordance with His plan." Not their plan but God's, about which the apostle elsewhere says [Rom. 9:11–12]:

> So that God's plan might stand in accordance with His election, Rebecca was told that the elder shall serve the younger, not because of their works but because of His call.

Elsewhere: "Not in accordance with our works but in accordance with His plan and grace" [2 Tim. 1:9]. Therefore, when we hear "Those whom He predestined He also called," we should recognize that they have been called in accordance with His plan. For the Apostle Paul began that passage by saying "God works everything for the good; they are called in accordance with His plan," and then he goes on to add: "For those whom He foreknew beforehand He also predestined to conform to the image of His Son, that he might be the firstborn among many brethren." To all the foregoing he then added: "Moreover, those whom He has predestined He also called." The apostle wants "those" to be understood as the ones whom God "called in accordance with His plan," so that we not think that some of them were called but *not* elected, in line with the Lord's pronouncement: "Many are called, but few are elected" [Mt. 20:16 and 22:14]. Anyone who has been elected has no doubt also been called. But anyone who has been called has not thereby been elected. The ones who have been elected, then, as is often said, are those who "are called in accordance with His plan," who also are foreknown and predestined. If any of them perishes, God is in error. But none of them perishes, since God does not err. If any of them perishes, God is overpowered by human vice. But none of them perishes, since God is not overpowered by anything. Furthermore, they have been elected to reign with Christ, not the way Judas was elected for the work to which he was suited. Judas, of course, was elected by Him Who knew well how to use even evil people, so that even through his damnable work He might bring to completion the work for which He came (which we hold in reverence). Thus when we hear: "Have I not elected you twelve? And one of you is a devil" [Jn. 6:70], we should understand that one of them was elected in judgment, the others in mercy. Therefore, He elected the latter to obtain His kingdom, but the former to spill His blood.

7.15    Deservedly does there follow the voice of those elected for the kingdom [Rom. 8:31–34]:

> If God is for us, who is against us? He did not spare His own Son, but delivered Him up for us all. How did He not give us all things along with Him? Who shall lay any charge against God's elect? It is God Who makes people just! Who condemns us? It is Jesus Christ who has died – or rather: It is Christ Who has risen again, Who is at the right hand of God, Who also intercedes for us!

Let them[34] go on to describe how they received the gift of steadfast perseverance up to the end [Rom. 8:35–39]:

> Who shall separate us from Christ's charity? Shall tribulation, distress, persecution, famine, nakedness, peril, the sword? As it is written: *For your sake are we put to death all the day long; we are reckoned as sheep for the slaughter* [Ps. 43:22 (44:22 RSV)]. Yet in all these things we more than conquer through Him Who loved us. For I am certain that neither death, nor life, nor angels, nor principalities, nor things present, nor things to come, nor power, nor height, nor depth, nor any other creature shall be able to separate us from God's charity, which is in Jesus Christ our Lord.

7.16    The elect are signified to Timothy, where, after it was declared that Hymenaeus and Philetus undermined the faith of some people [2 Tim. 2:17–18], it was quickly added: "But the foundation of God stands firm, having this seal: The Lord knew those who are His" [2 Tim. 2:19]. Their "faith which works through love" [Gal. 5:6], surely either does not fail at all, or, if there are any whose faith does fail, it is revived before this life is ended, and, since their intervening iniquity has been cleansed away, it is counted as perseverance up to the end.

   On the other hand, those who are not going to persevere, and so are going to fall away from Christian faith and conduct – and as a result the end of this life finds them such – then even while they are living well and religiously they should undoubtedly *not* be counted in the number of the elect. For God's foreknowledge and predestination has not singled them out from the mass of perdition,[35] and hence they are neither "called in accordance with His plan" [Rom. 8:28] nor, for that reason,

---

[34]  "Them": those elected for the kingdom.
[35]  See the note to 7.12 about the "mass of perdition" [Rom. 9:20–21].

are they elected. Instead, they were called along with those of whom it is said "Many are called," but not along with those of whom it is said "but few are elected" [Mt. 20:16 and 22:14]. Yet who would deny that they are elected while they believe, are baptized, and live according to God? Clearly, they are called "elect" by those who do not know what they are going to be, not by Him Who knows that they do not have the perseverance which brings the elect to the happy life, and Who knows that they stand in such a way that He will have foreknown that they are going to fall.

Suppose that at this point I am asked: "Why did God not give perseverance to those to whom He gave the love by which they might lead Christian lives?" 8.17

My reply is: "I do not know." Not with arrogance, but recognizing my limitations I heed the apostle, who says: "Who are human beings to answer back to God?" [Rom. 9:20] and "The depth of the riches of God's wisdom and knowledge! His judgments are inscrutable and His ways past finding out!" [Rom. 11:33]. To the extent that He deigns to make His judgments clear to us, let us give thanks; to the extent that He keeps them hidden, let us not grumble against His plan but rather believe that this too is the most beneficial for us.

But you – whoever you are, the enemy of His grace, you who raise the question like this – what do *you* say? It is well that you do not deny being a Christian, and take pride in being Catholic. Therefore, if you admit that persevering in the good up to the end is God's gift, then I think that you are as ignorant as I am why one person receives this gift and another does not. Neither of us at this point is able to penetrate the "inscrutable judgments" of God.

Alternatively, if you say that it depends on human free choice (which you defend not in accordance with God's grace but in opposition to it) whether each person perseveres or does not persevere in the good, doing so not by God's granting it but instead by human will, what are you going to come up with against His words: "I have prayed for you, Peter, that your faith may not fail" [Lk. 12:32]? Will you dare to say that, even with Christ petitioning that Peter's faith not fail, it would have failed if Peter had willed it to fail, that is, if he had been unwilling for it to persevere up to the end? As though Peter were somehow to will something other than what Christ petitioned for him to will! Who does not know that Peter's faith would perish if the very will by which he was faithful were to fail, and that it would stand firm if his selfsame will were to be steadfast? But since "the will is made ready by the Lord" [Prv. 8:35 LXX], Christ's prayer for him could not then be in vain. Therefore, when He petitioned that Peter's faith not fail, what else did he petition but that Peter have a completely free, strong, unconquered, persevering will in his faith? You see how the freedom of the will is defended in accordance with God's grace, not in opposition to it! The human will does not attain grace through its freedom, but rather attains its freedom through grace, and, so that it persevere, a pleasureable everlastingness and invincible strength.

8.18     It is indeed surprising – quite surprising – that God does not give perseverance to some of His children who were born again in Christ, and to whom He gave faith, hope, and love, whereas He forgives great wrongdoings in the children of others and makes them His own children by the grace he imparts. Who would not be surprised at this? Who would not be completely dumbfounded?

The following point is also no less surprising. Yet it is true and so clear that not even the enemies of God's grace are able to find a way to deny it: (*a*) God excludes some of the children of His friends (namely the faithful who are born again and are good) from His kingdom, although He sends their parents there; they are the young children who leave here without baptism, for whom He could surely procure the grace of this bath, were He to will it, because all things are in His power; (*b*) God makes some of the children of His enemies come into Christian hands, and through this bath He leads them into His kingdom, from which their parents are excluded – even though in the case of young children there are no evil deserts in (*a*), or good deserts in (*b*), that are due to their own will. Certainly God's judgments here, since they are just and deep, cannot be criticized or penetrated. Among them is His judgment about perseverance, which we are arguing over now. Concerning each, then, let us cry out: "The depth of the riches of God's wisdom and knowledge! How inscrutable are His judgments!" [Rom. 11:33].

8.19     Nor should we be surprised that we cannot find out. "His ways are past finding out" [Rom. 11:33]. I must also remain silent about countless gifts that are given to some people and not to others by the Lord God, "with Whom there is no distinction among persons" [Rom. 2:11], and are not handed out in line with the deserts of their wills. For instance: speed, strength, good health, physical beauty, extraordinary talent, a mind naturally gifted in various arts. Or gifts that come from outside, such as wealth, noble birth, honors, and other things like this, whose possession is entirely in God's power. Let us not delay even over the baptism of young children – which none of these people can say, like the latter gifts, does not pertain to the kingdom of God – namely, why [baptism] is given to this young child and not to that one, though each is in God's power and without this sacrament no one enters into God's kingdom. Let us say nothing about these matters, then, and leave them open.

Instead, let our opponents look at the case of those with whom we are now dealing. We are examining people who do not have perseverance in goodness, but instead die with their good will falling away from good into evil.

Let them say, if they can, why God did not snatch these people from the dangers of this life while they were leading faithful and religious lives, "so that wickedness not change their understanding and deceit beguile their souls" [Wis. 4:11]. Did He not have this in His power? Or did He not know their future evils? Surely each of these alternatives is a completely perverse and insane reply! Then why did He not do it? Let those who mock us say why, when in such matters we cry out: "How inscrutable are His judgments, and His ways are past finding out!" [Rom. 11:33]. For God indeed gives this gift to those whom He wills, or else Scripture lies when it says of the supposedly premature death of a just man: "He was snatched from this life so that wickedness not change his understanding and deceit beguile his soul" [Wis. 4:11]. Why then does God give so great a benefit to some and not to others? After all, "with Him there is no inequality nor distinction among persons" [Rom. 2:11],[36] and it is in His power how long anyone remains in this life, which has been called "a trial on Earth" [Job 7:1].[37]

Therefore, just as our opponents are forced to admit that it is God's gift that a person finishes this life before changing from good to evil, though they do not know why this is given to some and not to others, so too let them admit along with us that perseverance in the good is God's gift, according to Scripture (from which I have already cited many passages). And let them deign to be ignorant along with us why it is given to some and not to others, without grumbling against God.

---

[36] See also 2 Chr. 19:7: "With the Lord our God there is no inequality, nor distinction among persons."

[37] See 12.37 for a note on this passage.

9.20     Nor should it bother us that God does not give this perseverance to some of His children. (Of course this could not be so if they were among those predestined and "called in accordance with His plan" [Rom. 8:28], who are genuinely the "children of the promise.")[38] For while they lead religious lives they are called 'the children of God'; but since they are going to lead irreligious lives and die in that selfsame irreligiousness, God's foreknowledge does not declare them to be the children of God. There are children of God who are not yet such to us but who are such to God. John the Evangelist says of them: "Jesus was going to die for the nation, and not only for the nation but also that He gather together into one the scattered children of God" [Jn. 11:51–52]. Surely they were going to be the children of God by believing through the preaching of the gospel. Yet they were already the children of God before this was done, enrolled in the record-book of their Father with unwavering firmness.

    Again, there are some people whom we call 'the children of God' due to the grace they received for a time, yet to God they are not such. Of these people the selfsame John says: "They went forth from us but were not of us; for if they had been of us, they would surely have continued with us" [1 Jn. 2:19]. He does not say: 'They went forth from us but, because they did not remain with us, they were then not of us.' Rather, he says: "They went forth from us but were not of us," that is, even when they seemed to be among us they were not of us. And, as though he were asked for the grounds on which to prove it, he declares: "For if they had been of us, they would surely have continued with us." This is the voice of the children of God. John, who is set in the foremost place among the children of God, is speaking. Therefore, when the children of God say of those who did not have perseverance: "They went forth from us but were not of us," and they add: "For if they had been of us, they would surely have continued with us," what else are they saying but "They were not the children of God even when, by their profession [of faith], they were in name the children of God"? It is not because they were counterfeiting justice, but rather because they did not continue in it. John did not say: "For if they had been of us they would surely have kept genuine rather than imitation justice along with us." Instead, he says: "If they had been of us, they would surely have continued with us." He undoubtedly wanted them to continue in the good. Thus they were in the good, but since they did not

---

[38] See the note to 6.9 for this expression.

continue in it, that is, they did not persevere up to the end, "they were not of us" even when they were with us – that is, they were not included in the number of the children, even when they were in the faith of the children. For those who truly are the children of God are foreknown and predestined "to conform to the image of His Son" and "are called in accordance with His plan" so that they would be elected [Rom. 8:28]. The 'child of the promise' does not perish, but the child of perdition does.[39]

These people, therefore, were among the multitude of those who were   9.21 called, but not in the small number of the elect. Hence it is not that God did not give perseverance to His predestined children. They would have it if they were in the number of His children, and what would they have that they did not receive, in accordance with the true apostolic view?[40] For this reason, such persons would have been given as children to Christ the Son, just as He Himself says to His Father: "So that all those whom You have given to me" should "not perish but have life eternal" [Jn. 6:39 and 3:15]. Therefore, those who are ordained to eternal life are understood to be given to Christ. They are the ones who are predestined and "called in accordance with His plan" [Rom. 8:28], none of whom perishes. For this reason, none of them ends this life having changed from good to evil. Each is ordained, and hence given to Christ, so that he "not perish but have life eternal."

Again, any of those whom we call His enemies (or the young children of His enemies) who are going to be born again, so that they end this life in the "faith which works through love" [Gal. 5:6], even before this comes to pass, already are His children in that predestination. They have been given to Christ His Son so that they "not perish but have life eternal."

Finally, the Savior Himself declares: "If you continue in my word, you   9.22 are truly my disciples" [Jn. 8:31]. Are we to count among them Judas, who did not continue in His word? Are we to count among them the people of whom the gospel speaks, when, after the Lord had laid it down that His flesh was to be eaten and His blood to be drunk, the evangelist says [Jn. 6:59–66]:

> He said these things while teaching in the synagogue in Capernaum. Therefore, many of His disciples, hearing this, said: "This is a hard

[39]  See Jn. 17:12: "None of them is lost but the child of perdition." Augustine also uses this expression in 9.24, 13.40, and 15.48.
[40]  See 1 Cor. 4:7: "What do you have that you did not receive?"

saying; who can hear it?" When Jesus knew within Himself that his disciples grumbled at it, He said to them: "Does this scandalize you? Then what if you see the Son of Man ascending to where He was before? It is the Spirit that gives life; the flesh is useless. The words I have spoken to you are spirit and life. But there are some among you who do not believe." For Jesus knew from the beginning who would be believers and who would betray Him, and He said: "Thus did I say to you that no one comes to me unless it be given to him by my Father." From this time many of His disciples went back, and then they walked no more with Him.

Are not even these people [who "went back and walked no more with Him"] termed 'disciples' in the gospel? Yet they were not truly disciples, for they did not continue in His word, in accordance with what He said: "If you continue in my word, you are truly my disciples" [Jn. 8:31]. Therefore, since they did not have perseverance, just as they were not truly disciples of Christ so too they were not truly children of God, even when they seemed to be and were so called. For our part, then, we name them "elect" and "disciples of Christ" and "children of God," since those whom we see to be born again and to lead religious lives should be so named. But they truly are what they are named at that time only if they continue in the condition due to which they *are* so named. If they do not have perseverance, that is, if they do not remain in that condition which they began to be in, then they are incorrectly named what they are named, and are not [what they are named]. For to Him Who knows what they are going to be (namely to become evil from good) they are not these things.

9.23    For this reason, once the Apostle Paul had said: "We know that God, along with those who love Him, works everything for the good" [Rom. 8:28], knowing that some love God and yet do not continue in this good up to the end, immediately added: "with those who are called in accordance with His plan" [Rom. 8:28]. For the latter remain in their love of God up to the end, and those who stray from it for a time come back to the love of God in order to continue to the end in the good in which they began. Showing what it is to be called in accordance with His plan, the apostle quickly added what I have already cited [Rom. 8:29–30]:

> For those whom He foreknew beforehand He also predestined to conform to the image of His Son, that he might be the firstborn

among many brethren. Moreover, those whom He has predestined He also called [namely in accordance with His plan], and those whom He called He also made just, and those whom He made just He also glorified.

All these things have already been done: "foreknew," "predestined," "called," "made just" – these things were already foreknown and predestined, and many people were already called and made just.

Yet what Paul put at the end, "He also glorified" – if we are here to understand the selfsame glory of which the apostle says: "When Christ, who is your life, shall appear, then you too shall appear with Him in glory" [Col. 3:4] – this has not yet been done. However, even the latter two things, namely having been "called" and "made just," have not been realized in all those of whom they are said, for all the way up to the end of the world many people shall yet be called and made just. Nevertheless, the Apostle used past-tense verbs with regard to events still to come, as though God had already done the things He already arranged from eternity to take place. Hence the prophet Isaiah also says of Him: "He has done what will be" [Is. 45:11 LXX]. Therefore, anyone who in the most provident arrangement of God has been foreknown, predestined, called, made just, glorified – I am not speaking only about those not yet born again, but even about those not yet born – are already the children of God, and cannot perish at all. They truly come to Christ, because they come in the way He describes: "All that the Father gives me shall come to me; and I shall not cast out one who comes to me" [Jn. 6:37]. And shortly afterwards: "This is the will of the Father who sent me: that I lose nothing of what He has given me" [Jn. 6:39]. Therefore, perseverance in the good up to the end is given by Him. It is given only to those who will not perish, since those who do not persevere will perish.

"God, along with" people of this sort "who love Him, works everything for the good" [Rom. 8:28]: 'everything' even up to this point, that even if some of them stray and wander off the path, He makes this too contribute to their good, because they return humbler and wiser. They learn that they should rejoice in this just life with trembling, not arrogating to themselves confidence in their continuing [on the path] as though of their own power, nor declaring in their fullness "I shall never be moved" [Ps. 29:7 (30:6 RSV)]. For this reason, they were told: "Serve the Lord with fear and rejoice in Him with trembling, lest the Lord at some time be

9.24

angered and you perish from the just path" [Ps. 2:11–12]. The Psalmist does not say "lest you not *come to* the just path" but "lest you *perish from* the just path." What does this show but that those who are already walking along the just path are warned to serve God in fear, that is, "not to be highminded but instead to fear" [Rom. 11:20] – which means that they not be proud but humble. Accordingly, he says elsewhere: "Not to be highminded but to feel things along with the humble" [Rom. 12:16]. Let them rejoice in God, but with trembling, not glorying in anything, since nothing is ours; "Let the one who glories glory in the Lord" [1 Cor. 1:31 and 2 Cor. 10:17], so that they not "perish from the just path" along which they have already started to walk, when they take the credit themselves for the fact that they are on it.

The apostle also used these words when he said: "Work out your own salvation with fear and trembling" [Phl. 2:12]. He shows why it is "with fear and trembling" when he says: "God is the one Who works in you both willing and doing works in conformity with good will" [Phl. 2:13]. For the one who said in his fullness "I shall never be moved" [Ps. 29:7 (30:6 RSV)] did not have this fear and trembling. But since he was a child of the promise, not a child of perdition, he experienced what he was when God left him for a short time: "Lord, by Your will You gave strength to my adornment; You turned Your face aside, and I was confounded" [Ps. 29:9 (30:8 RSV)]. Look here! More wise, and for that reason even more humble, he held to the path, now recognizing and acknowledging that God gave strength to his adornment by His will. When he attributed to himself the adornment which God had given him, crediting himself in his fullness and not Him Who provided it, he declared "I shall never be moved." Thus was Peter confounded in order to find himself and to learn, in humble wisdom, in Whom to put hope not only of eternal life but also of religious conduct and perseverance in this life.

This could also be the voice of the Apostle Peter. He had said in his fullness: "I shall lay down my life for You" [Jn. 13:37], hastily attributing to himself what was later to be bestowed upon him by the Lord. The Lord turned His face aside from him, and confounded him, so that he denied Him three times, being afraid to die on His behalf. But the Lord again turned His face to him, and he washed his sin away with his tears. For what else is "He looked upon him" [Lk. 6:22] but that He turned His face to him again, which He had turned aside from him briefly? Thus was he confounded.[41] But since he learned not to trust in himself, even this was turned into good for him, by the agency of Him Who, "along with those who love Him, works everything for the good." For Peter "was called in accordance with His plan" [Rom. 8:28] and no one can tear him away from the hand of Christ, to Whom he had been given.[42]

Therefore, let no one say that a person who wanders off the just path is 9.25 not to be reprimanded, and that we should only entreat the Lord for his return and perseverance. No one who has prudence or faith should say this. For if this wanderer has been "called in accordance with His plan," then doubtless "God works along with" him even his being reprimanded "for the good" [Rom. 8:28]. Now since the one who offers the reprimand does not know whether the wanderer is called in this way, let him do with charity what he knows ought to be done. For he knows that such a person ought to be reprimanded, with God the one Who is going to give mercy or judgment: Mercy if the person who is reprimanded has been singled out from the mass of perdition by the bestowal of grace, and he is not among the "vessels of wrath fitted for perdition" but among "the vessels of mercy which He prepared for glory" [Rom. 9:22–23]; judgment if he has been damned with the former and not predestined with the latter.

Here another question arises, one that certainly should not be scorned. 10.26 With the assistance of the Lord, "in Whose hand are we and our words" [Wis. 7:16], we should attack and solve it. We ask, insofar as it is relevant to this gift of God (namely perseverance in the good up to the end), what we should think of the First Man,[43] who surely "was made upright" [Ecl. 7:30 (7:29 RSV)] without any vice. I am *not* asking: If he did not have perseverance, how was he without vice, when he lacked so necessary a gift of God? An answer is easily given to this query. He did not have perseverance, since he did not persevere in this good in which he was without vice. Indeed, he began to have vice, through which he fell. And if he *began* [to have vice], then before he had begun he was, in any event, without vice. It is one thing not to have a vice, another not to continue in that goodness in which there is no vice. By the very fact that Adam is not said to have never been without vice, but rather is said not to have *remained* without vice, he is undoubtedly shown to have been without vice. And he is blamed for not remaining in this good.

---

41  For Peter's denial, see Mt. 26:71–75, Mk. 14:66–68, Lk. 22:57–59, Jn. 18:15–18.
42  See Jn. 10:29: "No one can tear him away from the hand of my Father."
43  "The First Man": Adam.

The following question should be further investigated and treated more diligently. How are we to reply to those who say: "If Adam had perseverance in that uprightness in which he was made without vice, he doubtless persevered in it. If he persevered, he surely did not sin, nor did he abandon that uprightness and God. Yet the truth cries out that he *did* sin, that he *did* abandon the good. Therefore, Adam did not have perseverance in that good. And if he did not have it, he surely did not receive it. For how could he have received perseverance and not have persevered? Furthermore, if he did not have it precisely because he did not receive it, how did he sin in not persevering, since he did not receive perseverance? Nor can it be said that he did not receive it for the reason that he was not separated from the mass of perdition by the bestowal of grace. For in humankind there did not yet exist that mass of perdition before Adam sinned, from which our vice-ridden origin is derived."

10.27    Consequently, we confess in the most beneficial way what we believe most rightly. God, the Lord of all things, Who created all things quite good,[44] Who foreknew that evils would emerge from good things, and Who knew that it pertained to His most omnipotent goodness to make good use even of evils rather than not permitting evils to exist, put the life of humans and angels in order, so that He might show in it what their free choice could do, and then what the benefit of His grace and the judgment of His justice could do. Then indeed some angels, whose leader is the one called the Devil, became fugitives from the Lord God by their free choice. Yet while fugitives from His goodness, by which they had been happy, they could not escape His judgment, by which they became thoroughly unhappy. But the others were steadfast in the truth by their selfsame free choice. They deserved to know as the most certain truth that they would never fall. For if we were able to know from Scripture that no holy angels are now going to fall, by how much the more do they themselves know this, since the truth is revealed to them in a higher way! An endless happy life is promised to us, of course, and equality with the angels.[45] From this promise we are certain that, when we come to that life after judgment, we are not going to fall from there. Yet if the angels do not know this about themselves, we shall be not their equals, but happier than them. Truth, however, promised us equality with them. Hence

---

[44] See Gen. 1:31.    [45] See Mt. 22:30.

it is certain that they know through sight[46] what we know through faith, namely that no holy angel will be brought to ruin from now on.

Although the Devil and his angels were happy before they fell and did not know that they were going to fall into unhappiness, there was still something further that could be added to their happiness. Suppose that they had been steadfast in the truth by their free choice until they received the fullness of supreme happiness as a reward for their constancy, namely as the great abundance of God's charity given through the Holy Spirit. Then in that case (a) they would have been completely unable any longer to fall, and (b) they would have known this with certainty about themselves. They did not have this fullness of happiness [described in (a)–(b)]. But since they did not know about their future unhappiness, they enjoyed a lesser happiness, but one still without any defect. For if they had known of their future fall and eternal punishment, they surely could not have been happy. The fear of such a great evil would even then have forced them to be unhappy.

So too did God make a human being with free choice. Although igno-   10.28
rant of his future fall, Adam was happy because he was aware that it was in his power both not to become unhappy and not to die. If he had willed to remain in this upright condition without fault, then by merit of this constancy, without any experience of death and unhappiness, he would surely have received the fullness of happiness by which the holy angels are happy too: namely, that he could not fall any longer, and that he would know this with certainty. For he could not be happy even in Paradise – in fact, he would not be there where it is not appropriate to be unhappy – if the foreknowledge of his fall were to make him unhappy due to his fear of so great an evil. But since he abandoned God by his free choice, he experienced God's just judgment. As a result, he was damned along with all his descendants, who sinned along with him while still wholly contained in him. As many of his descendants who are set free by God's grace are also surely set free from the damnation in which they are now kept bound. Accordingly, even if none were set free, no one would justly criticize God's just judgment. Therefore, the fact that few are set free – few in comparison with those perishing, but many in their own number – happens by grace: It happens gratuitously, and thanks are to

---

[46] Presumably, through their experience of the Beatific Vision, the good angels now know that they will never fall.

be given.[47] Let no one be filled with pride over his own merits, but rather "every mouth may be stopped" [Rom. 3:19] and "let the one who glories glory in the Lord" [1 Cor. 1:31 and 2 Cor. 10:17].

11.29   What then? Did Adam not have God's grace? Rather, his grace was great, but different. He was amidst goods that he had received from the goodness of his Creator. Not even Adam merited these goods by his deserts, goods in which he suffered no evil. But, in this life, the saints who have this grace of being set free are amidst evils, out of which they cry to God: "Free us from evil!" [Mt. 6:13]. Adam in the midst of those goods did not need the death of Christ, whereas the blood of the Lamb[48] washes from the saints both their hereditary and their personal guilt. Adam had no need of the assistance that those saints implore when they say [Rom. 7:23–25]:

> I see another law in my members, warring against the law of my mind, and holding me captive in the law of sin which is in my members. How unhappy I am! Who shall set me free from this body of death? The grace of God, through Jesus Christ our Lord.

In the saints, "the flesh has lusts against the spirit, and the spirit against the flesh" [Gal. 5:17]. Laboring away and endangered in this struggle, they ask that they be given the strength to fight and win through the grace of Christ. Adam, however, was neither tempted nor upset by any such conflict of himself against himself – in that place of happiness[49] he enjoyed peace with himself.

11.30   Consequently, the saints now do not need a more joyous grace for the time being. Instead, they need a more powerful grace. And what grace is more powerful than the only-begotten Son of God, equal to and co-eternal with the Father? For them was He made human. Without any original or personal sin of His own, He was crucified by human sinners. Although He rose up on the third day never to die again, He nevertheless suffered death on behalf of mortals. He gave life to those who were dead so that, redeemed by His blood and having received such a great guarantee, they might say: "If God is for us, who is against us? He did

---

[47] "It happens gratuitously, and thanks are to be given": There is some complicated and untranslatable wordplay here. The word for grace (*gratia*) is the root form of the adverb "gratuitously," and it also occurs in the idiom 'to give thanks (to).'

[48] "Blood of the Lamb": Christ as the sacrificial "lamb of God."

[49] "That place of happiness": Paradise.

not spare His own Son, but delivered Him up for us all. How did He not give us all things along with Him?" [Rom. 8:31–32]. Therefore, God took on our nature – namely the rational soul and the flesh of Christ the human being – in a manner uniquely marvelous, or marvelously unique, so that, without any preceding deserts of His own justice, He was the Son of God from the moment He began to be human, so that He[50] and the Word which has no beginning were a single person. Obviously, no one is so blinded with such great ignorance of this matter and of the faith as to dare say that, although the Son of Man was born of the Holy Spirit and the Virgin Mary, He nevertheless deserved to be the Son of God through His free choice, by leading a good life and doing good works without sin. The Gospel is against this, saying: "The Word was made flesh" [Jn. 1:14]. For where did this occur but in the Virgin's womb, in which Christ had His beginning as a human being? Again, when the Virgin asked how what the angel announced to her would come to pass, the angel replied: "The Holy Spirit shall come upon you and the power of the Highest shall overshadow you; consequently, the Holy One to be born of you shall be called the Son of God" [Lk. 1:35]. He does not say "consequently" on account of works; one who is not yet born surely has none. Rather, he said it because "the Holy Spirit shall come over you and the power of the Highest shall overshadow you," and *consequently* "the Holy One to be born of you shall be called the Son of God." That birth (which was surely gratuitous) conjoined, in the unity of a person, human being to God, flesh to Word. That birth was followed by good works; it was not deserved by good works. Nor was it to be feared that human nature, taken up in this indescribable way by God the Word into the unity of His person, would sin through free choice of the will. For the very 'taking up' was such that the nature of the human being thus taken up by God would admit in itself no movement of an evil will. Through this Mediator,[51] God has shown that He makes those whom He redeemed through His blood[52] to be made good, ever after, out of evil. God took Him[53] up in such a way that He would never be evil; He would always be good without having been made good out of evil.

---

[50] "He": Jesus in his human nature.     [51] "This Mediator": Jesus. See 7.12.
[52] "His blood": Christ's blood, that is.
[53] "Him": Augustine is referring to "the rational soul and the flesh of Christ the human being" as he says above: the particular human nature that God the Word takes up. Likewise the later occurrences of "He" in this sentence.

11.31    The First Man did not have this grace by which he would never will to be evil. But he definitely had grace (*a*) in which, if he had willed to continue, he would never be evil; (*b*) without which he could not have been good, even with free choice; but (*c*) which he could have abandoned through free choice. Therefore, God did not want Adam, whom He left to his free choice, to be without His grace, seeing that free choice is sufficient for evil, but hardly for good, unless it is assisted by the omnipotent Good One. And if Adam had not abandoned this assistance through free choice, he would always be good. But he abandoned it, and he was abandoned. In fact, the assistance was such that he abandoned it whenever he willed to, and in which he would continue if he willed to – not that by which it would come to pass that he willed to. This is the first grace which was given to the First Adam.

In the Second Adam[54] [grace] is stronger than this. For the first grace is that by which it comes to pass that a human being has justice if he wills to have it. The second grace, then, is more potent, by which it also comes to pass that one wills, and wills so greatly, wishing with so strong an ardor, that he overcomes, by the will of the spirit, the pleasure of the flesh which desires contrary things.

The first grace, in which the power of free choice was disclosed, was not small. For Adam was assisted in such a way that, without this assistance, he would not continue in the good, although he could abandon this assistance if he willed to. But the second grace is greater to this extent: The first grace is not sufficient to restore lost freedom to someone.[55] Again, the first grace is not sufficient for someone who lacks the second grace to be able either to grasp the good or to continue in the good if he so wills, unless the second grace also brings it about that he does so will.

11.32    At that time, then, God had given Adam a good will. He Who had "made him upright" [Ecl. 7:30 (7:29 RSV)] had made him in that [good will]. He had given the assistance without which Adam could not continue in it were he to so will, but He left it to his free choice that he so will. Thus Adam would have been able to continue if he willed to, since the assistance was available through which he could (and without which he could not) steadfastly hold on to the good he willed. But since Adam was unwilling to continue, it was surely his own fault. It would have been

---

[54] "The Second Adam": Christ.
[55] The second grace is sufficient to restore lost freedom to someone.

to his credit had he been willing to continue, as the good angels did. When the other angels fell through free choice, the good angels stood fast through the selfsame free choice. They deserved to receive the reward due to their persistence, namely the full abundance of happiness in which they are completely certain that they will always remain in it. But if this assistance had been unavailable to angels or to human beings when they were first made, then indeed they would not have fallen by their own fault, since their nature was not made such that it could continue, if it willed to, without divine assistance. They would have lacked the assistance without which they could not continue. Now, however, for those to whom such assistance is unavailable, it is the present penalty for sin. For those to whom it is given, it is given in accordance with grace and not as something owed. And it is given so much the more through Jesus Christ our Lord, to those to whom it pleased God to give it, that not only is there present that without which we cannot continue even if we will to, but also it is so great and of such a sort that we *do* will to. For through this grace of God in receiving the good and holding on to it with perseverance, there comes to pass in us not only that we are capable of what we will, but also that we will what we are capable of.

This was not the case with the First Man. He had one of these but not the other. Surely he did not require grace in order to receive the good. He had not yet lost it. But in order for him to continue in it he did require the assistance of grace, without which he could not do so at all. He received *being able were he to so will*, but he did not have *willing what he could do*. If he had had it he would have persevered. For he could have persevered had he willed to. The fact that he was unwilling proceeds from his free choice, which was then so free that he could will both good and evil. Yet what shall be more free than free choice when it is unable to be enslaved to sin? This was going to be for Adam the reward of his deserts, as was done for the holy angels. But now, since his good deserts are lost through sin, what was going to be the reward of deserts is realized instead as the gift of grace in the case of those who are set free.

Consequently, there must be a careful and attentive examination of 12.33 what the difference is between the elements in these three pairs:

- to be able not to sin – not to be able to sin
- to be able not to die – not to be able to die
- to be able not to abandon the good – not to be able to abandon the good

The First Man was able not to sin, able not to die, able not to abandon the good. Shall we say: Adam, who had such free choice, was not able to sin? Or: Adam, to whom it was said "If you sin you shall die the death" [Gen. 2:17], was not able to die? Or: Adam was not able to abandon the good, although he did abandon it by sinning, and hence died? The first freedom of the will was therefore to be able not to sin; the final freedom will be much greater: not to be able to sin. The first immortality was to be able not to die; the final immortality will be much greater: not to be able to die. The first power of perseverance was to be able not to abandon the good; the final happiness of perseverance will be not to be able to abandon the good. The final goods will be better and more powerful. Were the first goods thereby little or nothing?

12.34    Again, we should distinguish these two types of assistance: that *without which* something does not happen; and that *by means of which* something happens. We cannot live without things to eat, but, even when things to eat are available, it does not happen through them that someone lives who wills to die. Therefore, the assistance provided by things to eat is that without which it does not happen that we live, not that by means of which it comes about that we live. On the other hand, when the happiness which someone does not have is given to him, he becomes happy right away. For it is an assistance not only without which it does not happen, but it is also the reason why that by which it happens is given. Accordingly, this is an assistance both by means of which it happens and without which it does not happen, since if happiness is given to someone he becomes happy right away, and if it is never given to him he will never be happy. But things to eat do not bring it about that someone lives as a result. Yet without them one cannot live.

Thus the First Man, who in that good condition in which he was "made upright" had received the power not to sin, the power not to die, and the power not to abandon the good, was given assistance towards perseverance: not the assistance *by means of which* it would happen that he persevere, but the assistance *without which* he could not persevere through free choice.

Now, however, such assistance towards perserverance is not given to the saints predestined by God's grace for His kingdom. Instead, perseverance itself is given to them as assistance. Not only could they not persevere without this gift, but also they do indeed persevere through this gift. For not only did He say, "Without me you can do nothing" [Jn. 15:5], He also said, "You have not elected me, but I have elected you and appointed you to go forth and bear fruit, and that your fruit remain" [Jn. 15:16]. In these words, He showed them that He had given them not only justice, but perseverance in it as well. For with Christ appointing them so that they go forth and bear fruit, and that their fruit remain, who would dare to say: "It will not remain"? Who would dare to say, "Perhaps it will not remain"? "For the gifts and calling of God are without repentance" [Rom. 11:29], and the 'calling' is of those "who are called in accordance with His plan" [Rom. 8:28]. Since Christ intercedes on their behalf so that their faith will not fail, undoubtedly it will not fail up to the end, and through this it will persevere up to the end. The end of this life will find their faith remaining.

In fact, greater freedom is necessary against so many great tempta- 12.35 tions that did not exist in Paradise – a freedom defended and fortified by the gift of perseverance, so that this world, with all its loves and terrors and errors, may be overcome. The martyrdom of the saints has taught us this. In the end, using free choice with no terrors and moreover against the command of the terrifying God, Adam did not stand fast in his great happiness, in his ready ability not to sin. The martyred saints, though, have stood fast in their faith, even though the world – I do not say "terrified" them, but rather savagely attacked them – in order that they not stand fast. Adam saw the present goods that he was going to leave behind. The martyred saints did not see the future goods that they were going to receive. Where does this come from, if not by God's gift? From Him the saints obtained mercy, that they might be faithful.[56] From Him they received not the spirit of fear, by which they would give in to their persecutors, but the spirit of virtue and charity and continence,[57] by which they might overcome all the threats and all the blandishments and all the torments.

Therefore, free will was given to Adam, who was without any sin when he was created, and he made it a slave to sin. But the will of the martyred saints, although it had been a slave to sin, was set free by Him Who said: "If the Son sets you free, then you shall truly be free" [Jn. 8:36]. They have received such great freedom through this grace that, although as long as they live here they struggle against the urgings of sins (and not

---

[56] See 1 Cor. 7:25: "From the Lord I have obtained mercy that I might be faithful."
[57] See 2 Tim. 1:7: "For God has not given us the spirit of fear, but the spirit of virtue and charity and continence."

a few such steal upon them so that every day they say "Forgive us our trespasses" [Mt. 6:12]), nevertheless they are no more the slaves of 'the sin that is unto death.' The Apostle John says of this sin: "There is a sin unto death; I do not say that one should pray for that" [1 Jn. 5:16]. There can be many different views about this sin, since it is not made explicit. For my part, I say that it is the sin of abandoning "the faith which works through love" [Gal. 5:6] up to death. To this sin the martyred saints are no more the slaves. They are not free in their first condition, like Adam, but they have been set free by God's grace through the Second Adam,[58] and by this liberation they have free choice, through which they may serve God, not through which they may be captured by the Devil. "Being set free from sin, they became the servants of justice" [Rom. 6:18], in which they will stand up to the end. For they were given perseverance by God, Who foreknew and predestined them, and called them "in accordance with His plan" and "made them just and glorified them" [Rom. 8:28–30]. Indeed, He has already done even the future things He promised in their regard. And "Abraham believed" His promise, "and it was credited to him as justice" [Rom. 4:3]. For he gave "glory to God, believing completely that what He promised He is also able to perform" [Rom. 4:20–21] (as it is written).

12.36     Thus He made them good that they may do good. Nor did He promise them to Abraham precisely because He foreknew that they would be good of their own accord, for if so, what He promised is not His but theirs. Not thus did Abraham believe. Instead, "he was not weakened in his faith, giving glory to God, believing completely that what He promised He was also able to perform" [Rom. 4:20–21]. This does not say: "what He foreknew He was able to promise" or "what He foretold He was able to reveal" or "what He promised He was able to foreknow," but "what He promised He was also able to *perform*." Hence He Who makes them good makes them persevere in the good.

Those who fall and perish, however, were not in the number of the predestined. Therefore, although the Apostle Paul was speaking about all who have been born again and lead religious lives when he said, "Who are you to judge another's servant? He stands or falls to his own Lord" [Rom. 14:4], nevertheless he immediately turned to those who are predestined and said: "But he shall stand fast." And so they would

---

[58] For "the Second Adam", see 7.12.

not arrogate this to themselves, he said: "For God is able to make him stand fast" [Rom. 14:4]. Thus God gives perseverance. God is able to make those who are standing to stand fast, so that they stand fast with the utmost perseverance, or to make those who have fallen stand upright again, for "The Lord helps up those who have been thrown down" [Ps. 145:8 (146:8 RSV)].

Therefore, the will of the First Man, which was created without any 12.37 sin, had such powers that it did not receive this gift of God (namely perseverance in the good). It was instead left up to his choice to persevere or not to persevere. Of itself, nothing offered resistance to him by way of urgings, so that it was appropriate that the choice of persevering be entrusted to such great goodness and such ready ability to lead a good life. Although God foreknew what Adam was going to do unjustly, His foreknowledge did not force him to do it. At the same time, He knew what He would do justly regarding it. But now, ever since that great freedom was deservedly lost for his sin, a weakness has remained that must be aided by even greater gifts.

In order to extinguish the pride of human presumption completely, it pleased God "that no flesh should glory before Him" [1 Cor. 1:29], that is, no human being. Why "should flesh not glory before Him," except on account of its own deserts? It was able to have such deserts but it lost them. And it lost them through that by which it was able to have them, namely through free choice. Accordingly, for those who need to be set free there remains only the grace of Him Who sets them free. So it is, then, "that no flesh should glory before Him." The unjust do not glory, for they have no grounds. Neither do the just, because they have their grounds from Him. Nor do they have glory of their own apart from Him to Whom they say: "My glory, the One Who lifts up my head" [Ps. 3:4]. For this reason, the saying "That no flesh should glory before Him" is relevant to all human beings, whereas "Let the one who glories glory in the Lord" [1 Cor. 1:31 and 2 Cor. 10:17] is relevant to the just. The Apostle Paul shows this explicitly. Once he had said "That no flesh should glory before Him," in order that the saints not think they were left without glory he immediately added [1 Cor. 1:30–31]:

> But from Him you are in Jesus Christ, Whom God made wisdom and justice and sanctification and redemption for us, so that, as it is written, *Let the one who glories glory in the Lord* [Jer. 9:24].

Hence it is that in this place of miseries, where human life upon the Earth is temptation,[59] "virtue is made complete in weakness" [2 Cor. 12:9] – and what is virtue if not that "one who glories glory in the Lord"?

12.38   On this account, even as regards perseverance in the good, God did not want His saints to glory in their own powers but rather in Him. God not only gives them assistance of the sort He gave the First Man, without which they cannot persevere even if they so will, but He also works in them the willing.[60] As a result, since they will not persevere unless they are able to and will to persevere, the possibility of persevering, and the will to do so, is given to them by the bestowal of divine grace. Their will is set afire by the Holy Spirit to such an extent that they can do so precisely because they will to, and they will to do so precisely because God works it that they so will. Now it is fitting in the great weakness of this life[61] for virtue to be made complete so as to curb our pride. Nevertheless, if in this life (*a*) their will were left up to them to remain in God's assistance, should they will to, without which they could not persevere; and (*b*) God did *not* work in them that they will – well, then, the will would give way in its weakness among so many great temptations. Hence they would not be able to persevere. Failing due to their weakness, they would not will to do so. Or at least, due to the weakness of their will, they would not will in such a way that they would be able to persevere.

Hence support was given to the weakness of the human will, so that by divine grace it moves unchangeably and insurmountably.[62] And so, although it is weak, in spite of that it does not fail, nor is it overcome by any adversity. This is done so that the human will, which is unhealthy and feeble, may still persevere in its still meager good through the power of God. The will of the First Man, which was healthy and strong, did not persevere in its more ample good. He had the power of free choice and, although he was never going to lack the assistance of God without

---

[59]  See Job 7:1: "Human life upon the Earth is hard service (*militia*)," a synonym for Augustine's *tentatio* (though he reads it as 'temptation [to sin]' instead).

[60]  See Phl. 2:13: "God is the one Who works in you both willing and doing works in conformity with good will."

[61]  "The great weakness of this life": See the beginning of 12.37.

[62]  "So that by divine grace it moves unchangeably and insurmountably": *ut diuina gratia indeclinabiliter et insuperabiliter ageretur.* Augustine's phrasing neatly splits the difference between 'divine grace moves the will' (which seems to cancel freedom) and 'the will moves itself in accordance with divine grace' (which seems to render grace ineffective).

which he could not persevere if he willed to, he nevertheless did not have the assistance by which God worked in him that he will to. Indeed, He turned the strongest one loose and permitted him to do what he willed. God looked after the weak, so that with His gift they unconquerably willed what is good, and unconquerably refused to abandon it. Thus when Christ says [to the Apostle Peter]: "I have prayed for you that your faith may not fail" [Lk. 22:32], let us understand that this was said to one who is 'built upon rock.'[63] Thus let the man of God "who glories glory in the Lord" [1 Cor. 1:31 and 2 Cor. 10:17], not only because he obtained mercy that he might be faithful, but also because his faith does not fail.

I am saying these things about those people who have been predes- 13.39 tined for the kingdom of God, whose number is settled, so that no one is added to them or taken from them. I am not speaking about those people who, after His announcement was given utterance, "are multiplied beyond number" [Ps. 39:6 (40:5 RSV)]. They can be described as "called," but not as "elected," since they are not "called in accordance with His plan" [Rom. 8:28].[64] The number of the elect is settled, not to be increased or diminished. John the Baptist suggests as much when he says [Mt. 3:8–9]:

> Then bring forth fruits for repentance, and be unwilling to say to yourselves: We have Abraham as our father. For God is able to raise up children of Abraham out of these stones.

He shows here that they are to be cut off if they do not bring forth fruit, but in such a way that the number promised to Abraham will not fall short. It is declared more explicitly, though, in the Apocalypse: "Hold fast to what you have so that no one else receive your crown" [Rev. 3:11]. If one person is going to receive it only if another has lost it, the number is settled.

Now these things are also said to the saints who are going to persevere, 13.40 as though the fact that they are going to persevere were considered something uncertain. Those for whom it is beneficial "not to be high-minded but instead to fear" [Rom. 11:20] should not hear them in any other way. For who among the many faithful, while given life in this mortal condition, would presume to be in the number of the predestined? That fact must be hidden in this place, where we should be on guard

---

[63] See Mt. 16:18: "You are Peter, and upon this rock [=Peter] I shall build my church" (punning on Peter's name).
[64] See 7.13–16 above for this distinction.

against pride – seeing that even Paul, the great apostle, was buffeted by a messenger of Satan so that he would not be filled with pride.[65] On these grounds the Lord said to the apostles: "If you continue in me" [Jn. 15:7], although when He was speaking He surely knew that they were going to continue. And through the prophet Isaiah: "If you are willing and obedient" [Is. 1:19], although He knew in whom He would work the willing.[66] There are many similar passages.

Because of the usefulness of this matter being secret – namely that no one be filled with pride, but everyone, even those who are running well, be fearful as long as it is hidden who reaches the goal – because of the usefulness of this matter being secret, then, we must believe that some of the 'children of perdition,'[67] who have not received the gift of persevering up to the end, begin to live in the "faith which works through love" [Gal. 5:6]; they live justly and with faith for a time, but afterwards fall, and they are not taken from this life before they fall. If this had not happened to any of them, people would have that healthful fear which quells the vice of pride up to the time at which they arrive at the grace of Christ (by which a religious life is led), and from then on would be secure that they would never fall away from Him. But this presumption is not beneficial in this place of temptations, where our weakness is so great that security can engender pride. In the end there will be this security too. What is already the case in angels will also hold for human beings then, when there cannot be any pride.

Therefore, the number of the saints predestined for the kingdom of God by God's grace, since perseverance even up to the end is given to them, will be brought there undiminished, and it will be preserved there in wholly complete happiness without end. The mercy of their Savior supports them when they are converted, when they are struggling, and when they are crowned.

13.41     God's mercy is necessary for them even at that time,[68] as Scripture attests where the saint speaks to his soul about the Lord God, "Who crowns you in compassion and mercy" [Ps. 102:4 (103:4 RSV)]. The Apostle James also says: "Judgment without mercy for one who showed no mercy" [Jas. 2:13], where he makes it clear that even in that Judgment

---

[65] See 2 Cor. 12:7: "So that I not be filled with pride … a messenger of Satan was sent to buffet me."
[66] "Work the willing": see Phl. 2:13.     [67] See 9.20, 9.24, and 15.48.
[68] "At that time": when the elect are 'crowned,' that is, at the Last Judgment.

in which the just are crowned and the unjust are damned, some are going to be judged with mercy and others without mercy. On this score, even the mother of the Maccabees said to her son: "That I may receive you in compassion along with your brothers" [2 Mac. 7:29]. As it is written [Prv. 20:8–9 LXX]:

> When the Just King shall be seated on His throne, there will be no evil standing in opposition before Him. Who shall glory that he has a chaste heart? Who shall glory that he is clean of sin?

For this reason, God's mercy will be necessary even at that time, the mercy by which it happens that "happy is the one to whom the Lord has not imputed sin" [Ps. 31:2 (32:2 RSV)].

But mercy itself will also be granted at that time by His just judgment for the deserts that belong to good works. For when it is said: "Judgment without mercy for one who showed no mercy" [Jas. 2:13], it is made clear that judgment with mercy comes to pass in the case of those in whom are found good works of mercy. Accordingly, that mercy itself is also rendered for the deserts that belong to good works.

This is not the case now. At present, His mercy comes not only to human beings who have no preceding good works, but even to those with many preceding evil works, in order to set them free from evils: (*a*) those which they have done; (*b*) those which they were going to do were they not guided by God's grace; (*c*) those they were going to suffer in eternity were they not delivered "from the power of darkness and transferred to the kingdom of the Son of God's charity" [Col. 1:13]. Yet nonetheless, eternal life, which is certainly rendered as what is owed for good works, is called a grace of God by the great Apostle Paul,[69] despite the fact that grace is not rendered for works but is given gratuitously. Thus we must undoubtedly admit that eternal life is called a "grace" precisely because it is rendered for those deserts which grace has conferred on someone. This is the correct understanding of what we read in the gospel: "Grace for grace" [Jn. 1:16], that is, for the deserts which grace confers.

Now the people who do not belong to the number of the predestined – 13.42 the predestined, whom God's grace brings to His kingdom, whether they do not yet have any free choice of their will, or with choice of the will

---

[69] See Rom. 6:23: "Eternal life in Jesus Christ our Lord is a grace of God."

that is genuinely free since it has been set free by that grace – the people, then, who do *not* belong to that completely settled and happiest number, are judged most justly for their deserts. Either (*a*) they lie fallen under the sin which they originally contracted at their birth, and depart from here with that hereditary debt which was not forgiven by rebirth. Or (*b*) they go on to add other sins [to Original Sin] by their free choice. A choice, I say, that is 'free' but not set free, free of justice but enslaved to sin.[70] By this choice they indulge themselves in various harmful desires, some people more evil and others less, but all evil, and in accordance with their variety they are to be judged with a variety of punishments. Or (*c*) they receive God's grace but have it only for a time and they do not persevere, they abandon it and they are abandoned. For, by the just and hidden judgment of God, they have not received the gift of perseverance and are left to their free choice.

14.43     Therefore, let people suffer to be reprimanded when they sin. Let them not use this reprimand to argue against grace, nor use grace to argue against the reprimand. For sins deserve a just penalty, and a just reprimand is part of that. It is administered medicinally, even if the recovery of the patient is uncertain, so that if the one reprimanded belongs to the number of the predestined the reprimand is a healthful medicine for him, whereas if he does not belong to their number it is a painful penalty for him. In this uncertainty, then, a reprimand, whose outcome is unknown, should be administered with charity; one should offer prayers that the person to whom it is administered may be healed. After all, when people come (or come back) to the path of justice through a reprimand, who works health in their hearts but God? Whenever anyone plants and waters, whenever anyone works in the fields or the groves, it is God who imparts growth.[71] No human choice resists Him when He wills salvation. For *being willing* or *being unwilling* is in the power of the one who is willing or unwilling in such a way that it does not get in the way of the divine will, nor surpass His power. He does what He wills even when it comes to those who do what He does not will.

14.44     What is written, that "God wills all people to be saved" [1 Tim. 2:4] and yet not all are saved, can be understood in many ways. I have

---

[70] See Rom. 6:20: "When you were enslaved to sin, you were free from justice."
[71] See 1 Cor. 3:7: "Neither the one who plants nor the one who waters is anything; rather, it is God who imparts growth."

mentioned some of these ways in other works of mine.[72] Here I shall describe this one: "He wills all to be saved" was said in such a way that all the predestined are understood [in 'all'], since every kind of human being is among them. Likewise, to the Pharisees it was said: "You pay tithes on every herb" [Lk. 11:42], where one should understand only every herb they had, for they did not pay tithes on every herb there was in the whole world. In this manner of speaking the Apostle Paul said: "Even as I please all in all things" [1 Cor. 10:33]. Did the man who said this also please his many persecutors? Rather, he pleased every kind of person which the Church of Christ was gathering together, whether they were already within it or to be brought into it.

Thus there should be no doubt that human wills cannot resist the will 14.45 of God, Who "did whatever He willed in heaven and on Earth" [Ps. 134:6 (135:6 RSV)] and Who has even "done what will be" [Is. 45:11 LXX]. They[73] cannot prevent Him from doing what He wills, seeing that He does what He wills when He wills even in the case of human wills themselves. When God willed to give Saul the kingdom – to mention one of the many examples – was it perhaps in the power of the Israelites to make themselves the subjects of Saul, or to not make themselves his subjects? This [power] was surely located in their will. Were they, as a result, able to resist even God? However, God did this precisely by human wills themselves, having, as He undoubtedly does, the most omnipotent power over human hearts that they be inclined to whatever He pleases. For so is it written [1 Sam. 10:25–27]:

> And Samuel sent the people away, and each went into his own house. And Saul went into his own house in Gibeah; and valiant men, whose hearts the Lord had touched, went with Saul. And the children of Belial said: How will this man save us? And they dishonored him, bringing him no gifts.

Surely no one is going to claim that any of the people whose hearts the Lord had touched so that they would go with Saul was *not* going to go with him, or that any of the children of Belial, whose hearts the Lord had not touched that they do this, went with him.

---

[72] For example, in *Enchiridion* 27.103 Augustine suggests that it might mean that (*a*) no person is saved unless God wills it; (*b*) that all kinds of people will be saved; (*c*) the human race will not perish as a whole.

[73] "They": human wills.

Again, there is the case of David, whom the Lord set up in the kingdom with greater success, as we read: "David went on growing, and was magnified, and the Lord was with him" [1 Chr. 11:9]. A little after this passage it is said: "The spirit came upon Amasai, leader of the thirty, and he said, 'We are yours, David, and we are going to be with you, son of Jesse. Peace, peace to you, and peace to your helpers, for God has helped you'" [1 Chr. 12:18]. Could Amasai be opposed to the will of God and instead *not* do the will of Him Who worked in his heart through His spirit, which came upon Amasai, that he would will this, say this, and do this?

Again, slightly later the same Scripture says: "All these soldiers arrayed for battle came to Hebron, in hearts filled with peace, to set David up over all Israel" [1 Chr. 12:38]. Surely they set David up as king by their own will. Who does not see this? Who would deny it? For they did not do this "in hearts filled with peace" unintentionally or without good will. Yet He Who works what He wills in human hearts brought this about in them. For this reason, Scripture put first: "David went on growing, and was magnified, and the almighty Lord was with him" [1 Chr. 11:9]. Accordingly, "the almighty Lord" Who "was with him" brought these soldiers so that they set David up as king. And how did He bring them? Surely He did not bind them with any physical chains. He acted within: He held their hearts; He moved their hearts; and He drew them on by their wills, which He worked in them. Therefore, when God wills to set up kings on the Earth, He has human wills more in His power than human beings do in their own power. Who else, then, makes a reprimand to be healthful, and correction to come about in the heart of the one who was reprimanded, so that he may be set up in the heavenly kingdom?

15.46 And so, let the brothers be reprimanded by the superiors to whom they are subject, as long as the reprimands stem from charity, and differ as lesser or greater in accordance with differences in the faults. For even the penalty called "damnation" pronounced by episcopal judgment, a penalty than which there is no greater in the Church, can, if God wills, turn into a most healthful reprimand and be beneficial. In fact, we do not know what may happen tomorrow. Either we are to despair of someone before the end of his life on this Earth, or it can be said contrariwise that God may take notice and give him repentance and, receiving "the sacrifice of a troubled spirit and a contrite heart" [Ps. 50:19 (51:17 RSV)], absolve him from the guilt of even a just damnation, so that He not damn the one who has been damned. Now to keep a dire contagion from spreading through many, it is a matter of pastoral necessity to separate the ailing sheep from the healthy ones. Yet perhaps the ailing sheep is going to be healed through this very separation, by Him for Whom nothing is impossible. Not knowing who belongs and who does not belong to the number of the predestined, we ought to be so affected by the affection of charity that we will everyone to be saved.

This happens when we try to bring each and every one of the people we encounter, and with whom it is possible, to the point that they are made just by their faith, and have the peace with God[74] which the Apostle Paul was preaching when he said: "Thus we are the ambassadors for Christ, as though God did appeal to you by us; we pray for you, on behalf of Christ, to be reconciled to God" [2 Cor. 5:20]. What is being reconciled to Him but having peace with Him? For this peace even the Lord Jesus himself spoke to his disciples: "Into whatever house you enter, first say 'Peace to this house!'; and if a child of peace be there, your peace shall rest upon it, but if not it shall return to you" [Lk. 10:5–6]. Once those of whom it was foretold: "How beautiful are the feet of those who announce good tidings, who announce peace!" [Is. 52:7] proclaim this gospel of peace, then everyone begins to be a 'child of peace' to us at the time when he believes and obeys this gospel. Having been made just by his faith, he begins to have peace with God. However, he already was a child of peace according to God's predestination. For Scripture does not say: "The one upon whom your peace shall rest is going to be a child of peace," but rather: "If a child of peace be there, your peace shall rest upon that house" [Lk. 10:6]. Therefore, a child of peace was already there even before this peace was declared upon the house, as he was known and foreknown to be: not by the evangelist, but by God.

Therefore, it is up to us – we who do not know who might or might not be a child of peace – not to exclude anyone or single anyone out, but instead to will that all those to whom we preach this peace be saved. We need not fear that we might lose it, due to our not knowing that the one to whom we are preaching is not a child of peace. It returns to us, that is, this preaching will benefit us, though not him. If the peace we have preached rests upon him, then it will benefit both us and him.

---

[74] See Rom. 5:1: "Being made just by our faith, we have peace with God through Jesus Christ our Lord."

15.47     Therefore, because God bids us, in our ignorance of those who are going to be saved, to will that all to whom we preach this peace be saved, and He works this [willing] in us by "shedding His charity abroad in our hearts through the Holy Spirit, Who has been given to us" [Rom. 5:5], the words "God wills all people to be saved" [1 Tim. 2:4] can also be understood as follows: He makes us will this by making us call it out, just as "He sent the Spirit of His Son calling out 'Abba Father!'" [Gal. 4:6], that is, making us call it out. In fact, He says about this Spirit in another passage: We have received "the Spirit of adoption of children, in which we call out 'Abba Father!'" [Rom. 8:15]. Thus we for our part call out, but He is said to call out because He brings it about that we call out. If Scripture was correct to say that the Spirit is calling out in bringing it about that we call out, then God is likewise correctly said to will when He brings it about that we will.

    Accordingly, since in giving reprimands we should do nothing but make sure that there is no falling away from this peace with God, or that the one who has fallen away returns to it, let us do what we are doing without despairing. If the one whom we reprimand is a child of peace, our peace will rest upon him. If not, it will return to us.

15.48     Thus even when "the faith of some is undermined, the foundation of God stands firm" because "the Lord knew those who are His" [2 Tim. 2:18–19]. Yet we should not for that reason be negligent or remiss in reprimanding those who ought to be reprimanded. For this was not said in vain: "Evil conversations corrupt good morals" [1 Cor. 15:33], and "Shall the weak brother, for whom Christ died, perish in your knowledge?" [1 Cor. 8:11]. Let us not argue against these precepts and a healthful fear[75] by saying: "Let evil conversations corrupt good morals, and let the weak one perish; what is it to us? The foundation of God stands firm, and no one perishes but a 'child of perdition.'"

16.48     Perish the thought that while babbling these things we believe that we ourselves ought to be secure in the midst of this negligence! It is true that no one perishes but a child of perdition. But God says through the prophet Ezekiel: "He will indeed die in his sin, yet I shall require his blood at the hand of the watchman" [Ez. 3:18 and 33:6].

16.49     To the extent that it is up to us, we who are not capable of singling out the predestined from those not predestined (and consequently ought to

---

[75] "A healthful fear": see 13.40.

will that all be saved), a severe reprimand should be administered to all medicinally in order that they not perish or not ruin others. It is up to God, however, to make the reprimand useful "for those whom He foreknew and also predestined to conform to the image of His Son" [Rom. 8:29]. If we sometimes do not offer a reprimand out of fear that someone might thereby perish, why do we not also offer a reprimand out of fear that someone might thereby perish all the more? For we do not bear greater visceral love than the blessed Apostle Paul, who says: "Reprimand the unruly, succor the timid, support the weak; be patient towards all; see that none renders evil for evil unto anyone" [1 Ths. 5:14–15]. Here we should understand that evil is rather rendered for evil if, when someone should be reprimanded, he is not reprimanded but instead is neglected in blameworthy feigned ignorance. For the apostle says: "Reprimand sinners in front of all, that the rest may have fear" [1 Tim. 5:20]. This should be taken with regard to sins that are not private, so that it not be thought that his statement is contrary to the view of the Lord, Who says: "If your brother sins against you, reprimand him between you and him alone" [Mt. 18:15]. Nonetheless, He Himself carries the severity of a reprimand to the point where he says: "If he will not hear the Church, let him be to you as a heathen and a publican" [Mt. 18:17]. And who loved the weak more than He did? He Who for the sake of all was made weak, and for the sake of all was crucified through His very weakness![76] Since these things are so, grace does not prevent reprimand, nor does reprimand deny grace. Hence (*a*) justice should be prescribed [in the reprimand], such that (*b*) God is petitioned in faithful prayer for the grace by which what is prescribed may be done. Both of these should be done in such a way that the just reprimand is not neglected. But "let all your deeds be done with charity" [1 Cor. 16:14], for charity does not produce sin, and it "covers a multitude of sins" [1 Pet. 4:8].

---

[76] See 2 Cor. 13:4: "Though He was crucified through weakness, He lives through the power of God."

# On the Gift of Perseverance, 8.16–13.33

8.16
Objection: "Why isn't the grace of God given in accordance with human deserts?" I reply: because God is merciful. Objection: "Then why not to all?" I reply: because God is a judge. Accordingly, grace is given by Him gratuitously, and His just judgment in other cases shows what grace confers on those to whom it is given. Thus let us not be ungrateful that the merciful God, "according to the pleasure of His will, to the praise of the glory of His grace" [Eph. 2:5–6], sets so many free from a perdition that is owed to such an extent that He would not be unjust if He did not set anyone free from it. From one[1] all have been sentenced to undergo a condemnation that is not unjust but just. Therefore, anyone who is set free should take delight in grace; anyone who is not set free should recognize what is owed. If there is goodness in remitting what is owed, and equity in exacting it, then iniquity is never found in God.[2]

8.17
Objection: "Why is His judgment so different not only in the case of young children, but in one and the same case of twins?" Is that not similar to the question: Why is His judgment the same in different cases? Let us recall, then, those workers in the vineyard. Some toiled the whole day long, some worked for a single hour.[3] To be sure, the cases differ in the expenditure of labor. Yet in the payment of their wages the judgment is the same. The workers who grumbled about this heard only the following reply from their Master: "I will it." His generosity towards some people was such that there was no inequity towards the others, and

---

[1] "From one": from Adam.
[2] See Rom. 9:14: "What shall we say then – is there injustice in God? By no means!"
[3] The Parable of the Vineyard is recounted in Mt. 20:1–16.

each of these⁴ is counted among good things. Nonetheless, inasmuch as one looks both to justice and to grace, it can rightly be said to the guilty one who is damned and of the guilty one who is set free: "Take what is yours and go your way!" [Mt. 20:14]; "to this one I will to give" what he is not owed. "Am I not permitted to do as I will? Or are you envious because I am generous?" [Mt. 20:14–15].⁵

In this case, if he were to object, "Why not to me too?" he will deservedly hear the reply: "Who are human beings to answer back to God?" [Rom. 9:20]. You see clearly that He is surely the most generous benefactor to one of you, while He is the most justly exacting to the other. Yet he is unjust to no one. For since He would be just even if He punished both, then the one who has been set free has grounds for giving thanks, and the one who was damned has no grounds for complaint.

8.18 Objection: "If it were appropriate for God to show what is owed to all by damning some people, but not all, and thus to commend His grace as the more gratuitous to the 'vessels of mercy' [Rom. 9:23], then why, in the selfsame case, will He punish me rather than another, or set free another rather than me?"

I do not say. If you ask why, I admit that I do not find anything to say. If *then* you ask why – well, it is because in this case, even as His anger is just, even as His mercy is great, so "His judgments are inscrutable" [Rom. 11:33].

8.19 The objector may still persist and object: "Why did He not give perseverance up to the end to some who worshipped Him with good faith?"

Why do you think? After all, he does not lie who says: "They went forth from us but were not of us; for if they had been of us, they would surely have continued with us" [1 Jn. 2:19]. "Are there then *two* human natures?"

Perish the thought! If there were two natures, there would not be any grace, for *being set free gratuitously* would be granted to no one if it were rendered as something owed to their nature. Now it seems to human beings that all who appear to be good and faithful ought to receive perseverance up to the end. But God judged it better that some who will not persevere be mixed in with the definite number of His saints, so that those for whom security amidst the temptations of this life is not useful

---

⁴ "Each of these": generosity and equitable treatment.
⁵ Literally, "Is your eye evil because I am good?"

cannot be secure. For what the Apostle Paul said holds back many people from pernicious pride: "Accordingly, let the one who thinks he stands take heed not to fall" [1 Cor. 10:12]. The one who falls, falls by his own will. The one who stands, stands by the will of God, "for God is able to make him stand fast" [Rom. 14:4] – therefore, *he* does not make himself stand fast, but rather God does. Nonetheless, it is good "not to be high-minded but instead to fear" [Rom. 11:20]. But anyone who stands or falls does so by his own thinking. As I mentioned earlier in *On Grace and Free Choice* 7.16, the apostle said: "Not that we are sufficient of our own selves to think anything; our sufficiency is rather from God" [2 Cor. 3:5]. Following the apostle, the blessed Ambrose dares to declare: "For our hearts and our thoughts are not in our power."[6] Everyone who is humble and genuinely religious recognizes that this is entirely true.

Furthermore, to explain this point, Ambrose talked about it in his   8.20 book *The Escape From the World*, declaring that we should escape from this world not with the body but with the heart, maintaining that this requires God's assistance. He says:

> We often speak about escaping from this world. If only our state of mind were as cautious and circumspect as our speaking is easy! But what is worse, often the allure of earthly desires creeps in and a flood of vanities takes hold of the mind, so that you think about and ponder what you are eager to avoid. It is difficult for a human being to avoid such thoughts and impossible to cast them off. In consequence, the Prophet bears witness that it is more a matter of wish rather than of attainment, saying: "Incline my heart to your testimonies and not to covetousness" [Ps. 118:36 (119:36 RSV)]. For our heart and our thoughts are not in our power. When they flood in unexpectedly, they confound the mind and spirit, and drag you elsewhere than you intended to go: They call you back to worldly things, they entangle you in earthly matters, they suggest voluptuous pleasures, they weave their allure, and, at the very moment when we are getting ready to raise up our mind, we are entangled in vain thoughts and often thrown down into earthly matters.[7]

Thus it is not in human power but rather in God's power for human beings to have "the power to become the children of God" [Jn. 1:12]. They

---

[6] Ambrose, *Escape From the World* 1.2 (163), cited in context in 8.20.
[7] Ambrose, *Escape From the World* 1.1 (163).

receive it from Him Who gives to the human heart the religious thoughts through which one has "faith which works through love" [Gal. 5:6]. To get and to hold onto this good, and to advance in it with perseverance up to the end, "we are not sufficient of our own selves to think anything; our sufficiency is rather from God" [2 Cor. 3:5], in Whose power are our heart and our thoughts.

9.21 Why then, out of two young children equally bound by Original Sin, is one taken up and the other left behind? And why, out of two irreligious adults, is one called in such a way that he follows the one who is calling, and the other is not called, or not called in such a way? "The judgments of God are inscrutable" [Rom. 11:33]. Why, out of two religious people, is one given perseverance up to the end and the other is not given it? The judgments of God are even more inscrutable. Yet this point should be most certain to the faithful: One of them is among the predestined, but the other is not. For "if they had been of us," says one of the predestined who drank in the secret at God's breast, "they would surely have continued with us" [1 Jn. 2:19].

I ask: What does it mean to say, "They were not of us, for if they had been of us, they would surely have continued with us"? Were not both created by God? Were not both born of Adam? Were not both made from the Earth? Did they not receive souls of one and the same nature from Him Who said, "I have made all breath" [Is. 57:16 LXX]? Finally, were not both called, and did not both follow the one who called them? Were not both made irreligious and then made just? Were not both made anew through the bath of rebirth?[8]

Well, if the one who knew without a doubt what he was saying were to hear these things, he could reply by saying: "These claims are true. According to these criteria, those [who did not persevere] were of us. But nonetheless, according to some other criterion they were *not* of us. For 'if they had been of us they would surely have continued with us.'"

What finally is this criterion?

The books of God are open; let us not turn our gaze away! Divine Scripture is calling out; let us listen to it! They were not of them, because they were not "called in accordance with His plan" [Rom. 8:28]. They were not "elected in Christ before the foundation of the world" [Eph. 1:4]. They did not "obtain an inheritance" [Eph. 1:11] in Him. They were not

---

8 "The bath of rebirth": baptism.

"predestined in accordance with the plan of Him Who works all things" [Eph. 1:11]. For if they had been, they would be of them, and without a doubt would have continued with them.

So as not to explain how it is possible for God to turn human wills to   9.22
faith in Him which are turned away in opposition, and to work in their hearts so that they neither give in to any adversities nor are overcome by any temptation to abandon Him (since He can do what the apostle says, namely not allow them "to be tempted beyond what they can do" [1 Cor. 10:13]) – so as not to explain these things, then, certainly God, foreknowing that they would fall, could have taken them from this life before this took place.

Or are we returning to this point, so that we keep on arguing over how absurd it is to say that the dead are judged even on the sins God foreknew they would commit if they were to have lived? This is so abhorrent to Christian sensibilities, or rather to human sensibilities, that it is embarrassing even to refute it. Why not say that the gospel itself was preached with such great effort and sufferings on the part of the saints, and even still is preached, in vain? Human beings could be judged, even without having heard the gospel, on the grounds of the rebelliousness or obedience which God foreknew they would have if they had heard it. Nor would Tyre and Sidon be damned, even if damned more lightly than cities in which miraculous signs were performed for non-believers by the Lord Jesus Christ, on the grounds that if they had been performed in Tyre and Sidon "they would have repented in sackcloth and ashes" [Mt. 11:21 and Lk. 10:13], as the declaration of Truth has it, in which words of His own the Lord Jesus Christ shows us more deeply the mystery of predestination.

Suppose that we are asked why such great miracles (*a*) were performed   9.23
among those who, upon seeing them, were not going to believe them, and (*b*) were not performed among those who would believe them if they saw them. What reply shall we offer? Are we going to give the reply put forward in my book *Six Questions Against the Pagans*?[9] (This reply does not judge in advance other reasons [for the divine judgments] which the prudent can investigate, of course.) As you know, when the question was raised why Christ came after so long a time, I replied: "Because

---

[9] This book, catalogued as *Letters* 102 (409/410) since it answers six questions sent by a friend in Carthage, offers the reply sketched in the remainder of 9.23 in 102.14.

He foreknew that in the times and places in which His gospel was not preached, everyone would react to the preaching of Him the way many did in His physical presence, namely those who were not willing to believe in Him, even after He raised the dead" (§14). Likewise, a bit later I said: "Is it surprising that Christ knew that in earlier times the world was so full of non-believers that He was rightly unwilling to be preached to those people, whom He foreknew would believe neither His words nor His miracles?" (§14). We certainly cannot say these things about Tyre and Sidon, though. In their cases we know that these divine judgments pertain to the reasons for predestination (at the time I said I was addressing these [divine judgments] without judging in advance these hidden reasons).

To be sure, it is easy for us to blame the Jews for their disbelief stemming from free will. For they were unwilling to believe such great and mighty deeds performed among them. The Lord reproached and censured them, saying: "Woe to you, Corazin and Bethsaida! For if the mighty deeds that were performed in you had been performed in Tyre and Sidon, they would have repented long ago in sackcloth and ashes" [Mt. 11:21 and Lk. 10:13]. But can we really say that even the people of Tyre and Sidon were unwilling to believe such mighty deeds performed among them, or that they would not have believed them if they had been done? For the Lord Himself bears witness for them that they would have repented with great humility if those signs of mighty divine deeds had been performed among them. And yet on the Day of Judgment they will be punished, although with a lesser punishment than the cities that were unwilling to believe the mighty deeds performed in them. The Lord goes on to say: "Nonetheless I say to you, it shall be more moderate for Tyre and Sidon on the Day of Judgment than for you" [Mt. 11:22 and Lk. 10:14]. Therefore, the latter cities will be punished more severely, the former more moderately, but they will be punished nevertheless.

Next, suppose that the dead are judged also according to the deeds they would have done if they continued living. Then surely they ought not to be punished, since they were going to be believers if the gospel had been preached to them along with such great miracles. But they will be punished. Hence it is false that the dead are judged also according to the deeds they would have done had the gospel reached them while alive. And if this is false, there is no reason to say of infants who perish (because they die without baptism) that they perish deservedly, on the

234

grounds that God foreknew that if they had lived and the gospel had been preached to them, they would have heard it without believing it. Hence it remains that they are held in bondage by Original Sin alone, and for this alone they depart into damnation. What we see given to others in the same condition results only from rebirth through God's gratuitous grace. And by His hidden but just judgment – for there is no iniquity in God[10] – some who would perish even after baptism by living very bad lives are kept in this life until they perish, though they would not perish if bodily death came to assist them before their fall. For none of the dead is judged on the basis of the good or bad deeds he would have done if he had not died. Otherwise, the people of Tyre and Sidon would not have paid the penalty according to what they did, but instead they would have obtained salvation through great repentance and faith in Christ, according to what they would have done if those mighty evangelical deeds had been performed among them.

A certain distinguished Catholic commentator[11] explained this passage 10.24 from the gospel as follows. The Lord foreknew that the people of Tyre and Sidon were later going to fall away from the faith after having believed the miracles performed among them. Out of mercy, He did not perform miracles there, since they would have become liable for a more serious penalty if they gave up the faith which they had held than if they had never embraced it.

Why should I say which points in the view of this learned and quite clear-sighted man still need to be investigated properly? His view supports us in the matter we are dealing with. Suppose that it was out of compassion that the Lord did not perform mighty deeds in Tyre and Sidon through which the people could become believers, precisely so that they would not be punished more severely when they became non-believers afterwards, as He foreknew they would. Then it has been clearly and sufficiently shown that the dead are not judged on the basis of the sins which He knew they would commit if they were helped in some way not to commit them – just as Christ is said to have helped the people of Tyre and Sidon (if that commentator's view is true), since He preferred them not to come to the faith rather than to commit the much more serious crime of abandoning it, which He had foreseen they would do if they had come to it.

---

[10]  See the note to 8.16.
[11]  The commentator to whom Augustine is referring has not been identified.

However, suppose the question were raised: "Why did it not happen that they were instead brought to believe and then, before they gave up the faith, they were allowed to depart from this life?"

I do not know what reply is possible. Anyone who says that a benefit was granted to those who were going to leave the faith behind, namely that they not begin to have what they would have abandoned with more serious irreligiousness, sufficiently indicates that a person is not judged on the basis of what evildoing it is foreknown he would perform, if he is assisted, by any benefit whatsoever, to not do it. Hence the one who "was snatched from this life so that wickedness not change his understanding" [Wis. 4:11] was given assistance. But why were the people of Tyre and Sidon not so assisted to believe and then be snatched from this life so that wickedness would not change their minds? Perhaps someone who endorsed this way of resolving the question might offer a reply. For my part, to the extent it pertains to the problem I am dealing with, I see that it is sufficient according to that view as well that it is shown that people are not judged for the things which they did not do, even if they were foreseen to be going to do them. However, as I said [in 9.22], it is embarrassing even to refute the view that the dying or the dead are punished for the sins they were foreseen to be going to commit if they had lived. However, let it not seem that we think it to be of any importance, despite the fact that we did argue against it rather than passing over it in silence.

11.25   Next, as the Apostle Paul says, "It does not depend on the one who is willing or on the one who is running, but on God, Who shows mercy" [Rom. 9:16]. On the one hand, God comes to the assistance of the young children whom He is willing [to assist], even though they neither will nor run. He elected them in Christ before the foundation of the world,[12] and He is going to give them grace gratuitously, that is, with no preceding deserts that come from faith or works. On the other hand, He does not give assistance to adults whom He is not willing to assist, even those whom He foresaw would believe His miracles if they had been performed among them. In His predestination He judged them otherwise – [a judgment] hidden [from us], but justly, to be sure, for there is no iniquity in God.[13] Rather, "His judgments are inscrutable and His ways past finding out" [Rom. 11:33], "but all the ways of the Lord are mercy

---

[12] Eph. 1:4: "[God] has elected us in Him [=Christ] before the foundation of the world."
[13] See the note to *On Grace and Free Choice* 21.43.

and truth" [Ps. 24:10 (25:1 RSV)]. Therefore, the mercy by which "He has mercy on whom He will" [Rom. 9:18], with no preceding deserts on their part, is "past finding out." And the truth by which "He hardens whom He will" [Rom. 9:18], even with preceding deserts on his part, deserts which he generally shares with the person on whom God has mercy, is "past finding out." For example, in the case of twins where one is taken up and the other left behind, the outcome is disparate but their deserts are the same. Yet one of them is set free by God's great goodness in such a way that the other is damned, with no iniquity on His part. For "is there iniquity in God? By no means!" [Rom. 9:14]. But "His ways are past finding out" [Rom. 11:33].

Thus let us not hesitate to believe in His mercy in regard to those He sets free, and in His truth in regard to those who are punished. Let us not try to scrutinize what is inscrutable or to find out what is past finding out. "Out of the mouth of babes and sucklings has He perfected His praise" [Ps. 8:2 (8:3 RSV)], so that we do not doubt in any way at all that what we see in regard to those whose liberation is not preceded by any good deserts on their part, and those whose damnation is preceded only by the original deserts common to both, also happens in the case of adults. That is, we do *not* think either that grace is given to people in accordance with their deserts, or that people are punished only for their deserts, whether those who are set free and those who are punished are in the same or in different evil straits. And so, "let the one who thinks he stands take heed not to fall" [1 Cor. 10:12], and "let the one who glories glory in the Lord" [1 Cor. 1:31 and 2 Cor. 10:17], not in himself.

But why do these brothers "not allow the case of young children to be used as an example for adults," as you write?[14] They have no doubt, in opposition to the Pelagians, that there is Original Sin which "entered the world through one man" [Rom. 5:12],[15] and "from that one all have gone into condemnation" [Rom. 5:16]. 11.26

The Manichaeans also do not accept this. Not only do they not hold all the writings of the Old Testament to have any authority, they also accept those belonging to the New Testament such that by a kind of 'privilege' (rather sacrilege!) of theirs they take what they want and reject what they

---

[14] Augustine directly addresses here a problem raised by Hilary in *Letters* 226.8: Some monks thought the case of infants differed from that of adults.
[15] See the note to *On Reprimand and Grace* 6.9.

do not want. I opposed them in *On the Free Choice of the Will*, and on the basis of this work of mine these [brothers] think they should raise an objection against me. Precisely in order not to make this work too long, I was unwilling to resolve quite laborious incidental questions in detail when the authority of Divine Scripture gave me no help against such perverse people. And whichever of them may be true, which I did not declare explicitly, I was nevertheless able, as I did, to come by certain reasoning to the conclusion that God should be praised in all things without any need to believe, as the Manichaeans hold, that there are two thoroughly intermixed co-eternal substances of Good and Evil.[16]

11.27    In point of fact, in my *Reconsiderations* – a work of mine you have not yet read – when I had come to looking again at *On the Free Choice of the Will*, I declared [1.9.2]:

> So many issues were examined in these books that I postponed some incidental questions – which either I could not untangle or which demanded a lengthy discussion – so that when it was not clear what came closer to the truth, our reasoning then would nonetheless draw the conclusion from each side (or from all the sides) of these selfsame incidental questions, in order that whichever of them may be true, we could believe, or even prove, that God ought to be praised.

> The discussion was undertaken on account of those who deny that the origin of evil lies in the free choice of the will, and who contend that, if this is so, God as the Creator of all natures ought to be blamed; as a result, they want to introduce some unchangeable nature of evil that is co-eternal with God in accordance with their irreligious error (for they are Manichaeans).

Again, a bit later in another passage [*Reconsiderations* 1.9.6]:

> Then I said that the grace of God sets sinners free from the misery that is most justly inflicted upon them. For of our own accord we were able to fall, namely by free choice, but not also to rise up. And this misery of our just damnation includes ignorance and trouble, which every human being suffers from the first moment of his birth. No one is set free from this evil except by God's grace.

---

[16]  See *On the Free Choice of the Will* 3.12.35.121 (repeated briefly at 3.16.46.159) for the argument to which Augustine is alluding here. The first part of this sentence closely paraphrases a remark in *Reconsiderations* 1.9.2, which Augustine cites in the next paragraph, 11.27.

The Pelagians are not willing for this misery to stem from a just damnation, since they deny Original Sin. However, as I argued in Book 3, even if ignorance and trouble were primordial features of the nature of human beings, God still ought to be praised rather than blamed.

This discussion was directed against the Manichaeans, who do not accept the Old Testament, in which Original Sin is described, as Scripture, and who contend with despicable shamelessness that whatever is read about it in the New Testament was inserted by people who corrupted the text of Scripture, as if these things had not been said by the apostles at all. Against the Pelagians, by contrast, we need to defend what both the Old Testament and the New Testament say, since they claim to accept each of them.

I said these things in *Reconsiderations* 1.9, while reviewing *On the Free Choice of the Will*. Nor are they the only things I said there about it. There were many other things, but I thought it would be tedious and unnecessary to put them into this work for you. I think you will judge likewise once you have read them all.

Therefore, although I argued about the case of young children in *On the Free Choice of the Will* Book 3 in such a way that even if what the Pelagians say were true – that ignorance and trouble, without which no human being is born, are primordial features of our nature and not punishments – the Manichaeans, who hold that there are two co-eternal natures (namely Good and Evil), would still be defeated. Should then our faith be called into doubt or given up? The Catholic Church defends it against the Pelagians. It asserts that there is original sin, and the guilt belonging to it, contracted by birth, must be dissolved by rebirth. But if even these brothers[17] confess this with me, so that together on this score we may destroy the error of the Pelagians, why do they think it should be doubted that God also delivers young children, to whom He gives His grace through the sacrament of baptism, "from the power of darkness and transfers them to the kingdom of the Son of God's charity" [Col. 1:13]? Therefore, given the fact that He gives grace to some and He does not give it to others, why are they unwilling "to sing of mercy and judgment to the Lord" [Ps. 100:1 (101:1 RSV)]? Why is it given to some people

---

[17] See the start of 11.26: the brothers mentioned by Hilary who thought the case of young children to differ from that of adults.

rather than others? Who knows God's intent? Who can scrutinize what is inscrutable? Who can find out what is past finding out?

12.28    Thus it is settled. God's grace is not given according to the deserts of the recipients, but instead "according to the good pleasure of His will, to the praise and glory of His grace" [Eph. 1:5–6], so that "the one who glories may glory in the Lord" [1 Cor. 1:31 and 2 Cor. 10:17] and not in himself at all. He gives it to those human beings to whom He wills to give it, because He is merciful. Even if He does not give it, He is just. And He does not give it to whom He does not will to give it, "so as to make known to the vessels of mercy the riches of His glory" [Rom. 9:23]. For by giving to some what they do not deserve, He wanted His grace surely to be gratuitous, and for this reason genuine grace. By not giving it to all, He shows what all deserve. He is good in His benefit to some, just in His punishment of the rest. He is good in all things, since it is good when what is owed is paid back; He is just in all things, since it is just when what is not owed is given without wrongdoing.

12.29    God's grace without deserts – that is, genuine grace – is maintained even if baptized young children, as the Pelagians hold, are not delivered "from the power of darkness" (since the Pelagians think that they are not in bondage to sin) but are only "transferred to the kingdom of God" [Col. 1:13]. Even then, the kingdom is given to those to whom it is given, without any good deserts [on their part]; and it is not given to those to whom it is not given, without any evil deserts [on their part]. This is the answer we typically give to those selfsame Pelagians when they object to us that we are attributing God's grace to Fate in saying that it is not given according to our deserts. Rather, it is they themselves who are attributing God's grace to Fate in the case of young children, for they call it Fate where there are no deserts. In fact, even according to the Pelagians themselves, no deserts can be found in young children as to why some of them are sent to the kingdom [of God] while others are kept apart from it.

Just as here,[18] to show that God's grace is not given according to our deserts, [in *On the Free Choice of the Will*] I preferred to defend the point in line with both views: (*a*) our view, which declares that young children are bound by Original Sin; (*b*) the Pelagian view, which denies that there is Original Sin. However, I need not thereby doubt that young children

---

[18] "Just as here": namely, in *On The Gift of Perseverance*. Augustine is still defending his procedure in *On the Free Choice of the Will* ("I *preferred*…").

have what they are forgiven by Him Who "saves His people from their sins" [Mt. 1:21]. Thus in *On the Free Choice of the Will* Book 3 I resisted the Manichaeans in line with both views, namely whether ignorance and trouble, with which every human being is born, are punishments or primordial features of our nature. Yet I hold one of these views. I also expressed it clearly enough there,[19] namely that it is not the nature of human beings as created but rather our penalty as damned.

Thus it is useless for them to object to me, on the score of that old book of mine, that I do not deal with the case of young children as I ought to, and thence that I do not prove in the light of clear truth that God's grace is not given according to human deserts. Well, I began *On the Free Choice of the Will* as a layman and finished it up as a priest. If I were still in doubt about the damnation of infants who are not reborn and the liberation of those who are reborn, no one, I think, would be so unjust and envious as to prohibit me from making progress, and to judge that I should remain in this state of doubt. But it might be more correct to understand that there is no need to believe me to have been in doubt about this matter. For I directed my aim against those who, it seemed to me, should be refuted, such that, whether the punishment of Original Sin is present in young children (as Truth holds) or is not present (as some people erroneously think), nevertheless there is no way one should believe in the complete mixture of two natures, namely Good and Evil, which the Manichaean error introduces. Far be it from us to abandon the case of young children, so that we declare ourselves uncertain whether those who are reborn in Christ, if they die as young children, enter into eternal salvation, whereas those who are not reborn enter into a second death! There is only one way to understand this passage correctly: "By one man sin entered into the world, and death by sin; and so death passed on to all human beings" [Rom. 5:12]. Nor is anyone, young or old, set free from the everlasting death that is the completely just repayment for sin, except by Him Who died for the remission of our sins, both original and personal, without having any original or personal sin of His own.

But why does He set free *these* rather than *those*?

Again and again we reply (and it does not bother us): "Who are human beings to answer back to God?" [Rom. 9:20]. "His judgments are inscrutable and His ways past finding out!" [Rom. 11:33]. And let us add

---

[19] See, for example, *On the Free Choice of the Will* 3.20.55.186.

to this: "Do not seek for things too high for you; neither look into things beyond your strength" [Sir. 3:22 (3:21 RSV)].

12.31    For do you see, dear brothers, how absurd it is and far removed from the soundness of faith and the purity of truth for us to say that young children who have died are judged according to the deeds they are foreknown to be going to do if they were to go on living? But those people who wanted to be set far apart from the error of the Pelagians were compelled to adopt this view, which is certainly abhorrent to all human sensibilities that rely on reason, no matter how little, and especially to Christian sensibilities. Yet they adopted it in such a way that they still continue to think they must believe, and what is more defend by arguments, that God's grace through Jesus Christ our Lord, in which alone we are given succor after the fall of the First Adam (in which all human beings fell), is given to us according to our deserts. Pelagius himself damned this view before the eastern bishops who were his judges,[20] fearing his own damnation. However, suppose that one did not make this claim about the works of the dead – namely about the good or the evil works they would do if they were to go on living, and consequently are not 'works' at all, and are not going to be in God's foreknowledge – suppose that one therefore did *not* make this claim (and you recognize the great error with which the claim is made). What will be left but for us (*a*) to acknowledge, once the shadows of controversy are cleared away, that God's grace is *not* given according to our deserts, as the Catholic Church maintains in opposition to the Pelagian heresy; and (*b*) to recognize it especially and with more evident truth in the case of young children?

God is not forced by Fate to give succor to some infants but not to others, since the case is common to both. Either we shall hold the view that human affairs in the case of young children are managed not by divine providence but rather by chance events, despite the fact that they are rational souls which are to be damned or to be set free (seeing that not a sparrow falls to the ground without the will of our Father Who is in Heaven);[21] or we shall hold the view that the fact that young children die without baptism should be attributed to the negligence of the parents, so that heavenly judgments have nothing to do with it – as though the

---

[20]   At the Council of Diospolis: See the note to *On Grace and Free Choice* 5.10.
[21]   Mt. 10:29: "A sparrow shall not fall to the ground without your Father."

children who die in this evil way elected for themselves, by their own will, the negligent parents from whom they would be born.

What shall I say to the fact that sometimes a young child expires before it can be succored by the ministration of baptism?

Often the parents make haste and the ministers are ready for baptism to be given to the child. Yet if God is unwilling, baptism is not given [in time], for He does not keep the child in this life a bit longer so that it may be given.

What shall I say, furthermore, to the fact that sometimes it has been possible for children of unbelievers to be given the succor of baptism, so that they not enter into perdition, whereas it was not possible for children of the faithful?

This case certainly shows that "with God there is no distinction among persons" [Rom. 2:11].[22] Otherwise, He would set free the children of His followers rather than of His enemies.

But now, since we are dealing here with the gift of perseverance, why 13.32 is it that succor is given to an unbaptized person about to die, so that he not die without baptism, whereas succor is not given to a person about to fall, so that he dies before [it is given]? Unless perhaps we are still giving our ear to that absurdity which says that it does not help anyone to die before he falls, since he will be judged according to those acts God foreknew he would do if he continued living. Who can stand to listen to this perversity, which is so violently opposed to the soundness of faith? Who can bear it? Yet those who do not admit that the grace of God is not given according to deserts are pushed into saying this!

However, those who are unwilling to say that any of the dead are judged according to the deeds God foreknew that they would do had they continued living – seeing the clear falsity and great absurdity in saying it – for them, there is no reason left to say what the Church condemned in the Pelagians and made Pelagius himself condemn, namely that God's grace is given according to our deserts. They see that some young children who have not been reborn are taken from this life into eternal death, while others who have been reborn are taken from this life into eternal life. They see that some of those who have been reborn go from here persevering up to the end, while others, who would surely not have

---

[22] See also 2 Chr. 19:7: "With the Lord our God there is no inequality, nor distinction among persons."

fallen if they had departed from here before they lapsed, are kept here until they fall. Again, they see that some lapsed people do not depart from this life before they return [to the faith], people who would surely perish if they had died before their return.

13.33 Accordingly, it has been shown quite clearly that God's grace – both of beginning and of persevering up to the end – is not given according to our deserts, but is given according to His most hidden and at the same time most just, wise, and beneficent will. For "those whom He has predestined He also called" [Rom. 8:30], by that calling of which it is said: "For the gifts and calling of God are without repentance" [Rom. 11:29]. Human beings should not claim with certainty that any person has a share in this calling until he has departed from this world: "In this human life upon the Earth, which is temptation" [Job 7:1].[23] "Accordingly, let the one who thinks he stands take heed not to fall" [1 Cor. 10:12]. Hence, as we already said above, the most provident will of God mixes together those who are not going to persevere with those who are going to persevere, so that we learn "not to be highminded but to feel things along with the humble" [Rom. 12:16] and to "work out our own salvation with fear and trembling; for God is the one Who works in us both willing and doing works in conformity with good will" [Phl. 2:12–13]. Therefore, we will, but God "works the willing in us." We do works, but God "works in us" our "doing works in conformity with good will." It is useful for us to say and to believe this; it is religious; it is true; so that our confession should be humble and submissive, and all should be attributed to God. We are thinking when we believe; we are thinking when we speak; we are thinking when we do whatever we do. But in what touches upon the religious path and the true worship of God, "we are not sufficient of our own selves to think anything; our sufficiency is rather from God" [2 Cor. 3:5]. For "our heart and our thoughts are not in our power."[24] Accordingly, the same person who said this, Ambrose, also says:

> Who is so happy as one who always ascends in his heart? But without divine assistance who can make it happen? Surely there is no way. And indeed the same book of Scripture says earlier: "Happy is the one whose help is from You, Lord; he ascends in his heart" [Ps. 83:6 (84:5 LXX)].[25]

[23] See the note to *On Reprimand and Grace* 12.37.
[24] Ambrose, *Escape From the World* 1.1 (163), cited in 8.19.
[25] Ambrose, *Escape From the World* 1.2 (163–164).

Indeed, for Ambrose to say this he not only read it in Scripture but, as we should undoubtedly believe of this man, he also felt it in his own heart. Therefore, that we turn our hearts upwards to the Lord, as instructed in the sacraments of the faithful, is a gift of the Lord. Those to whom these words are addressed are prompted by the priest, after these instructions [to turn our hearts upward], to give thanks to the Lord our God for this gift; the [congregation] replies that it is right and just.[26]

For "our heart … is not in our power" but instead is lifted up by divine assistance so that it may ascend and heed "those things which are above, where Christ sits at the right hand of God" [Col. 3:1], "not things of the Earth" [Col. 3:2]. To whom then should thanks be given for this great deed if not to the Lord our God Who does it, and Who, in setting us free from the depths of this world through such a great benefit, elected and predestined us before the foundation of the world?[27]

---

[26] Augustine is describing the congregation's responses to the priest's prayers at the beginning of the Mass (the "sacraments of the faithful").

[27] See the note to 11.25.

# Index of works cited

# Index of works cited

## New Testament

# Index of names

# Index of subjects

# Cambridge Texts in the History of Philosophy

*Titles published in the series thus far*

Hume *An Enquiry Concerning Human Understanding* (edited by Stephen Buckle)
Kant *Anthropology from a Pragmatic Point of View* (edited by Robert B. Louden with an introduction by Manfred Kuehn)
Kant *Critique of Practical Reason* (edited by Mary Gregor with an introduction by Andrews Reath)
Kant *Groundwork of the Metaphysics of Morals* (edited by Mary Gregor with an introduction by Christine M. Korsgaard)
Kant *Metaphysical Foundations of Natural Science* (edited by Michael Friedman)
Kant *The Metaphysics of Morals* (edited by Mary Gregor with an introduction by Roger Sullivan)
Kant *Prolegomena to any Future Metaphysics* (edited by Gary Hatfield)
Kant *Religion within the Boundaries of Mere Reason and Other Writings* (edited by Allen Wood and George di Giovanni with an introduction by Robert Merrihew Adams)
Kierkegaard *Concluding Unscientific Postscript* (edited by Alastair Hannay)
Kierkegaard *Fear and Trembling* (edited by C. Stephen Evans and Sylvia Walsh)
La Mettrie *Machine Man and Other Writings* (edited by Ann Thomson)
Leibniz *New Essays on Human Understanding* (edited by Peter Remnant and Jonathan Bennett)
Lessing *Philosophical and Theological Writings* (edited by H.B. Nisbet)
Malebranche *Dialogues on Metaphysics and on Religion* (edited by Nicholas Jolley and David Scott)
Malebranche *The Search after Truth* (edited by Thomas M. Lennon and Paul J. Olscamp)
*Medieval Islamic Philosophical Writings* (edited by Muhammad Ali Khalidi)
*Medieval Jewish Philosophical Writings* (edited by Charles Manekin)
Melanchthon *Orations on Philosophy and Education* (edited by Sachiko Kusukawa, translated by Christine Salazar)
Mendelssohn *Philosophical Writings* (edited by Daniel O. Dahlstrom)
Newton *Philosophical Writings* (edited by Andrew Janiak)
Nietzsche *The Antichrist, Ecce Homo, Twilight of the Idols and Other Writings* (edited by Aaron Ridley and Judith Norman)
Nietzsche *Beyond Good and Evil* (edited by Rolf-Peter Horstmann and Judith Norman)
Nietzsche *The Birth of Tragedy and Other Writings* (edited by Raymond Geuss and Ronald Speirs)
Nietzsche *Daybreak* (edited by Maudemarie Clark and Brian Leiter, translated by R.J. Hollingdale)
Nietzsche *The Gay Science* (edited by Bernard Williams, translated by Josefine Nauckhoff)
Nietzsche *Human, All Too Human* (translated by R.J. Hollingdale with an introduction by Richard Schacht)
Nietzsche *Thus Spoke Zarathustra* (edited by Adrian Del Caro and Robert B. Pippin)
Nietzsche *Untimely Meditations* (edited by Daniel Breazeale, translated by R.J. Hollingdale)
Nietzsche *Writings from the Early Notebooks* (edited by Raymond Geuss and Alexander Nehamas, translated by Ladislaus Löb)